The Revelation of the Breath

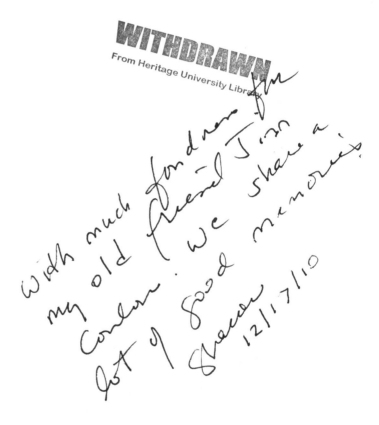

WITHDRAWN
From Heritage University Library

With much fondness for
my old friend Jim
Conlon. We share a
lot of good memories.
Sharon 12/17/10

SUNY series in Transpersonal and Humanistic Psychology

Richard D. Mann, editor

The Revelation of the Breath

A Tribute to Its Wisdom, Power, and Beauty

Edited by

SHARON G. MIJARES

excelsior editions

State University of New York Press
Albany, New York

Cover image: Gabo Carabes (www.haiku.com.mx). Reprinted by permission of the artist.

Published by
State University of New York Press, Albany

© 2009 State University of New York

All rights reserved

Printed in the United States of America

No part of this book may be used or reproduced in any manner whatsoever without written permission. No part of this book may be stored in a retrieval system or transmitted in any form or by any means including electronic, electrostatic, magnetic tape, mechanical, photocopying, recording, or otherwise without the prior permission in writing of the publisher.

For information, contact State University of New York Press, Albany, NY
www.sunypress.edu

Excelsior Editions is an imprint of State University of New York Press

Production by Eileen Meehan
Marketing by Fran Keneston

Library of Congress Cataloging-in-Publication Data

The revelation of the breath : a tribute to its wisdom, power, and beauty / edited by
  Sharon G. Mijares.
      p. cm. — (SUNY series in transpersonal and humanistic psychology)
  Includes bibliographical references and index.
  ISBN 978-1-4384-2877-2 (hbk. : alk. paper)
  ISBN 978-1-4384-2876-5 (pbk. : alk. paper)
    1. Breathing exercises.   2. Respiration—Religious aspects.   3. Mind and body.
  4. Healing.   I. Mijares, Sharon G. (Sharon Grace), 1942–

RA782.R48 2009
613'.192—dc22   2009005311

10 9 8 7 6 5 4 3 2 1

This book is dedicated to
Connie, Raphael, Heather, Hollie, Lisa and their children.
May each member of my family
—and the entire human family—
open to the healing power of the breath

Contents

Acknowledgments

Religious and spiritual teachings all acknowledge our connectedness with one another. This understanding became a visible reality when so many friends, old and new, came together to make this book a reality. I am especially grateful to the contributing authors. Each one has shared his or her unique knowledge and training. We wanted to convey the healing power of the breath and believe that we have accomplished our goal.

My spiritual teacher, Neil Douglas-Klotz, has guided me in my learning process with the breath for the last twenty years. He was my field supervisor for my master's research and thesis on the healing power of the breath. He introduced me to Samuel Lewis's unpublished manuscript, 101 Suras on the Breath, and supported my explorations in this essence of life. He continues to guide and support my process. For this, I am eternally grateful.

Once again, I express my gratitude for the excellent grammar and insight of Dania Brett. She has a great editorial eye and has made excellent editorial suggestions in my own chapters. Dania is able to hold my vision in her own mind and then make excellent recommendations. Also, I would like to acknowledge Sharon van den Berg for her appreciation and support. It was helpful to have an "average reader" respond to various chapters in the book. My long-time friend and Sufi sister Malika Merrill Endres has decades of training in yogic teachings. Her review of the final version of my yoga chapter is highly valued.

The staff at SUNY Press has been great! Jane Bunker has been a very pleasant and supportive presence. I appreciated the original reviewers. Their comments and suggestions strengthened the end result. I also give my appreciation to Andrew Kenyon, who quickly responded to my emails and questions, enabling me to flow through the early phases of the publication process. Much thanks to Eileen Meehan for bringing this book through the editorial, marketing, and design processes into its completed form. Her work has been greatly appreciated. In short, it is an honor to have this book published by the State University of New York Press.

Foreword

In the universe of eternity, an element represents the whole while the whole is the complete mirror of the element.

The *Revelation of the Breath* collects a diversity of essays on the vital subject of breath, something in which every being on our planet has a share. This collection includes perspectives of mystics, spiritual guides, psychologists, scientists, and historical researchers who have studied ancient texts from various traditions. Written in English, this compilation is especially valuable to Western readers who have become increasingly open to the ancient wisdom of the East. At a time when much of the world, including the East, races to adopt a consumer-driven lifestyle, the opposite is also true. More and more people in the West wish to adopt a simpler lifestyle where attention to the act of breathing is recognized as an essential means of achieving inner peace. Such practice increases attention, and such attention cannot help but lead to a more harmonious global society.

The desire for peace, love, and wisdom and the search for knowledge of *Being* are fundamental to human nature; it does not belong to any one culture or era. Traditionally, the East has been the seat of wisdom primarily because the environment is conducive to a slower and more meditative lifestyle.

Although the Middle Eastern culture is changing, at one time Islamic societies looked to the *hakim* ("the wise one") for guidance in all affairs. All of knowledge was unified under *hekmat* ("wisdom"). The community's hakim had experience of the divine qualities and had access to the wisdom of the first movement of creation and was thus knowledgeable about all other movements. To reach the station of hakim and serve one's society took years of inner practice; only when wisdom was garnered through concentrated daily practice was such a person eligible to serve. But that was long ago. Wisdom rarely guides a society today, and human knowledge has become ever diversified into narrowly defined branches and categories. While many scientists, psychologists, spiritual practitioners, and others are looking for the "secret" of life and a unifying theory—and their search brings incredible advances to civilization—the one point, the wisdom of the hakim, is hidden. Now more than ever, as suffering and pain caused by conflict and ignorance increases, we need the unifying wisdom of the hakim. This book is a testament to the search for that unifying wisdom as found through the breath.

The great physicist Albert Einstein searched for a unifying theory, although he never found it. He also wrote in his memoirs that he wanted to know the mystery beyond the creation of every creature he saw. Not surprisingly, he felt that the most mysterious of all creatures is humankind, for he saw the depth of our potential for knowledge of both creation and destruction and the terrible responsibility such knowledge carries. The main difference between Einstein and the Hakim, the wise mystic, is that the mystic searches for unity and the source of creation through the practice of meditation and inner traveling. There s/he experiences unity and witnesses that the surface of nature is simply a *reflection* of the source of Being, the first movement, the very first breath. Such a one strives to ascend to a state of purity in order to receive the first breath and experience unity.

Humans possess both the potential and the capacity to ascend to the state of the first pure breath, the source of Being. As my master Moulana Shah Maghsoud (1916–80), a great Sufi of the twentieth century, said, such potential and capacity makes humans the mirror of the divine. It is our potential to receive the first breath and our ability to both recognize and understand the source of our Being that sets us apart from the rest of creation, which may experience unity but not be able to name it. The Qur'an refers to such a state of recognition in Surah 38:71: "Behold the Lord said to the angels, I am about to create man from clay. When I have fashioned him and breathed into him from my spirit, fall ye down in obedience onto him." Let us be clear. It is not the man of clay to whom the angels bow. It is to the one who has reached the station of purity, received the divine animating breath, and cognized the source of *Being*. Such a one has been opened into the space of divinity and expanded into universal awareness. The prostration of angels means that this human has received the divine breath and, with it, all the pure divine qualities of the One.

As you read the following collection of essays and consider the practice of breath, the most important question to ask is: In what state and which station of being am I breathing? As you inhale and let your breath expire, consider: Breath of what, breath of when, how? If we pay attention to our breath in the physical state of being only, breathing in oxygen and carbon, our bodies are kept alive and our awareness is heightened to some extent. This is indeed beneficial. However, the best practice of all is to upgrade our being from the limitation of the "clay" (physicality) and qualify ourselves to receive the first pure breath, which is ever present beyond the limitations of time and space. While breath itself always carries the message of life, we ultimately have the capacity to receive the pure breath of divinity and thus to cognize the source of our being and the essence of unity. It is then that our breath truly has the capacity to manifest peace, love, and prosperity. In fact, it is then we have actualized our potential and fulfilled our capacity. We become fully human and can claim with certainty "*I am alive!*"

Shah Nazar Seyyed Ali Kianfar, Ph.D.
September 2, 2008 / Ramezan 2, 1924

From the first faint breath of the infant
to the last gasp of the dying man,
it is one long story of continued breathing.
Life is but a series of breath.

Ramacharaka, *The Science of Breath*
(Chicago: Yogi Publication Society, 1904), 8

Introduction

Breath is the very essence of life. Our entrance into life occurs with that first breath, and it is with a final breath that we depart. The breath we breathe contains the attributes of the Divine. Awareness of breath determines the level of our connection to the deeper meaning of life itself. It is an expression of our humanity, carrying our sighs, moans, subtle praising, and compassion. Breath changes with emotion, with threat, arousal, activity, and so on. When it is held, it can reflect our anger and our fear. The depth of breath, the ease of breath, the rhythm of breath, all change automatically with our condition and mood. A sudden shock brings a gasp or a momentary cessation of breathing. A sneeze is an eruption of breath that makes one so suddenly vulnerable that we wish the sneezer good health and blessings to ward off the incursion of malicious spirits. Recognition of the breath can also transform our lives. Its release can bring us greater emotional, mental and spiritual freedom. Its study can lead us to the source of life's secrets, and the more intention and focus we bring to breath, the more deeply we connect with our original nature.

Limited Breath, Limited Life

An infant enters life with a full, deep breathing pattern. Her whole being is involved as she takes in the world through her senses, for she is still connected to the unifying field. But as this infant grows and develops, she discovers that the world is not necessarily a safe place. Parental love and approval may be conditional, and the child learns to restrain natural curiosity and spontaneity—and, in so doing, the breath. This same pattern will, more often than not, be repeated as the child enters formal schooling and conventional religious training; as perceived criticisms and approvals of teachers and peers are integrated into the growing child's self-concept. If the child receives harsh, unloving discipline or encounters traumatic experiences, the breath will be further restrained as this natural life force and the body's musculature retract from full expression. Introjected influences will have entered into the child's intrapsychic world, dominating future beliefs and behaviors, inhibiting creative power, and limiting the ability to live an authentic life.

Television and various forms of electronic media comprise yet another form of introjected influences as people are told how to dress, what to buy, what to believe, and how to behave. According to Elena Serrano and Cindy Bardon's *Kids, Food and Electronic Media* (Virginia State University Publication #349-008, June 2004):

> The average American child between the ages of 2 and 17 spends 25 hours per week watching television (approximately 20 percent to 30 percent of their waking hours). One study showed that 19 percent of children between the ages of 2 and 17 watch more than 35 hours of television per week. Most children will have spent more time in front of a television than a teacher. It is estimated that kids will have seen at least 360,000 commercials before they graduate from high school.

As s/he is initiated into mass consciousness and the commercial empire, the child integrates the emotional, mental, and physiological intensity of fast-paced entertainment. In the process, s/he loses the capacity for a natural breath with its own unique rhythm.

These experiences have the power to block emotions and create negative mindsets, thereby contributing to problems in relationships with self and others. The loss of natural rhythm can also be the initiating cause of illness. The late Sufi master Hazrat Inayat Khan noted in his *Heart of Sufism* (Boston: Shambhala, 1999, p 275) that health depends "upon the rhythm of the breath." Breath has the power not only to restore physical health and free us from psychological limitations, it can also lead us into transformation and wholeness, as evidenced in the ancient writings and teachings on the breath from Eastern and Middle Eastern traditions.

A Brief History on the Breath:
Alchemy and the Deeper Side of Transformation

The first known written account of breath training occurred approximately three thousand years ago. However, humanity's reverence and respect for the breath has a longer history than evidenced in ancient writings, as teachings on the breath were originally given only to spiritual devotees. They were deemed secret teachings—only to be given to the initiated.

Eastern and Middle Eastern traditions typically included some form of breath practice as a catalyst for alchemical transformation on physical, emotional, mental, and spiritual levels. Even though explanations and spiritual exercises differed, each depth tradition had techniques for recognizing and integrating masculine (active) and feminine (receptive) energies, emphasizing methods for balancing these two poles as part of the journey to realizing one's unity with the divine. In particular, the ancient Hindu (Vedic) teachings known as the Upanishads were filled with references to the breath, acknowledging its relationship to creation itself. Alchemical practices of Pranayam (elementary breathing practices), such as alternate nostril breathing were intended to balance masculine and feminine (active and passive) energies.

Alchemy, the spiritual process of transmutation and transformation, is believed to be a Hermetic tradition, dating back to ancient Egypt. Although the deeper practices within yogic, Buddhist, and Taoist traditions are based on alchemical processes, the actual practitioners known as *alchemists* were primarily Sufi mystics and Jewish Kabbalists who had been influenced by Hermetic teachings. Some of these practices were also woven into Greek and Roman esoteric teachings, resurfaced during the Renaissance, and are now part of the tapestry of contemporary Western thought.

Carl Jung's *Collective Works*, volumes 13 and 14, reflect his research into alchemy and coniunctio, the union of the opposites, male and female, spirit and body. His research led him to study both Kabbalah and Sufi writings. Jung found that each of these schools of thought emphasized the process of unifying masculine and feminine energies as a prerequisite to achieving cosmic unity. His research led him to conclude that the awareness of the breath encouraged recognition of different ego states, sub-personalities, and archetypal forces. As with ancient traditions, the practitioner in more modern forms of breathwork is fully engaged in a journey toward wholeness.

While alchemical breath practices aid in the recognition and balancing of opposing poles, they also integrate the elements: air, fire, earth, water, and *Ether*. Teachings and rituals related to these elements are found in Eastern, Middle Eastern, and most, if not all, indigenous cultures. For example, most readers may be familiar with terms such as the "four corners of the earth," or "the four directions" more commonly used in Native American and other indigenous traditions. Each of these directions is equated to an element, either air, fire, earth, or water. Ether is representative of the unifying field.

In a sense, Ether is synonymous with *Om* (or *Aum*). Most Westerners are familiar with this Sanskrit mantra, which is often chanted with the intention of harmonizing with cosmic energy. Max Mueller, one of the first English translators of Eastern spiritual texts, explained the use of Om in *The Upanisads* (New York: Dover, 1962, pp xxv–xxvi) as the "symbol of all speech and all life. . . . Om means Ether (akasa) and that Ether is the origin of all things . . . and that Ether is in fact one of the earliest and less perfect names of the Infinite, of Brahman, the universal Self." It is the subtle field of creation—the place where all is united. It is the divine creative force.

Opening the Field

The very breath we breathe unites us with this universal mind and creative force; and yet we choose to limit our lives, trapped in pits of despair, mediocrity, and held breath. Our awareness of and connection to the life energy is forgotten, until that magical moment when a knowledge deep within us begins to awaken. We are stirred by an inner remembrance that there is something more than the mundane goals and unfulfilled aspirations that have entertained and limited our minds. It is at this moment that the process of attaining wholeness and reexperiencing a unifying breath begins.

This book provides a variety of theories and methods evidencing the wisdom, power, and beauty of the breath. The first three parts focus on Eastern, Western, and Middle Eastern breathwork, respectively, whereas part IV addresses further considerations of the miraculous power of the breath. Each chapter within these sections contributes to this kaleido-scopic view of universal perspectives on the breath. It is noteworthy that different forms of breathwork tend to elicit different responses in the breather. The results seem to mirror the tradition's intention. For exam-ple, rebirthing, a Western practice, leads one to early life traumas and heals them, whereas the Eastern yogic breathing practices can systemati-cally awaken the sleeping serpent (Kundalini) at the base of the spine, opening the psychic energy centers. These differences alone evidence the profound creative intelligence of the mysterious breath we breathe.

Breathing practices have the potential to reverse detrimental effects of the past, for the breath provides the impetus for healing, and for recon-necting to the fuller potential imparted by the gift of life. The following glimpse into the history of the breath has the potential to deepen our understanding of its power, while drawing us into ever expanding revela-tion. This revelation is the intention inherent in this book, a collection of essays on the various ways that breath can affect our lives. Each chapter encourages readers to rediscover the healing power of the breath, each page pays tribute to the immensity of this innate power, its wisdom, and its beauty.

As Puran Bair notes in the last chapter of this book, "the exhalation is one's primary means of affecting the world." Through our conscious breathing we can bring greater peace and harmony into the world, and, in so doing, benefit all sentient beings.

Part I

Eastern Breathing Practices

In meditating, a man must have a sort of conscious intuition, so that he feels energy and breathing unite in the field of the Elixir; he must feel that a warm release belonging to the true light is beginning to stir dimly. Then he has found the right space.[1]

Introduction

The *Science of Breath*, a classic yogic text on the breath, explains that *prana* is a "universal principle . . . the essence of all motion, force or energy, whether manifested in gravitation, electricity, the revolution of the planets, and all forms of life, from the highest to the lowest."[2] It is the breath that unites us to all.

The teachings of the Far East provide explicit directions for using the breath to awaken one's spiritual nature. Yogic traditions focus on awakening the Kundalini,[3] thereby initiating this purifying and illuminating force residing as a coiled serpent at the base of the spine. Yogic breath training, Pranayama, is a process of purification, preparing the way for the rising Kundulini by balancing the masculine (active) and feminine (receptive) energies within body, mind, and soul. In my chapter, "Ancient and Modern Yoga," I explain the practice of Pranayama and how it and other yogic disciplines pave the way for the Kundalini to rise.

This spiritual awakening enables the breather to live his or her life with greater authenticity, wisdom, and compassion.

Likewise, all Buddhist traditions focus on the breath. However, they differ in regard to the process and, even more subtly, on the purpose of breath practices. For example, Theravada Buddhism, a Hinayana school, uses mindful breathing practices with the goal of the individual attainment of nirvana (boundless life beyond all desire). Tibetan Buddhism, a Mahayana school, specifically focuses on opening the heart to compassion and obtaining enlightenment for the benefit of all living beings. Michael Essex, Timothy Laporte, and Drupon Samten Rinpoche discuss the relevance of the breath from a Tibetan Buddhist perspective in their chapter, "Buddhism and the Breath." The authors point out that as we deepen "our awareness of the breath, it is possible to ease our suffering, to clear away our ignorance, and to move ever closer to the limitless compassion and wisdom of the Buddha."

When Buddhism migrated from India into Asia, it embodied yogic methods for breath training, but these breathing techniques are also found in early Chinese texts. For example, *The Secret of the Golden Flower,* which contains the teachings of *The Book of Consciousness and Life* (an early Chinese text emphasizing a rotating mindful breath), discusses how "The rotation method makes use of breathing to blow on the fire of the gates of life; in this way one succeeds in bringing the true energy to its original place."[4] Although the terminology differs, there is a strong correlation to yogic teachings on the process of awakening Kundalini.

Taoism has specific breathing practices for balancing and working with ch'i. Dr. Benjamin Tong's chapter, "The Breath of the Tao and the Tao of Breathing," exemplifies the unique emphasis found in Chinese Taoist philosophy and its use of breath. It is a wholistic path, uniting the elements, body, mind, and spirit. Dr. Tong is a long-time practitioner and teacher of Taoism and its focus on the Tao (the Way).

Obviously, the above Eastern traditions have long recognized the power and presence of breath as the basic foundation of spiritual development. This recognition is also found at the heart of another Eastern tradition, the martial arts. In Chapter 4, "Breathing Respect: Breath and the Martial Way of Aikido," Sensei Darrell Bluhm, provides insight into the movement of breath as related to the martial arts. For instance, in his discussion of the process of working with the sword, Bluhm Sensei explains the importance of "inhaling with the upswing and exhaling with the downswing." The conscious awareness of the breath reinforces the art of martial movement.

The ancient Chinese wisdom recorded within *The Secret of the Golden Flower* shows the breath to be both our foundation and our liberation. This same teaching is found throughout the mystical teachings of the Far East. Enlightenment is not achieved through intellect alone, true spiritual awakening includes the body. Breathing practices bring mind and body into harmony, enabling a porosity of being through which the soulic *Ethers* enter into one's daily life. The chapters of part I offer an illuminating journey into the Eastern traditions that utilize this healing power of the breath.

Notes

1. Richard Wilhelm (ed.), *The Secret of the Golden Flower* (New York: Harcourt, Brace and World, 1962), 48.

2. Yogi Ramacharaka, *The Science of Breath* (Chicago: Yogi Publication Society, 1904), 19.

3. Kundalini is a Sanskrit term. It refers to a lock of hair from the beloved. In the Yogic tradition this strand represents a feminine energy coiled up like a snake at the base of the spine. Once aroused, typically through yogic breath and breathing postures, its purifying and enlightening energy rises through the chakras.

4. Richard Wilhelm (ed.), *The Secret of the Golden Flower* (New York: Harcourt, Brace and World, 1962), 61.

1

Ancient and Modern Yoga

A Science of Breath, Healing, and Enlightenment

SHARON G. MIJARES

Introduction

Seated in a half-yoga lotus position at a local athletic club, students slowly inhale through one nostril, hold the breath, and then slowly exhale through the opposite. They may hear the instructor call this practice pranayama, but the majority of these students have little, if any, understanding with regard to the translation and history of the term. They are unaware of the deeper intention within this ancient yogic practice.

This chapter addresses a process of spiritual awakening that had its beginnings in ancient Vedic teachings. It is an introduction to the spiritual and scientific yogic methods through which this awakening is obtained—specifically in the area of breath training.

Yoga's foundational practices and philosophy undergird the journey of awakening to one's divine nature, uniting mind, body, and spirit. The term "yoga" actually means to yoke or join together.[1] This unifying principle is manifest in the yogic understanding and practices related to the breath, postures, chants, and teachings as described in the following historical development.

Vedic Teachings on the Breath

There is no consensus as to when the Vedic-Yogic tradition began. Although there is historical confirmation that the Vedic religion was in place by 5000 BCE[2] differing yogic schools place its initial emergence at some time in between 8,000 to 10,000 years ago.[3] Ancient findings suggest the Vedic people of early India practiced shamanic, communal rituals intended to both heal and transcend ordinary human consciousness.[4] Early yoga continued to emphasize these ritual communal practices, incorporating and expanding upon the unique transcendent processes; but as yoga continued its development it gave less attention to shared ritual and, instead, placed increasing relevance on individual inner experience. In particular, it focused on practices that encouraged an inner realization of one's divinity. One sacred text, known as the *Rig Veda*, believed to be one of the oldest texts, in an Indo-European language (Sanskrit), referred to breath as the bringer of life, creator, and purifier (which is to say, prana).[5]

The mystical teachings of the Vedas were designed to evoke and affirm the divine presence to be found within each human being. A Sanskrit saying "Tat Twan Asi" (That thou art) conveys this understanding for it acknowledges a recognition that God is to be found within the human being. The breath is noted throughout the Vedic scriptures. Its authors knew the breath facilitated awareness of the innate divine nature.

Scriptural texts, known as the Upanishads, emerged later, some time between 1500 and 300 BCE (accounts vary). They expounded upon the doctrine of the Atman, the divinity within. For example, the Brihadaranyaka Upanishad advised its readers that,

> Whoever worships another divinity than his self, thinking, "He is one, I am another, knows not. . . . One should worship with the thought that he is one's self, for therein all these become one. This self is the footprint of that All, for by it one knows the All—just as, verily, by following a footprint one

may find cattle that have been lost. . . . One should reverence the self alone as dear. And he who reverences the self alone as dear—what he holds dear, verily, will not perish.[6]

Vedic Yoga emphasized a three-fold method for spiritual development.[7] The first aspect, *Mantra Yoga,* is a mantric practice that focuses on the sacred names of deities such as Shiva, Krishna, Ram,[8] and others and also the qualities of, and leading to, the divine. Often root sounds such as OM, AIM, HUM, HRIM, KRIM, and SHRIM are chanted.[9] These mantras are considered universal principles and convey divine qualities. Sacred sounds are both intoned and repeated in harmony with the breath. The intention is that these sacred mantras resonate with the vibration of the deity and/or quality of the divine. Just as the river eventually unites with the greater ocean, the chanter's mantric practice evokes a field of energy with the vibrational power to lead her into divine realization.

The second focus of Vedic Yoga is *Prana Yoga*, the yoga of the breath leading to the awakening of the internal pranic energy. The Prasna Upanishad[10] notes five different forms of prana in Hindu physiology, denoting directions of pranic movement. *Prana* is interpreted as "breathing forth," and the early teachings claimed this initial momentum to be based in the heart, dwelling place of the Atman. *Apana* is "breathing away." Its impetus is centered within the intestines and digestive system. *Vyana* is the breath that moves in differing directions, pervading the entire body. *Udana* is the "up" breath, initiated from the throat. *Samana* is "breathing together." It is a central breath, based within the navel. In short, these early yogis were researching the breath, and learning all they could about its flow. Mindfulness of the breath deepens one's emotional, mental and spiritual awareness. As one begins the practice of conscious breathing, the breather's sensory awareness expands. Many people have not experienced their capacity for breathing through and to different areas of the body. The following exercise, "Breath Awareness," encourages awareness of these differing movements:

Sit quietly with your spine erect.
Be aware of the originating impulse for your inhale.
Be aware of the originating impulse for your exhale.
Can you feel the space in between?
What else do you notice about its movement?

The last focus of this Vedic yoga triad is *Dhyana Yoga*,[11] wherein one meditates upon the Divine Self. The primary emphasis of Vedic yoga is mantra, breath, and meditation. Yogis recognize that mantric entoning, breathing practices and meditation bring the devotee into higher states of consciousness. Prana Yoga, the precise science of the breath, will be the topic of this chapter.

Classical Yoga: Patanjali's Yoga Sutras

Classical Yoga emerged shortly after the turn of the millennium. It was influenced by Patanjali's *Yoga Sutra* (200 CE)[12] and his related yogic model, Raja Yoga (*yoga-darshana*). Pantanjali's Yoga Sutra was comprised of 196 aphorisms, expounding upon the practices related to Raja Yoga, known as the "eight-limbed" path. Classical Yoga is founded precisely upon these eight limbs, a purification system intended to lead the practitioner to enlightenment. The first two limbs, restraint (*yama*) and observance (*niyama*) recognize the importance of developing a spiritual foundation based upon ethics and morality. The next three limbs are physical exercises, such as the postures (*asanas*), found in Hatha Yoga; control of prana through breathing practices (*pranayama*); and beginning meditation training (*pratyahara*). The final three limbs regard the training of the mind developed through concentration (*dharana*), meditation (*dhyana*), and, ultimately, the complete realization and union with the Divine (*samadhi*). In short, Patanjali's spiritual training model represents a path leading to Self-realization, freedom from the lesser self, and its illusions (*kaivalya*).

Prior to Pantanjali's Yoga Sutras, mind and body were seen as one, each manifested from the same primordial source (*prakriti*). The body was an extension of the Atman within. Classical Yoga was inherently dualistic in nature for it separated body/matter (*prakriti*) from pure spirit (*purusha*). Its overall goal was to train the body, and in so doing discover pure consciousness. As time passed Yogic practitioners began to focus more on concentration and meditation, while ignoring the body and yogic postures (*asanas*). In many ways this dualistic view paralleled Christianity's negation of the body, as both traditions emphasized a spiritual focus believed to be superior to life in the present moment.

Postclassical Yoga

A primary impetus of Postclassical Yoga was centered on the debate between dualistic and nondualistic views of spirituality. In response, Tantric, Kundalini, and Hatha Yoga traditions emerged, offering nondualistic yogic traditions.[13]

The dualistic view infers that humanity suffers from its disconnection with the Atman or higher Self, that suffering is the result of the attraction to the illusionary world (*maya*), and that liberation comes with the realization of the true Self. The nondualistic view presents a different slant on the issue. For example, suffering results when we make the distinction of a lesser self and a greater Self, and suffering occurs when we ignore the fact that we are part of a larger reality.

The dualist sees the world as a theater, the stage upon which we live out our illusionary dramas. The nondualist recognizes the element of reality within our everyday life for we are real people engaged in life experience. In this view, there is a recognition that the Divine, like the breath, is to be found within all experience.

Tantra Yoga, a nondualistic yogic practice, began some time before the turn of the millennium. Tantric Yoga had its foundations in the worship of the Indian deities, Shakti, the creative feminine life force, and her consort, Shiva, the passive masculine force. Tantric practices are geared toward awakening the enlightening force, the Kundalini, to be found within the human being. In this sense, Tantric Yoga is affiliated with the later development of what is now known as Kundalini Yoga. In its essence, Tantric Yoga is concerned with unifying the mind with experience, as the practitioner becomes at one with the prayer, meditation, and mantric and breathing practices. Tantric Yoga may also include knowing divine unity through sexual union.

Hatha Yoga, also a nondualistic tradition, emerged around the ninth century. Hatha Yoga is the practice of physical postures (*asanas*), and sessions usually include more basic breathing practices (*pranayama*). Today, besides the deeper teachings and advanced practices at ashrams and yoga centers throughout the world, Hatha Yoga classes are taught in neighborhood yoga studios and athletic clubs. The term "hatha" represents the unity of male and female in its name (leading to wholeness). This unity is inherent in the title for "ha" is the word for sun, and "tha" for moon.

The goal is one of uniting opposites, male and female, light and dark. The postures are intended to balance and lead the practitioner to wholeness. The tradition is based upon a guru-student relationship (*gurukhulu*) and includes a purification process of diet, ethics, etc., prior to engaging in pranayama and the asanas.

In recent times, there is an increasing interest in practicing the various asanas, and pranayama. For example, many persons practice Ashtanga Yoga, which emphasizes attaining power through strength and endurance; Iyengar Yoga whose focus is alignment and balance; the classical yoga rooted in Sivananda Yoga, a traditional and holistic approach; and a Yoga known as Bikram, which is practiced in a heated room with the belief that heat accelerates physical flexibility. Many are training in these disciplines. Yet it can also be somewhat overwhelming to the beginner, who is confronted with the array of choices. I would suggest that there is no "superior" form, but rather it is best to visit various schools to find which one most resonates with one's own preferences, and to find the teacher(s) who exemplifies the type of yoga one wishes to learn.

As noted at the beginning of this chapter, training in yogic postures, along with a brief introduction to breathing exercises, has become a traditional part of many holistic health programs. Many Westerners see yoga as exercises promoting health, strength, and relaxation. The deeper journey includes spiritual realization, with a greater emphasis on meditation and breathing practices as discussed in the following sections.

Yoga and the Western World

Numerous yogic traditions have influenced the development of yoga in the Western world. For example, Swami Vivekananda (1863–1902), a disciple of the late Hindu saint, Ramakrishna, brought Ramakrishna's yogic teachings into the West and supported the development of the Vedanta Society in America. Vivekananda made quite an impression on all attendees of the first Parliament of World Religions, convened in Chicago in 1893. One attendee, Professor John Henry Wright of Harvard University respectfully exclaimed, "To ask you, Swami, for your credentials is like asking the sun about its right to shine."[14] Vivekananda introduced many Americans to yogic *pranayama*, the path to divine realization through the breath.

The Yogi Publication Society in Chicago published *The Science of the Breath*[15] in 1904, openly providing instruction on breathing practices. The text classified respiration into four different manners of breathing; namely, (1) high breathing, (2) mid breathing, (3) low breathing, and (4) Yogi complete breathing. The first three were deemed as incomplete breathing methods. A complete breath includes the positive points of high, mid, and low breathing and does so in a way that allows a maximum amount of benefit to be achieved using the least amount of energy. The following exercise, "Complete Yogic Breath," is an example from this treatise:

> Sitting erect, inhale steadily through the nostrils, filling the lower, middle and higher portions of the chest.
>
> Feel your entire chest expand, until the lower part of the abdomen is slightly drawn in.
>
> Retain the breath for a few seconds
>
> Exhale very slowly, holding the chest up in a firm posture. Draw the abdomen in and upward as the air slowly leaves the lungs.
>
> Relax the abdomen and the chest. (Adapted from *The Science of Breath*)

Paramahansa Yogananda (1893–1952) founded the Self Realization Fellowship (SRF) in 1920. His teachings of *Kriya Yoga* are widely practiced and taught in various SRF ashrams throughout the United States. Kriya Yoga is a breathing method that draws on energy deep within our spines. Using awareness and will, the yoga student mentally draws this energy up and down the spine. These techniques are shared with their students, but not publicly.[16]

Sri Aurobindo (1872–1950) established what is known as Integral Yoga, which is tantric in nature. He noted the *ascent* of consciousness through the chakra system, and also pointed out the relevance of the *descent*. He pointed out that one could not control the process of illumination; it is ordained by the grace of the Mother (supreme power). Aurobindo believed "it was the destiny of the body to grow into a divine body; its purpose is to pour out and breathe forth the delight of being and becoming."[17] The practices of pranayama, mantra, asanas and meditation enable the body to develop a porosity enabling oneness with Spirit.

Kundalini Yoga is a tantric tradition in that it views the body as a means, rather than an opposition, to enlightenment. Understanding and respecting the deeper nature of the body, the late Yogi Bhajan (1929–2004) introduced American students to Kundalini Yoga in the early 1970s, establishing a training school known as the 3-H Foundation (Happy, Healthy, and Holy). Yogi Bhajan broke the long tradition of secrecy concerning these deeper yogic teachings, when he introduced the yoga exercises to all who sought them. In particular, he was a teacher of teachers, intending these teachers to extend this yoga tradition to others. Yogi Bhajan declared the body to be a temple, "in which you can deposit the treasure of happiness of life."[18] He presented a program for Kundalini awakening, including the disciplines of diet, ethics, asanas, mantras, and breathing practices.

The Deeper Side of Yoga

We have entered an era that recognizes the importance of unifying body, mind, and spirit. Yoga represents an important influence in helping to heal the split between mind and body, heaven and earth, male and female. Thanks to the above yoga masters, and many more not listed, we have the teachings to both understand and apply the methods that enable healing and enlightenment. The following pages provide a yet deeper investigation into yoga.

According to yogic philosophy there are seven primary psychic energy centers located in specific areas of the human body. These centers are known as chakras (Sanskrit for wheels). The yogic practices, in particular, breathing processes, encourage an increasing movement of pranic energy throughout the body. This process represents a purifying journey that eventually awakens the sleeping serpent, the Kundalini, the enlightening power coiled at the base of the spine. Once awakened, this powerful energy, moves through the chakras clearing the path for enlightenment to take place as the body receives the spiritual force hidden deep within.

First chakra, the Muladhara, is located at the base of the spine, between the anus and the genitals. It represents a basic grounding in the body, and one's sense of security in life.

Second chakra, the Svadhistana, is located in the area of the genitals. It is related to sexuality, balance of polarities and creative energy.

Third chakra, the Manipura, is located at the navel and is corresponds to the solar plexus area. It is related to fear, courage and centeredness.

Fourth chakra, the Anahata, is the region of the heart center. It is related to our capacity to open to love.

Fifth chakra, Vishuddha, is located at the base of the throat. As it opens one develops the ability to speak authentically.

Sixth chakra, the Ajna, is in the space between the eyebrows, known as the third eye. As this power center is activated, the awakening human being's perception is exhilarated. This can increase the capacity for intuitional knowledge.

Seventh chakra, Sahasrara, is at the crown of the head, corresponding to the pineal gland. This opens like a flower to receive the grace inherent within the Divine. It is the center of pure consciousness.

The Alchemy of Illumination

The Yoga tradition recognizes 72,000 energy meridians, comprising a subtle nervous system flowing throughout the human body. It also recognizes three specific meridians/nerves, known as the ida, pingala, and sushumna (Sanskrit), all corresponding to the column of sensory and motor fibers in the spine. The ida is a neural pathway associated with the receptive, feminine aspect of our nature, flowing from the left nostril to the right side of the base of the sushumna, whereas the pingala is associated with the active, masculine side and moves from the right nostril to the left side of the sushumna.

Nitya Chaitanya Yati explains in his book, *Pranayama*, that the "Pingala is life-consuming and is called solar" whereas the "prana that operates the ida is life-generating and called lunar."[19] The goal of the following "Pranayama Exercise" is to stimulate and clear these channels through alternate nostril breathing. This particular form of pranayama encourages a balancing of masculine and feminine energies deep within the body. The sushumna is the central stem, connected to the ida and pingala. As the lunar and solar energies flowing through the ida and pingala are purified and balanced, they have an effect upon the sushumna, which moves through the central axis of the chakras (psychic energy centers).

> Using the right hand place your thumb over your right nostril, your index and middle fingers at the brow chakra, and your ring finger over the left nostril.
>
> Releasing the thumb, breath in the right nostril to a slow count of four.
>
> Hold for four counts.
>
> Release slowly out the left nostril while closing the right nostril with your thumb (to a count of four)
>
> Now repeat, but breathe in through the left nostril, hold and release through the right one.
>
> Repeat this entire process four times on each nostril.
>
> Now release your hands and simply breathe in through both nostrils simultaneously in the same rhythm of four counts, hold, and then release.
>
> Do this phase four times and then sit quietly aware of your natural breath, feelings, and sensations.

Elementary pranayama, alternative nostril breathing, represents a scientific method established to prepare the devotee for the illuminating experience of Kundalini, the awakening of the *coiled serpent* residing deep at the base of the spine. As the Kundalini activates and psychic energy enters into the sushumna, it rises through the chakras, illuminating the devotee's consciousness.

The word, Kundalini, actually refers to a snake. *Kundal* can be translated as "the coil in the hair of the beloved." This refers to the long hair of the ancient yogic ascetics, which was coiled up in a bun on top of their heads. The *ini* at the end of the word provides its feminine connotation.

This is the experience inherent within the metaphor of Shakti and Shiva. Kundalini Shakti is asleep at the base of the Muladhara. Up until now, the human being has been thus unaware of his or her larger identity, seeing only the outer world, but as Shakti awakens and unites with Shiva, the supreme consciousness, the human being is awakened to the divine nature, thereby experiencing a oneness with all life, heaven, and earth.

The awakened devotee manifests kindness and compassion. There is a greater clarity of mind, with intention and will directed toward good. The Kundalini awakening brings one into spiritual awareness and its accompanying development.

In fact, this illuminating healing process is portrayed in a well-known image, the medical symbol, known as the caduceus. The central stem of the caduceus represents the *sushumna*, with the healing influence of the Kundalini. The two coiling snake forms weaving up the central stem are archetypically related to the ida and the pingala. The caduceus represents what heals and makes whole, and, likewise, the awakening of the Kundalini embodies the way of healing and wholeness. And this is the greater intention in the breathing practices taught in yoga classes.

No one knows when the Kundalini experience will manifest, but when it awakens it brings one into a unitive experience, and is considered an act of divine Grace. The breath and other exercises prepare the way, but the timing is in the hands of the Divine.

Guidance on the Path

Overall yoga classes represent a positive trend, as participants are focusing on strengthening their bodies, disciplining their minds, and experiencing a greater sense of peace. They also learn to inhale and exhale with the extending and contracting movements. This balance of breath and movement creates a sense of well-being, but it can also increase pranic energies and unleash unresolved emotional issues.[20] Sometimes the yoga exercises can help integrate these energies; whereas at other times it may simply increase the problem. Along these lines, there is some concern regarding the numerous yoga classes led by yoga teachers who may have certifications for teaching the asanas, but who lack an in-depth understanding and training in the inherent power within these yoga disciplines. In other words, they may lack the personal experience of the phenomena associated with Kundalini.

This is the challenge of our current era. Previously yogic exercises were held sacred, and only given to disciples immersed in yoga training. Teachers trained in the mysteries, knowledgeable on a variety of levels watched over the student's development. This paradigm is changing. We are in the midst of this change, as secret teachings are the way of the past. The patriarchal relationship of guru over student is also undergoing an immense transformation, and yet it is fair to say that there are those who have more knowledge and experience than others. It is a blessing to receive the guidance of those who know the way to a fuller and healthier life. The loss of the guru's knowledge would be a great loss indeed! So the current transformation is a matter of finding a right balance, one of "power with" rather than "power over."

The Inner Guru

There is an inner guru guiding the process, and once the Kundalini has awakened, the devotee is aware of the divine Yogi within. This is the point when one truly becomes a Yogi, having achieved Self-Knowledge, and a renewed understanding of the universe. He or she is now dedicated to serving life. Yogi Bhajan claimed that "the sign of the Kundalini energy is the expansive consciousness, the compassion, and the practicality of the being who acts in humility before the Infinite Creator."[21] The Yogi's breath is at one with the Divine.

In summary, the breath is a guide. The yoga of awareness and attention to the breath is the path leading to realization of the Divine. As we bring our breath into alignment with our movements, our vocalizations, and our meditative concentration we live the yoga of life.

Notes

1. Eleanor Criswell and Kartikeya Patel, "The Yoga Path: Awakening from the Dream," in *Modern Psychology and Ancient Wisdom: Psychological Healing Practices from the World's Religious Traditions*, ed. Sharon Mijares (Binghamton, NY: Haworth Press, 2003), 201–36.

2. Geoffrey Parrinder (ed.), *World Religions from Ancient History to the Present,* (New York: Facts on File, 1971).

3. Research in this area reveals there is no historical consensus providing a concise time for its emergence.

4. Mircea Eliade, *A History of Religious Ideas: From the Stone Age to the Eleusian Mysteries,* trans. Willard R. Trask (Chicago: University of Chicago Press, 1978).

5. Joseph Campbell, *The Mythic Image,* (Princeton, NJ: Princeton University Press, 1974).

6. Brihadaranyaka Upanishad, in Joseph Campbell, *The Mythic Image,* (Princeton, NJ: Princeton University Press, 1974), 278–79.

7. Based on Sri Aurobindo's (1872–1950) philosophy and practice of Integral Yoga.

8. Various yogic traditions entone the names of particular deities, but in concern for gender balance it is important to note that each of these named male deities has a female consort—Durga, Radha, and Sita, respectively.

9. Although numerous sources expound on these mantric sounds, the following website offers concise descriptions and is a good resource: Mantras and Vidyas: Godhead as Sound (1975–2007), http://www.shivashakti.com/mantra.htm.

10. Eknath Easwaran and Michael N. Nagler, *The Upanishads,* trans. Eknath Easwaran (Tomales, CA: Nilgiri Press, 2007).

11. Ian Whicher with contributions from Ian Whicher and Julius Lipner, *Yoga: Tradition and Transformation* (New York: Routledge, 2000).

12. Max Mueller, *Six Systems of Indian Philosophy; Samkhya and Yoga, Naya and Vaiseshika* (Calcutta: Susil Gupta). Originally published as *The Six Systems of Indian Philosophy,* 1899.

13. K. A. Jacobsen (ed.), Theory and Practice of Yoga: Essays in Honour of Gerald James Larson (Boston: Brill, 2005), 210.

14. http://www.ramakrishna.org/sv_sa.htm.

15. Yogi Ramacharaka, *The Hindu-Yogi Science of Breath* (Chicago: Yogi Publication Society, 1904).

16. It is fair to note that numerous yogic schools have been established in the last century. All those known and unknown are acknowledged in this short chapter whether mentioned or not.

17. Vasant V. Merchant and Sri Aurobindo, "The Tantra and Kundalini," in *Kundalini, Evolution and Enlightenment,* edJohn White (New York: Paragon House, 1990), 77.

18. Gurucharan Singh Khalsa, *Sadhana Guidelines* (Los Angeles: Kundalini Research Institute, 1974 [1988]), 4.

19. Nitya Chaitanya Yati, *Pranayama* (India. Mangala Press, 1979), 7 and 23.

20. Examples of this are included in chapter 15, "Be Wary When You Breathe."

21. Gurucharan Singh Khalsa, "Exploring the Myths and Misconceptions of Kundalini," in *Kundalini, Evolution and Enlightenment*, ed. John White (New York: Paragon House, 1990), 133.

2

Tibetan Buddhism
and the Breath

MICHAEL ESSEX AND TIMOTHY LAPORTE
WITH DRUPON SAMTEN RINPOCHE

Introduction

Of all our physical activities, it is the simple act of breathing that is most capable of linking our physical and psychological natures. As we move through the ups and downs of life, the quality of our mental states extends an active influence over our breathing patterns, and our ever-changing state of being is constantly reflected through the mirror of our respiration. Although the breath is such a natural part of us, it is easy to lose contact with this aspect of ourselves in our increasingly fragmented and frenetic modern world. Ultimately, this too is reflected in our breathing: the breath becomes weak, shallow, and uneven, and our minds quickly follow suit, overwhelming us with random, erratic thoughts, anxiety, and the inability to concentrate. Clearly, there is a need to reconnect with this essential part of ourselves—the breath—and in so doing, to reclaim a basic sanity and peace of mind.

For centuries, the spiritual tradition of Tibetan Buddhism has recognized the interrelated nature of the breath and mind, and it has developed countless methods that harness the power of the breath in order to facilitate a deeply transformative spiritual practice. Practicing high in the spectacular, yet unforgiving terrain of the Himalayan Mountains, generations of Tibetan yogis have utilized the breath as a powerful tool in the quest for enlightenment, and they have transmitted this wisdom down to the present time through unbroken lineages of teacher-disciple relationships. Some practices are simple and can be undertaken by anyone, while others require years of mental and physical training under the supervision of an accomplished master. Nevertheless, the basic message remains the same: by deepening our awareness of the breath, it is possible to ease our suffering, to clear away our ignorance, and to move ever closer to the limitless compassion and wisdom of the Buddha. Given how disconnected we often feel in modern society—from ourselves, from others, and from our spiritual nature—it seems there is much that we can learn from this ancient Tibetan wisdom of the breath.

In this chapter, we will explore a few different Tibetan Buddhist meditations that involve the breath and explain how they fit within the larger scope of Buddhist understanding. We remind the reader that this chapter is nothing more than an introduction to the subject, and that he or she should seek guidance from a qualified teacher in order to put such techniques into practice. Finally, we hope that these practices will be of benefit to sentient beings, especially to those who have lost touch with the deeper dimension of life, and those who are seeking to rekindle the light of the sacred within themselves.

Breath as Tool, Breath as Teacher

From its inception, the Buddhist tradition has employed the breath in a dual manner as a means for imparting its teachings. On one hand, the breath is utilized as an effective tool to help the student gain leverage in his or her quest for meditative stabilization. Simultaneously, however, the breath also functions as a kind of teaching-in-action that helps to reveal the Buddhist truth (Sanskrit. *Dharma*, Tibetan pronunciation. chö, Tibetan. *chos*) in active process. According to the Pali scriptures, which comprise the oldest complete canon of Buddhist teachings that are still extant, the deep connection between the breath and Buddhist teachings finds its origin in the *Satipatthana-sutta*, which is one of the primary meditation manuals that is utilized today by the Theravada school of Buddhism in Sri Lanka and Southeast Asia. In this famous discourse on meditative technique, the Buddha forever cemented the importance of the breath as an object of meditation by describing it first in his exposition. He is reported to have spoken:

> Here *Bhikkhus*, a *bhikkhu* having gone to the forest, to the foot of a tree or to some empty place, sits down with his legs crossed, keeps his body straight and his mindfulness alert.
>
> Ever mindful he breathes in, and ever mindful he breathes out. Breathing in a long breath, he knows "I am breathing in a long breath;" breathing out a long breath, he knows "I am breathing out a long breath;" breathing in a short breath, he knows "I am breathing in a short breath;" breathing out a short breath, he knows "I am breathing out a short breath."
>
> "Experiencing the whole body, I shall breathe in;" thus he trains himself. "Experiencing the whole body, I shall breathe out;" thus he trains himself. "Calming the activity of the body, I shall breathe in;" thus he trains himself. "Calming the activity of the body, I shall breathe out;" thus he trains himself.
>
> Thus he lives observing (the activities of) the body internally, or . . . externally, or . . . both internally and externally. Or his mindfulness is established to the extent necessary just for knowledge and awareness that the body exists, and he lives unattached and clings to naught in the world.[1]

The Buddha therefore encouraged his disciples to utilize the breath both as a tool for "calming the activity of the body," and also as a means for revealing the true way for an earnest disciple to live: "unattached," and clinging to "naught in the world."

We find a similar attitude toward the breath, as both a meditative tool and a form of teaching-in-action, in Japanese Zen Buddhism as well, which utilizes concentration upon the breath as a method for directly discerning the type of "non-dual" reality espoused by this tradition. This form of meditation, known as zazen, also fosters a direct experience of the Buddhist teaching of emptiness of the self. The twentieth century Zen roshi, Shunryo Suzuki, who helped to plant Zen Buddhism in America, describes this process as follows:

> When we practice zazen our mind always follows our breathing. When we inhale, the air comes into the inner world. When we exhale, the air goes out to the outer world. The inner world is limitless, and the outer world is also limitless. We say "inner world" or "outer world," but actually there is just one whole world. In this limitless world, our throat is like a swinging door. The air comes in and goes out like someone passing through a swinging door. If you think, "I breathe," the "I" is extra. There is no you to say "I." What we call "I" is just a swinging door which moves when we inhale and when we exhale. It just moves; that is all. When your mind is pure and calm enough to follow this movement, there is nothing: no "I," no world, no mind nor body; just a swinging door.[2]

The Tibetan Buddhist tradition utilizes the breath in a similar manner as both an object of meditative concentration, and also more subtly as an expedient for revealing the essence of the realizations that it seeks to convey. In comparison with the two traditions mentioned above, however, the Tibetan understanding of breath is somewhat more complicated because it is dependent upon a conception of the universe which, in many respects, is deeply divergent from the Western worldview. Moreover, the breath is an important issue in Tibetan thought that has ramifications across a diverse spectrum of fields ranging from cosmology and philosophy to medicinal theory and anatomy, and, of course, the theory and practice of meditation. Therefore, understanding the role of the breath in Tibetan Buddhism requires that we grasp its inherent interrelatedness with these deeper issues.

Breath, Wind, and Mind

From the standpoint of Tibetan Buddhism, the breath is far more than a simple physiological mechanism that sustains our respiratory and organic processes. Indeed, the Tibetan tradition regards the breath as possessing an almost magical quality that serves to connect us with a vibrant and profound world that lies directly beneath the pain and confusion which are pervasive throughout the conditions of our mundane existence. This mystical understanding of the breath derives specifically from its close connection with two other important concepts in Tibetan thought: wind and mind. Comprehending these subtleties will give us a better grasp of its precise role in the meditation practices that we will discuss toward the end of this chapter.

In Tibetan, the word for respiration is *dbugs* (which is pronounced roughly "oog" or "woog," depending on where the speaker comes from in Tibet). However, this term refers not only to the literal physical breath that moves in and out during our respiration, but also to a type of "subtle breath" that courses through the entirety of our body via a network of similarly subtle channels (Skt. *nadi*, Tib. tsa, *rtsa*).

This understanding of the subtle breath is intimately related with another important Tibetan concept, that of air or wind. The Tibetan word for wind is *rlung* (pro. loong), and this has at least three important meanings. On the first level, *rlung* refers to the element of air, which is one of the five basic elements from which the universe (including human beings) is constructed. In this context, *rlung* refers to the principles of lightness and movement in all things and it is the translation for the Sanskrit term *vayu*. In another sense, *rlung* refers more broadly to a type of subtle energy that is pervasive throughout the universe and has properties of consciousness, and here it is the translation of the Sanskrit word *prana*. In this second context, *rlung* could be associated with *any* of the five elements that construct the world.[3] Also, according to Tibetan medical theory *rlung*, or wind, is one of the three humors that work together to produce the overall state of health in the human body (the other humors are bile [tipa, *mkhris pa*] and phlegm [bekan, *bad kan*]).

Furthermore, the wind itself is intertwined with the Tibetan under-standing of mind, or awareness.[4] Though the distinction between mind and wind is subtle, it is important for correctly understanding the pre-cise meaning of breath in Tibetan Buddhism. To be specific, the mind is the relatively passive "knowing" aspect of consciousness, but the wind is a motive force that situates this awareness in a particular location. Traditionally, the mind (*sems*) is described as riding upon the wind as an equestrian upon a horse. To illustrate this point, let us use the example of a virtuoso guitarist. While performing, this excellent musician will be intently focused on the sensations of his fingers plucking the strings and moving around on the fretboard, and he will also be aware of more general sensations such as the positioning of his arms and the basic state of his body as it anchors into the chair in which he sits. From the standpoint of Tibetan Buddhism, this display of precision and mastery is made possible by the mind and wind acting together in perfect concert. The guitarist's mind, or knowing aspect, rides on the wind into his arms and hands, enabling him to make such precise and intricate movements. The wind brings his awareness into the place of concentration, but the mind is the quality of awareness itself.

Breath and Cosmology

These three interrelated concepts—breath, wind, and mind—are products of a worldview that is quite different from that which is predominant in the West, and thus a few words on these critical differences in perspective are merited. Indeed, the role of the breath in Tibetan Buddhism is an issue that impinges directly upon the constituents of the universe itself as understood by Tibetan cosmology. As opposed to the Western scientific worldview, which primarily views the universe from a materialistic perspective, the Tibetan understanding is inclined to view the universe from the standpoint of consciousness. Therefore, while the West tends to round out its materialistic conception of the universe by dividing inert matter into smaller and smaller constituents until one arrives finally at the world of atoms and subatomic particles, the Tibetan view, on the other hand, attempts to analyze the phenomenon of consciousness in a similar way until one can ultimately discern the fundamental constituents of consciousness. Viewing the universe from this different perspective is what unlocks the great power of the breath in the Tibetan tradition because, as we will see, the breath serves as a mediator between ordinary physicality and the subtler levels of consciousness that lie beneath it.

The basic outlines of this cosmology of consciousness follow a general threefold classification. This understanding is perhaps most clearly expressed in the doctrine of the "three bodies of the Buddha."[5] According to this theory, the Buddha is said to possess three different, yet interconnected "bodies." The actual physical body of the Buddha is referred to as his "manifestation body," (Skt. *nirmanakaya*, Tib. tulku, *sprul sku*). Beneath this physical existence is a subtler body known as the "complete enjoyment body" (Skt. *sambhogakaya*, Tib. longcho dzok pay ku, *longs spyod rdzog pa'i sku*), which is composed out of a collection of subtle energies and "winds" that are at least somewhat independent of the physical body. Subtler still and lying beneath the *sambhogakaya* is a third "body," which is really not a body in the conventional sense. This "body" is pervasive throughout the entire universe and is said to have the properties of clear light and innate wakefulness. It is referred to as the "truth body" of the Buddha (Skt. *dharmakaya*, Tib. cho kyi ku, *chos kyi sku*).

It is important to understand that this teaching on the Buddha's three bodies is really a description of the universe itself. The material world with which we are familiar, and which is the object of study for Western science, is only the grossest level of manifestation and has its equivalence in the Buddha's *nirmanakaya*. Lying beneath this is a world of subtle energies that can be broken down into five fundamental "elements"—earth, water, fire, air, and space. Subtler still is the final level of reality, which is the basis of everything in the universe. This is often referred to as the "nature of mind," and it is identical with the *dharmakaya* that we have just described.

This most basic level of mind is of utmost importance in Tibetan Buddhism. It is simultaneously the ultimate nature of reality, the fundamental essence of the universe, and the highest good. Despite its centrality to Tibetan Buddhist thought, or perhaps because of it, the nature of mind is a very subtle concept that is difficult to articulate precisely and that tends to resist simple classification. A seventeenth century Tibetan text expresses it as follows:

> Mind has no form, color, or concrete substance.
> It is not to be found anywhere outside or within your body, nor in between.
> It is not found to be a concrete thing,
> Even if you were to search throughout the ten directions.
> It does not arise from anywhere, nor does it abide and disappear at any place.
> Yet, it is not nonexistent, since your mind is vividly awake.
> It is not a singularity, because it manifests in manifold ways.
> Nor is it a plurality, because all these are of one essence.
> There is no one who can describe its nature.

> But, when expressing its resemblance, there is no end to what
> can be said.
> It may be given many kinds of names such as "mind essence,"
> "I," or the "all-ground."
> It is the very basis of samsara and nirvana.[6]

Despite the fact that mind "is not found to be a concrete thing," it is nevertheless regarded as the fundamental basis for all phenomenal manifestations. This has profound implications that extend throughout Tibetan thought, and these are especially apparent in the Buddhist teaching of reincarnation. The death of the physical body, which is often viewed as the absolute cessation of existence in our culture, is considered from this different perspective as merely the dissolution of the outermost layer of manifestation. The subtlest levels of consciousness persist after the breaking up of the body and provide the cause for future incarnations in different bodies.

In Buddhist thought, this transference of consciousness from one life to the next is believed to happen repeatedly to all sentient beings, and this overall process is known as samsara (Tib. khorwa, 'khor ba). Formally, samsara refers to the circling of the stream of consciousness through many births and deaths in six different "realms" of existence, which are inhabited by gods, jealous gods, humans, animals, hungry ghosts, and hell beings, respectively. Beyond this technical definition, samsara is also the ultimate existential dilemma because the continual and repeated transmigration from life to life and realm to realm is considered to be extremely unpleasant and dissatisfying on the whole. Even the god realms, where the inhabitants are believed to live enormously long lives filled with tremendous pleasure, are not viewed optimistically because these beings too must eventually die and fall again into the lower levels of existence, which are plagued by overt suffering. From the Buddhist standpoint, the only acceptable aim is to seek nirvana (Tib. nya-ngen le de-pa, mya ngan las 'das pa), which refers to release from any kind of future rebirth, and according to the Tibetan tradition, this is attained by recognizing and resting in the ultimate nature of mind.

A further consequence of this cosmology concerns the inherent spiritual capacities of every human being. Because the nature of mind is the foundation of the phenomenal universe, all beings are therefore naturally endowed with this most basic aspect of mind. Following this logic, the same text quoted above informs us, in another passage, that "The essence of the mind of all sentient begins is, since the very beginning, the essence of the enlightened one . . . [It is], since primordial time, your natural possession."[7] Thus, in Tibetan Buddhism there is a definite sense of the unlimited spiritual potential of every human being because the highest good is also the "natural possession" of every being. This doctrine is referred to as "Buddha-nature" (San. *tathagatagarba*, Tib. de-zhin sheg-pay nying po, *de bzhin gshegs pa'i snying po*).

Unfortunately, it is said to be very difficult to actually realize this true nature of mind. One of the reasons for this is that the ordinary physical world that we experience on a regular basis acts to obscure the subtler levels of consciousness lying beneath it. Therefore, the true essence of consciousness, which is the basis of the phenomenal universe, goes unnoticed. This problem is compounded by our habitual tendencies and human nature which make us prone to seek fulfillment in the external and material world, all of which is necessarily subject to transience, suffering, and death. We lack the awareness that our only true fulfillment is to be found inwardly at the very root and essence of our own consciousness.

The power of the breath in Tibetan Buddhism lies in its ability to counteract this tendency at two levels. In the most basic sense, breathing practices can help the practitioner break this cycle by calming the mind, thereby enabling one to regain composure, stability, and peacefulness. Other practices utilize the breath as a tool for developing specific positive qualities, such as loving-kindness and compassion, or to eliminate harmful mental states such as hatred. These introductory meditations are essential because, without developing composure and peace of mind, any further practices are both impractical and impossible.

On a deeper level, however, the breath can help the practitioner to realize the nature of mind *directly* by using it to control and guide the subtle winds and consciousness with which it is so intertwined. These practices require an understanding of a detailed subtle anatomy of the human body that explains precisely how the wind and mind flow throughout the body. They are also quite advanced and are reserved for seasoned practitioners who have received direct instruction from a qualified lama. On this latter type our discussion will be limited, but we will describe the general understanding that informs these practices.

Foundational Practices

We have decided to refer to the first type of meditation, which is aimed at both calming the mind and cultivating positive qualities, as "foundational" meditation practices. These meditations are foundational in the sense that they encourage the development of mental qualities that are prerequisites for the more advanced practices that follow. We will discuss two such foundational meditation practices. The first is called "calm abiding" meditation (San. *shamatha*, Tib. *zhi gnas*) and is aimed at developing peace and mental focus, and the second is known as "giving and receiving" (Tib. *gtong-len*) and fosters loving kindness and compassion.

Developing Peace and Focus: "Calm Abiding" Meditation

The purpose of this kind of meditation is to allow the mind to focus and rest. This directly counters the tendency of the mind to be distracted and to wander around wherever the wind blows it. The Tibetan word for this kind of meditation is "zhi nay" (*zhi gnas*), which comes from the Tibetan words "zhi wa" (*zhi ba*), meaning peace or calm, and "ne pa" (*gnas pa*), which means to abide, to dwell, or to stay.

The goal of any specific meditation practice that aims at calm abiding is to choose a focus for the mind and to let it remain on this focus. When it wanders, notice this and bring it back to the object. When one attempts to do this for the first time, it will seem very difficult. In fact, the renowned American psychologist, William James, questioned the ability to achieve this:

> The faculty of voluntarily bringing back a wandering attention over and over again is the very root of judgment, character and will. An education which should improve this faculty would be the education *par excellence*. But it is easier to define this ideal than to give practical directions for bringing it about.[8]

Some approaches to developing calm abiding directly involve the breath. One very popular form is to sit calmly and direct attention to the sensations of breathing itself. We encourage the reader to try this exercise:

> Assume a comfortable, seated position, either cross-legged on a cushion or in a chair with the back upright but relaxed.

Place your hands on your thighs in a position that allows your shoulders to relax and your posture to remain erect. Now bring your awareness to the sensation of the breath as it passes in and out through the nostrils. When the mind wanders to other thoughts or sensations, simply notice this and bring it gently back to the breath.

After practicing this for a few minutes, shift your attention to the expansion and contraction of your abdomen during breathing. You may also like to count your breaths, which acts as a further reminder to remain focused on the object, and also helps to mark your progress as your ability to concentrate grows stronger.[9]

At first, most people notice that the mind will not cooperate. After a few breaths, it might spend the next half hour thinking about what happened on last night's television, the cute person sitting in front of you, or what is being served for lunch. Finally, you remember what you were supposed to be doing and again feel the breath several times. But then, without noticing, off you go again. This is when many people say, "I can't meditate."

However, if you stick with it on a regular basis, for instance for fifteen minutes several times a day, you will begin to experience periods of relative clarity. You may go through a period where you feel you are getting worse and the distractions are becoming more frequent, but this is just a sign that you are becoming more familiar with what goes on in your mind.

Then you may go through a stage where you can sit and watch the breath for more extended periods of time, but still there is a sense of distance, of the breath being the object and you being the observing subject. Later there may be a stage where this distinction fades away and "the mind becomes the breath." By this time, the mind is quite strong and flexible.

Developing Loving-Kindness and Compassion: "Giving and Receiving" Meditation

There are many techniques in Tibetan Buddhism for developing positive mental traits and eliminating negative ones. Loving-kindness and compassion are two closely related qualities. These terms have specific meanings to Buddhists. The term "loving-kindness" (San. *maitri*, Tib. jampa, *byams pa*) designates the overwhelming desire for others to have happiness and the causes of happiness. This has been likened to the feeling most people get when they hold a newborn baby. Compassion (San. *karuna*, Tib. nying je, *snying rje*) refers to the overwhelming desire for others to be free of suffering and the causes of suffering. It has been likened to the feeling you would have if you saw a loved one about to walk off the side of a cliff.

There are many different meditation techniques that are used to develop the qualities of love and compassion. One very popular one, known as "tong len" (Tib. *gtong-len*) or "giving and receiving," utilizes the breath directly. There are numerous variations of this technique. Here is one example:

> Sit in a chair or on a cushion and visualize all suffering beings in the various states of existence. Make sure to visualize your friends and loved ones, as well as people who antagonize you. While you are taking an in-breath, visualize that all the suffering is being taken out of sentient beings and brought into you in the form of black light that enters your nostrils with the breath. This goes down to your heart, and in the interval between breaths, is transformed from suffering into happiness and the color changed from black to white. On the out-breath, this light exits through the nose and goes out to all beings everywhere, replacing their suffering with happiness.

Because some people do not feel comfortable taking on the sufferings of other sentient beings when they are beginning this meditation, it is possible to practice another form of it as follows:

> As before, visualize all sentient beings and this time also visualize that all the Buddhas and bodhisattvas are in the sky in front of you, radiating white light. While taking an in-breath, bring this light into your body at the heart area. On the out-breath, the white light is radiated out to all sentient beings, removing their suffering and replacing it with happiness.

Advanced Practices

The advanced meditation practices aim at accessing very subtle states of consciousness that assist in directly realizing the nature of mind. These are perhaps best explained with reference to the Tibetan understanding of subtle human anatomy. Because the style of Buddhism that is practiced in Tibet originated in India, the Tibetan understanding of subtle anatomy has many points of congruence with the yogic physiology of Hinduism that Dr. Mijares detailed in chapter 1. Both systems, for instance, assert that the physical body is supported by a type of subtle energy (San. *prana*, Tib. *rlung*) or "wind" (San. *vayu*, Tib. *rlung*) that courses throughout the body via a network of 72,000 subtle channels (San. *nadi*, Tib. *rtsa*). Both systems also believe that three of these channels stand out as the most important: a central channel, which is generally described as being slightly anterior to the spinal column, and two subsidiary channels on either side, which crisscross the central channel in double helical fashion. (The Sanskrit and Tibetan names for these channels are listed below in table 1.) Furthermore, at each point of intersection with the central channel, both traditions teach that there are circular centers of psychic energy known as chakras (Tib. *rtsa 'khor lo*).

Beyond these basic similarities, however, the two systems begin to diverge. For example, although both traditions assert the existence of chakras, they differ in regard to how many there are. The standard Hindu system notes the existence of seven chakras, while the number referred to in the various Buddhist tantras varies between four and six. The teachings of the Hevajra Tantra, which are used by many Tibetan yogis, focus on four. Furthermore, there is a difference in perspective toward the chakras

Table 1. Sanskrit and Tibetan names of channels.

Language	Right channel	Central channel	Left channel
Sanskrit—Hindu	pingala	sushumna	ida
Sanskrit—Buddhist	rashanā	avadhūti	lalanā
Tibetan	ro ma	dbu ma	rkyang ma

Adapted from Alex Wayman, *Yoga of the Guhyasāmaja: The Arcane Lore of Forty Verses* (New York: Samuel Weiser, 1977), 65.

in the two systems. The Hindu conception tends to regard the chakras as centers of psychic energy that the yogi strives to "awaken" through rigorous religious discipline, and which are understood to endow the practitioner with supernormal psychic abilities (San. *siddhi,* Tib. ngo drup, *dngos grub*). Buddhist tantras, on the other hand, view the chakras as regions where the subsidiary channels constrict the flow of wind and mind through the central channel.

The central channel is of utmost importance in Tibetan Buddhism because a healthy flow of wind and consciousness through this channel sustains the continued physiological functioning of the body. Moreover, when the wind and consciousness dissolve in this channel, it is possible to experience the nature of mind directly. Because the chakras are considered to restrict the free flow of wind through the central channel, Tibetan Buddhism views them essentially as "knots" of psychic energy that the aspiring yogi must attempt to "untangle." If advanced practices to this end are performed successfully, then the wind and mind will be able to flow freely in the central channel, enabling the practitioner to experience the most basic levels of mind.

During our ordinary consciousness, the mind is traveling rather aimlessly on the winds throughout our body. It is only in very subtle states of consciousness that the mind and wind enter into the central channel, and when these happen in our daily life, we are generally unconscious of the event. In order to attain realization, however, you need to become aware of these subtle states of consciousness by intentionally bringing the mind and wind into the central channel.

There are numerous advanced practices that are directed toward this end, and many of them directly manipulate the breath in order to advance

Table 2. Sanskrit and Tibetan names of chakras.

Language	Head	Neck	Heart	Navel
Sanskrit, Hindu	ajña	vishuddha	anahata	manipura
Sanskrit, Buddhist	mahasukha	sambhoga	dharma	nirmana
Tibetan	bde chen	longs spyod	chos	sprul pa

Adapted from Alex Wayman, Yoga of the Guhyasāmaja: The Arcane Lore of Forty Verses (New York: Samuel Weiser, 1977), 66.

toward this goal. Some of these practices, such as the "Nine Rounds of Breathing," help to purify the channels by using the breath.[10]

This practice involves visualizing the three main channels while breathing in one nostril and out the other with specific amounts of intensity. Other practices, such "vase breathing," are directly involved in bringing the winds into the central channel.

In general, it is necessary to perform numerous preparatory practices before one is ready to move on to such advanced meditations. As a precursor, the practitioner is usually instructed to engage in numerous visualization-based meditations that serve to purify one's conception of oneself and the world. After extensive preparatory practice of this type, the meditator will be prepared to move on to the advanced practices that seek to realize the nature of mind directly.

In the end, one progressively realizes the stages of enlightened experiences by carefully examining what is happening to the mind and body, and all of these experiences are related to the breath. When one is able to voluntarily bring the winds into the central channel, one also gains the ability to perform physical and mental feats, eventually leading to blissful experience and realization. Moreover, when the central channel is closed to the wind, we will have ordinary experiences, but when the central channel is open to the wind, we will naturally have enlightened experiences. This leads to the realization that our everyday experience really has little to do with the external world, but is mostly dependent upon the movement of the wind energy and the power of the mind.

Conclusion

In this chapter, we have provided a basic outline of the Tibetan understanding of breath and its role in the transformative spiritual practices of Tibetan Buddhism, and we have described a few of these practices. In the beginning, the breath serves as an introduction to spiritual practice, but for the more advanced practitioner, it is a tool to engage in profound meditation. Eventually it leads to the experiences of enlightenment, in which the negative and positive emotions are identified as primordial wisdom.

We believe that the perspectives and practices outlined here could be useful in easing some of the more intractable existential dilemmas currently plaguing individuals in the modern West. In particular, the Tibetan Buddhist view is important because it offers an alternative to the materialist paradigm presently reigning in the West, and further because it directly attests to the fundamental sanctity at the root of every human being. In this context, the breath serves as an expedient to dispel our illusions and to reveal this inherent sacredness within. We hope that this chapter can serve as a small voice calling us back to this primordial purity.

Notes

1. This particular translation is taken from Walpola Rahula, *What the Buddha Taught*, rev. ed. (New York: Grove Press, 1974), 110. We have taken the liberty of removing a few of this translator's addendums to this passage.

2. Shunryu Suzuki, *Zen Mind, Beginner's Mind*, ed. Trudy Dixon, with a preface by Huston Smith and an introduction by Richard Baker (New York: Weatherhill, 1979), 29.

3. That *rlung* serves as a translation for both *vāyu* and *prāna*, depending on the circumstance, is implied from the discussion in Geshe Gedün Lodrö, *Walking Through Walls: A Presentation of Tibetan Meditation*, ed. and trans. Jeffrey Hopkins, Anne C. Klein, and Leah Zahler (Ithaca, NY: Snow Lion, 1992), 32–34.

4. The meaning of "mind" in Tibetan Buddhism is quite subtle and complex. For a clear and comprehensive treatment of this subject, the reader should consult Lati Rinbochay, *Mind in Tibetan Buddhism*, ed. and trans. Elizabeth Napper (Valois, NY: Snow Lion, Gabriel Press, 1980).

5. The Buddha, in this case, is not limited to the historical Śakyamuni Buddha, but refers to any sentient being which is in a state of complete awakening and liberation.

6. Chöki Nyima Rinpoche, *The Union of Mahamudra and Dzogchen*, ed. Marcia B. Schmidt, trans. Erik Pema Kunsang, (Hong Kong: Rangjung Yeshe, 1989), 122–23. The passage quoted is from the English translation of The Union of Mahamudra and Dzogchen, The Direct Instructions of the Great Compassionate One (phags pa thugs rje chen po'i dmar khrid phyag rdzogs zung 'jug gi nyams len snying po bsdus pa bzhugs so), written by Karama Chagmey the First (1605–1670), a prolific Tibetan author who has left a lasting impact on both the Kagyü and Nyingma lineages.

7. Ibid., 112–13.

8. William James, *Principles of Psychology* (New York: Dover, 1950), 424; cf. Daniel Goleman, "Tibetan and Western Models of Mental Health," in *MindScience: An East-West Dialogue*, ed. Daniel Goleman and Robert A. F. Thurman (Boston: Wisdom, 1991), 98.

9. For a general discussion of the physiological effects of similar techniques to calm the mind and body, see Herbert Benson with Miriam Z. Klipper, *The Relaxation Response* (New York: Avon, 1975).

10. For specific instructions on the Nine Rounds of Breathing from an authorized guru, see chapter 5, "Channeling the Breath," in Drikung Kyabgon Chetsang Rinpoche, *The Practice of Mahamudra*, ed. Ani K. Trinlay Chödron (Ithaca: Snow Lion, 1999), 33–35.

3

The Breath of the Tao
and the Tao of Breathing

BENJAMIN R. TONG

The Sage breathes down to his feet.[1]

The Universal Breath

In everyday Chinese and Chinese-American language, the word for breath or air is *ch'i*. In the Cantonese (southern Chinese) dialect spoken in Hong Kong and Chinatown communities all over the world, ch'i is pronounced as "hei"or "hay." At the end of a long, hard day, the frequent complaint is "Ngall moh sai jing sun hei, wah!" That is to say, "I'm so tired, the wind's knocked out of me!" or "I'm all out of breath!"

Interestingly enough, ch'i (or *hei*) is also the classical term for the "vital energy" that courses throughout the body's blood and organ systems. According to Traditional Chinese Medicine (TCM), illness is frequently traceable to depletion or abnormal movement of ch'i, or vital energy, in the body. In Western terms, we might say that Ch'i (with a capital C) refers to, or is synonymous with, *the Tao*—i.e., the Tao of the Taoists—the Universal Life Force that is both transcendent and imminent. It is the all-pervasive energy that sustains all that exists and has being.

A recurrent metaphor for this Big Ch'i is the Breath of God. The Divine as Cosmic Breath is found in the history of cultural traditions in many parts of the world. "God" in Hebrew, e.g., is sometimes spoken of in terms of His/Her/Its *ruahk* (roo-ock) or "breath." Similar to the Taoist account of Creation, the very first line in the Old Testament declares that "In the beginning when God created the heavens and the earth, the earth was a formless void and darkness covered the face of the deep, while *a wind from God* swept over the face of the waters."[2] In a number of known cultures, the Breath of the Universe has also been perceived as an instrument of divine intervention. At one point in the history of Japan, a great storm repelled military invasions ordered by the Mongol emperor of China, Kublai Khan—once in 1274 CE and again in 1281 CE. In both instances the Mongol armada was destroyed at sea by this "Fierce Breath of the Divine" (*kamikaze*). So much for the Big Ch'i. Our attention will be focused on the "small" ch'i.

In the human body, the Cosmic Breath is manifest in the form of ch'i, the vital energy that sustains all living beings within the canopy of Creation. In various meditation practices, ch'i in the organ systems and the blood is consciously directed to move along specific paths. This is known as *ch'i gung*, (or *Qigong*), which consists of *disciplined* activities that enhance, balance, and strengthen the ch'i in the body. In certain forms of sitting meditation, "following the breath" with the mind's eye represents a means to use the movement of incoming air to direct ch'i— both internal and external—to a specific bodily location.

The most important location is the "center" point (a.k.a. the *daan tien*, or the "sea of ch'i") in the lower abdomen. Specifically, we are referring to an imaginary point approximately 3.6 inches down from the navel and in front of the spine. *Proper breathing* takes the ch'i to where it belongs. Put another way, proper or natural or abdominal breathing is said to be a way to direct ch'i to its natural home, i.e., the daan tien.

Air flows like ch'i and ch'i flows like air. Without air and also without ch'i, a human being cannot live. However, despite the equivalency established by popular (folk) Chinese culture of long-standing, one is actually not the same as the other. Vital energy is like air, but it is *not* air. To add to the confusion, many in contemporary Western medical science choose to view ch'i as electromagnetic impulses (electricity) "naturally" produced by the body. Indeed, ch'i has some of the characteristics of electricity but, as with air, it is *not* identical to the body electric.

Ch'i in the body normally moves smoothly and vigorously along its preordained circuits or *meridians* without the help of directed breathing and other Qigong exercises. Movement of bodily ch'i, however, is more completely or consistently natural and beneficial with this kind of practice. This is particularly true in the case of harried and stressed contemporary life leading to all too many instances of stuck ch'i, ch'i depletion, and ch'i imbalance—the cumulative result being all manner of stress, ailments, and disease. (Apart from meditational work like directed breathing, "treatment" for ch'i flow problems also includes such TCM regimens as acupuncture, herbology, cupping, massage (*tier nah*), and external Qigong healing.)

Taoist breathing has two purposes, according to Loy Ching-Yuen. First, it is a means "by which we store chi in our bones, nourish the skin with healthy blood, and decrease calcification of the major joints."[3] Secondly, it is integral to the "path of enlightenment" that leads to increasing oneness with Tao. One is enabled to "embrace the emptiness of the unborn state."[4]

There are those who do not need to conscientiously practice "following the breath" in order to circulate internal ch'i as well as move incoming (external) Cosmic ch'i to the center point and elsewhere. *Diaphragmatic breathing*, or "natural breathing," is virtually intuitive in babies, animals, and Frank Sinatra. Furthermore, healing masters have taught that a lifetime of upper body (chest) breathing is not natural: It actually threatens human longevity.

The ancient Taoists taught that everything in Creation has its own color. The color of the Tao is said to be a light yellow gold. Likewise, all creatures and objects have distinctive individual rhythms or vibrations. The Tao, too, has its own rhythm. To the extent that one's breathing or ch'i movement pattern approximates that of the Tao, to that extent is the person's rhythm close to the Universal Rhythm itself. Correct, natural breathing, in short, leads to increasing rapport with the Force. Perhaps the proper response to someone saying "May the Force be with you" is "Thanks, I'm working at it."

Meditational breathing leads one to be centered while existing in the arena of stress-laden life situations. Stress is lowered to the extent that one is able to "*breathe like a dead man!*"[5] At this level, the state of *wu wei* is achieved: One acts in such a way that action itself feels like no action at all. This is effortless effort, the proverbial calm in the midst of a storm. To paraphrase St. Paul, one is in the world but not of it. This is what Taoists mean when they refer to the state of oneness with the Tao, the Universal Life Force.

Now one might entertain the question, "When one is 'with the Force,' what does that look like?" The spirit of centeredness and nonattachment in the state of *wu wei* can be illustrated, perhaps, in the following two stories that I have shared with students and colleagues over the years.

At the height of his activities to evict the British colonizer from India, Gandhi was followed about day and night by an ambitious white American reporter. One day the seemingly tireless young man said to Gandhi, "Sir, I am the kind of journalist who *always* gets his story when I am hot on the trail of one. I can dog just about anyone on the face of the earth! But, you, Mr Gandhi, I cannot keep up with. You are much older than me. And you walk slower than me. Yet half the time I am exhausted just trying to keep up—all the while you are besieged by a heavy political schedule, death threats, and racist violence. Mr. Gandhi, do you think maybe you might consider taking a vacation at some point? Gandhi looked calmly into the reporter's eyes and said, "Young man, I am always on vacation."

A student went to his meditation teacher and said, "My meditation is horrible! I feel so distracted, my legs ache, and I'm constantly falling asleep!"

"It will pass," said the teacher.

A week later, the student came back to his teacher. "My meditation is wonderful! I feel so aware, so peaceful, so alive!"

"It will pass," said the teacher.

The Tao of Breathing

Breathing is the foundation of meditation, Tai Chi Ch'uan, and the Shao Lin school of martial arts. Taoist breathing is also essential for maintaining the peak of health and wellness. "By using a combination of exercise and breathing, Taoist techniques provide an efficient and effective method for taking in . . . precious elements [such as iron, copper, zinc, fluorite, and quartz] and getting rid of wastes and poisons. These techniques, as Chuang Tzu says, 'expel the old (and) take in the new.' "[6]

It has been said that "the most important element of all is that *Taijiquan* (a Taoist practice) emphasizes long, profound breathing techniques that allow you to take in plenty of oxygen for action. . . . This will provide the best condition for blood and Qi [i.e., ch'i] circulation. In this manner, hypertension can be eased, the heart-beat slowed down, and high blood pressure can be lowered."[7]

Yang Cheng-Fu, one of the grandmasters of Classical Yang Style Tai Chi Ch'uan, wrote of the "ten essentials of Taijiquan practice." Principle Ten: "Seek stillness in motion." "When practicing slowly, the breathing deepens and lengthens, the qi [i.e., ch'i] sinks to the dantian. One avoids the harm of straining the blood circulation."[8] Furthermore, the *context* of Taoist breathing is Ch'i Gung in such modes as sitting, standing, lying down, or moving. Practiced in alternation, these activities resonate to the ever changing Way of Nature. "Passive (or sitting) meditation should be followed by dynamic exercise such as Tai Chi . . . then by further sitting meditation. Our personal energy is certain to be increased through this method."[9]

The reader will want to come away from this didactic discussion with something concrete and useful. In that spirit, let us consider a number of highly beneficial Taoist Ch'i Gung breathing exercises. We begin with a key, centuries-old, foundational Taoist meditation form:[10] Breathing incoming ch'i to the daan tien ("center point") while sitting.

> All breathing should be done through the nose. Use your belly
> to help you breathe, not your chest. This kind of breathing is
> sometimes called abdominal breathing. To maximize breathing
> capacity, relax your chest by sinking the sternum and dropping
> the shoulder. Then round your chest from the scapulas by

pushing your arms slightly forward and to the sides, creating a gap in the armpit.

The stomach expands as we breathe in, contracts as we breathe out. Sometimes it is referred to as Buddhist Breathing or Postbirth Breathing. When you have the chance, observe other animals as they breathe or even newborn babies. They breathe with their bellies naturally.

During inhalations of normal breathing, expand the belly on all four sides (forward, backward, and sideways). Sink both the thoracic diaphragm and the pelvic diaphragm. Inhale and gather the chi in the daan tien.

When exhaling, the belly contracts from all four sides. Both the chest diaphragm and the pelvic contract, lift upward pushing the air out. Breathe out thru the nose.

Waking Up the Upper Body Ch'i

The following exercise enables you to wake up or invigorate the ch'i in the entire upper body, most especially ch'i in the neck, shoulders, spine, and abdominal area. "Waking Up the Upper Body Ch'i (Lut Saow Wun Duung)" consists of a simple two-step movement executed in a standing position.[11]

Stand tall. Imagine your spine is a needle pointing to the heavens. Make your feet as wide as your shoulders. Place your mind's eye in your daan tien.

Now begin by moving both arms forward and up. Then push straight back with vigorous force, as though intending to slap a wall behind you with your open palms. Inhale air into your daan tien when doing this. Your heels may naturally lift off the ground from time to time during this first (yang) movement. Next, exhale and allow your arms to relax and swing forward (yin movement). Force them to come to a dead stop approximately seven inches in front of your upper thighs.

Repeat the first movement from that seven-inch point. Note: Do not allow your arms to start or arrive any higher.

Set aside a little time everyday to practice this form. Gradually work up to a minute and aim for an eventual maximum of ten continuous minutes. Taoist healers have maintained that consistent practice of Lut Saow Wun Duung is capable of acting as a preventive regimen for certain diseases and tumors.

Holding Large Breathing Bubble

Adopt any of three body positions—standing (with knees slightly bent), sitting (at the edge of an ordinary chair) or lying down. Choose the one that makes you feel most comfortable and relaxed.[12]

> Place your arms in front of your chest as though holding a large bubble the size of a basketball. Breathe down to your daan tien. Upon inhaling, allow your abdomen and the bubble to expand slightly. When exhaling, let abdomen and bubble contract a little.
>
> All the while try to maintain a gentle "just so" state of being (*wu wei*): Be aware that holding the bubble too firmly will cause it to pop, whereas too lightly will result in the bubble floating away. Therefore, you will want to hold it "just so," with just the right amount of energy—no more and no less than is required for it to remain in your hands.

For those with problems related to insomnia or gastrointestinal ailments, it is beneficial to do the exercise in the lying down position before going to sleep. When you feel a strong sensation of ch'i in you, put down your palms slowly and put them on your lower abdomen. Then concentrate your attention on the daan tien, which will enable ch'i accumulated in your hands to be stored in its natual home (the sea of ch'i) for future use by the body and the mind.

Wild Goose Spreads Its Wings

This breathing exercise is taken from that famous internal arts system known as Da Yaang Chi Gung, literally meaning Wild Goose Chi Gung.[13]

Developed centuries ago by the Taoist Kunlun School, Da Yaang consists of vigorous and gentle movements in which motion is alternated with stillness. Benefits range from promotion of blood circulation to delay of aging and prolonging of life.

> Raise both arms slowly to shoulder level, with palms facing each other. Then, as you go on raising arms, inhale and spread them out, rotating so that palms face upwards, chest is expanded, shoulders are relaxed, and elbows slightly bent. Meanwhile, bend body backward (not to an extreme) and lift heels slightly off floor with knees slightly flexed. Look to the sky. Hold for about 3 seconds. Fold back into the opening position (exhale) and repeat.

String-Blowing Exercise

This Chi Gung exercise is designed to help develop the ability to breathe out. This facilitates expulsion of waste air.[14]

> Simply hang a string about 18 inches from your face. Exhale strongly to make the string blow in the wind. As you get better at this, you can move the string (or yourself) farther and farther away.

Kick Lower Legs in Three Directions

While doing the following leg and torso strengthening Chi Gung exercise,[15] inhale and exhale with no thought of when you should do which.

> Stand upright with feet together and hands on hips. Raise left knee and kick lower leg forward, toes pointed. Set foot down. Repeat seven times. Kick left lower leg backward, so that heel touches right buttock, if possible. Set foot down. Repeat these movements with your right leg. Raise left knee and kick lower leg inward. Set foot down. Repeat seven times.

Breathe and Think

According to the creator of Tai Chi Chuan, Cheng Shen Feng, "It is said that when you breathe out you contact the Root of Heaven and experience a sense of openness, and when you breathe in you contact the Root of Earth and experience a sense of solidity. Breathing out is associated with the fluidity of a dragon, breathing in is associated with the strength of a tiger."[16]

We can draw to a close with the observation by my primary Taoist mentor, Grandmaster Kwong Gate Chan, that those who would have their lives resonate to the rhythm of the Universal Life Force need only do two things: "Breathe and think." We have just considered breathing, particularly breathing in the most appropriate and beneficial manner. To "think" correctly—in the words of Lao Tzu's contemporary, Confucius—is simply to ponder on the question, "What are the right things to worry about in life?" And that will be, to be sure, the subject of another essay, which very likely can only be written while inhaling and exhaling to move the ch'i along its natural path.[17]

Notes

1. This quote is a saying from my own teacher, Grandmaster Kwong Gate Chan (unpublished).

2. Genesis 1:1, emphasis added, New Revised Standard Version (NRSV).

3. Loy Ching-Yuen, *The Supreme Way: Inner Teachings of the Southern Mountain Tao,* trans. Trevor Carolan and Du Liang (Berkeley, CA: North Atlantic Books, 1999), 25.

4. Ibid., 44

5. This comment was made by Grandmaster Kwong Gate Chan in a personal communication.

6. Cited in Da Liu, *Tai Chi Ch'uan and Meditation* (New York: Shocken Books, 1986), 49. Cf. Fechter, 2003; Lewis, 1997, 2002, 2004.

7. Yang Jwing-Ming, *Tai Chi Secrets of the Yang Style* (Boston: YMAA Publication Center, 2001), 163.

8. Fu Zhongwen, *Mastering Yang Style Taijiquan,* trans. Louis Swaim (Berkeley, CA: North Atlantic Books, 1999), 19.

9. Loy Ching-Yuen, *The Supreme Way: Inner Teachings of the Southern Mountain Tao,* trans. Trevor Carolan and Du Liang (Berkeley, CA: North Atlantic Books, 1999), 24.

10. Instructions are from http://members.tripod.com/internalart/the%20art%20of%20meditation/breathing.htm.

11. Text is mine. Cf. *Knocking at the Gate of Life and Other Healing Exercises of China: The Official Handbook of the People's Republic of China,* trans. Edward C., Chang (Emmaus, PA: Rodale Press, 1985), 48.

12. Adapted and modified from *The Wonders of QiGong: A Chinese Exercise for Fitness, Health, and Longevity,* compiled by *China Sports Magazine* (Los Angeles: Wayfarer Publications, 1985), 80–81.

13. Ibid., 48.

14. *Knocking at the Gate of Life,* 97.

15. Modified from *Wonders* of *QiGong,* 68.

16. Daniel Reid, *Harnessing the Power of the Universe: A Complete Guide to the Principles and Practice of Chi-Gung* (Boston: Shambhala, 1998), 38–39.

17. Benjamin R. Tong, "Taoist mind-body resources for psychospiritual health and healing," in *Modern Psychology and Ancient Wisdom: Psychological Healing Practices from the World's Religious Traditions,* ed. Sharon G. Mijares (Binghamton, NY: Haworth Press, 2003); reprinted in Benjamin R.Tong, "Taoism: Concerned sbout wellness and then again not," *The Empty Vessel: A Journal of Contemporary Taoism* 6 (Fall 1999): 32–40.

4

Breathing Respect
Breath and the Martial Way of Aikido

DARRELL BLUHM

Breath as Rhythm

We live in a world of rhythm and cycle. The cycles of seasons, of light and dark, wet and dry, hot and cold, the rhythm of tides and storms all linked to the movement of the earth around its self, the sun and in relationship to the moon and the myriad celestial bodies that exert their influence upon it. Life in all its forms is adapted to our rhythmic world. Each of us expresses the billions of years of evolutionary relationship to these rhythms in our heartbeat, sleeping and waking, activity and rest, inhaling and exhaling. Breath is essential to living, and breath—synchronous with visceral, cardiac, and muscular-skeletal rhythms—is necessary for health. Our personal breath ties us to the breath of others and to the breathing of the world of which we are part.

This rhythmic connection to our world is inherent in our being and so fundamental to our well-being that it can't be dependent upon learning. We don't learn to beat our heart, fall asleep, digest our food, or breathe. However, each of these processes is subject to the influence of learning—our breath probably more so than any. Maladjustment of these primal patterns of interaction—pumping of blood, moving, digesting, breathing, etc.—arises through maladapted learned responses to the demands imposed by the physical and social environment.

A corrective strategy for addressing faulty habits of sensing, moving, and breathing lies in learning to stop interfering with the natural functioning of our nervous system and to allow the intelligence accumulated through the evolutionary history of our species to work for us.[1] This requires recognizing when and how we interfere with ourselves and learning to step out of our own way. Learning to avoid interference with one's self or others is also an integral element of the martial art of Aikido.

Martial Art as Adaptive Capacity

The term "martial" is derived from Mars, the Roman god of war, and refers to war or warrior. The martial arts are generally understood as systems of training to cultivate the skills requisite for success in combat. In a larger sense, all organisms are engaged in what Darwin called "the struggle for existence." The ability to fit an ecological niche or, in times of a changing environment to adapt to new circumstances, represents an organism's martial capacity. As humans, our ability to survive and ensure the survival of our offspring is determined by a multitude of factors and can be accomplished by means of a seemingly infinite variety of strategies as evidenced by the diversity expressed around us biologically and within human culture. A biological example of a martial system that operates within us yet outside of our conscious control is our immune system, which is continuously defending us against the invasion of environmental pathogens.[2]

All human cultures have developed martial systems for the protection of their members. The origins of these systems have roots in our species' unique evolutionary trajectory, especially with the emergence of upright posture and the hominid line (of which we are the remaining representatives). The shift to upright posture created advantages essential to the success of our species, such as the ability to orient easily and move readily in all directions with hands free to carry, manipulate, or (powered by a rotating pelvis and hip joints capable of full extension) throw objects with accuracy and power. These abilities combined with a keen intelligence and the development of language and a social structure to pass on and refine knowledge from generation to generation (culture) allowed our ancestors to emerge as the dominant predators on the planet. The experience accumulated through hunting beginning with the physical and perceptual ability to strike with or throw an object at a moving target underlies much of the increasingly sophisticated use of weapons that has followed. Many of the skills that are refined through martial training today, across all cultures, share commonalities with the skills employed in hunting and scavenging by our earliest ancestors.[3]

Our vertical organization in the field of gravity did not come free of liabilities. To maintain our balance over two feet requires a complex integrated function of our vestibular, visual, proprioceptive, and neuromuscular systems that even when operating optimally leave us fundamentally unstable. The psychomotor complex associated with the experience of anxiety is closely linked to the startle reflex and the fear of falling which distorts posture and disrupts breathing.[4] The ease with which we can be imbalanced, physically, emotionally, and psychologically is readily exploited in all martial traditions and consequently practices directed towards learning how to quickly reestablish balance when lost are taught.

Breath is of paramount concern for martial artists because of its relationship to movement and as an indicator of one's internal state of being as well as that of an opponent or partner to which one must respond. In this chapter I will explore the role breath plays in the practice of martial arts, especially the Japanese Martial Way of Aikido.

Breath, Posture, and Action

We can begin to appreciate the importance of breath in relation to well-coordinated action by understanding how its neuromuscular pattern is adapted to upright human posture, the advantages of which are strongly exploited in martial arts. The ability to stand upright exists through a complex scaffolding of ligaments, tendons, and muscle (or myofascial network) to support balance and move the spine as well as the myofascial organization of the pelvis, hip joints, legs, and feet to support, balance, and move the trunk (inclusive of the spine) and the head and arms above. The muscles that erect the spine and bend it backwards are referred to as the extensor muscles, and the muscles that bend the spine forward are the flexors; muscles that turn the spine are rotators and muscles that create side bending are lateral flexors.

Most muscles contribute to several of these actions at any given time. An even distribution of tone in these various muscle groups is necessary for balanced posture and freedom of movement. When we inhale, the diaphragm (the muscular structure that forms the floor of the thoracic cage and the roof of the abdominal cavity and is the primary engine of breath) contracts and is drawn downward. This increases the volume of the thorax resulting in a relative change of air pressure between the inside and outside that draws air into the lungs, where the exchange of gases from air to blood occurs; oxygen being absorbed into the blood and carbon dioxide released into the air. Simultaneous with the contraction of the diaphragm is an increase in tone of the extensor muscles of the back and a decrease in tone of the abdominal muscles, the primary flexors of the spine.

Conversely, when we exhale, the diaphragm relaxes and moves upward returning to its neutral position, decreasing the volume in the thorax, and through the resulting change in relative pressure inside and out, air is expelled from the lungs. As the diaphragm relaxes, the extensor muscles of the back decrease in tone and the tone of the abdominal muscles increases. This reciprocal pattern of activity and rest of muscles acting in antagonistic and synergistic ways is illustrative of the connection between the rhythm of breath and the larger rhythm of muscular skeletal action.[5]

A basic exercise in Aikido involves raising the hands overhead as if to raise a sword (or actually using a sword) and then swinging downward in an arc as if to cut. This is done in the standing position with one foot forward of the other with both feet in line (this stance is called *hamni* in Japanese, meaning "half body"). The breathing is coordinated with the movement so that one inhales with the upswing and exhales with the downswing. The movement is initiated with the shifting of weight from the back foot to the front as the hands swing upward, the thumbs leading fingers well extended to a point well over the head, all the while drawing the breath in. At the apex of the movement the point at which the decend of the arms begins one should sense the activation of the lower abdomen (*tanden*) in conjunction with the release of the breath outward as the hands return downward, the little fingers leading and weight shifts back to the back foot. Each repetition of this movement should be done imagining that the in-breath is drawn in through the fingers down the spine to the center of oneself and the out-breath is released from the center out through the spine and the fingertips. Consciously directing our breath with our movement (and imagination) in this way reinforces the natural link between them.

The action of breathing is quite plastic and capable of change in response to different circumstances. The forces that can distort or interfere with either the ability to breathe fully and easily or to change appropriately as circumstances dictate are many, such as injury or illness, chronic anxiety or prolonged emotional trauma, or poorly learned habits of self use. In order to develop skill in any martial discipline the fullness and flexibility of the breathing apparatus must be strongly established. The fact that our breathing is available to us by means of attention and active control provides the necessary resources for correcting faulty habits and developing the potential for the use of our breath to powerfully assist any action. The link between breath and vocal expression exemplified in the roar of an attacking lion or the focused shout of an attacking swordsman (known in Japanese as a *kiai*) gives outward confirmation of these resources.

Ki and Martial Arts

The development of martial arts is widespread throughout China, Korea, Japan, and other parts of Asia. While there are many aspects that differentiate these arts both within and between the different cultures, there are certain shared commonalities. Some of these commonalities lie in the mutual influences within the cultures of Taoism, Confucianism, and Buddhism. Important among the philosophy espoused within these traditions is the theory of yin and yang that recognizes the inherent unity of opposing elements such as male and female, up and down, light and dark, expansion and contraction, etc., and the creative force generated by the interaction of these pairs.

The relationship of humanity to the larger realm of nature expressed within the construct of the Tao (or Way), in which humanity exists as a part of, rather than apart from, nature is also integral to most Asian martial arts. Closely associated with both of the above examples is the idea of a vital force that moves through all of nature within and between the myriad forms animate and inanimate of existence known in Chinese as *qi* and Japanese as *ki*. (Dr. Tong elaborates on qi, or ch'i, in his chapter "The Breath of Tao and the Tao of Breathing.") The close connection between the phenomenon expressed by this term and the practice of Asian martial arts, in particular, the Japanese Martial Way of Aikido, makes it especially important to this discourse.

The art of Aikido is one of the modern forms of Japanese *Budo,* or Way of Martial Arts, developed in the twentieth century by Morihei Ueshiba (1883—1969). Aikido is an art that is born of the profound martial culture of Japan and the unique genius of its founder. The name Aikido (pronounced eye-key-doe) is made up of three kanji: (1) *ai* meaning "harmony" or "to join with," (2) *ki* meaning "fundamental creative principle" or "life force," and (3) *do* meaning "a way" or "path." Aikido then translates as the Way of Harmony with *ki*. In the Japanese language the concept of *ki* is incorporated in many words, such as *seiki* (vital), *genki* (healthy), *yoki* (cheerful), and *kibun* (feeling).

There is no single English word that can serve as an equivalent for *ki*, but depending on what dimension of *ki* is emphasized, different choices can be made. If we stress the spiritual aspect of *ki* then we can use the word "spirit" (a life-giving force), derived from the Latin *spiritus,* meaning breath, and found in words such as "inspire," "respire," "aspire," etc. If we want to bring forward the affective element, we can use the words "feeling," "intuition," or "sense." In the psychological domain words like "intention" or "consciousness" work, and in the physiological realm, "breath."[6]

The modern biological view of living systems rejects the notion of life arising from a vital force (vitalism) in favor of an explanation that recognizes the unique qualities of living organisms are due to their organization (organicism) and that the genetic program of any organism directs its development and activity through a dynamic interaction with its environment. Each organism has a constellation of capacities shared by all living systems, such as the capacity to evolve, to reproduce, to grow and differentiate, to bind and release energy (metabolism), to respond to environmental stimuli by means of perception, and to self-regulate by means of homeostatic and allostatic mechanisms.[7] However, at the level of experience we feel life moving in and through us. It is this phenomenological reality of life force that is important to the martial artist as experienced in the energy generated with movement (kinetic energy), and in the flow of blood, sensation, breath, and consciousness.

In the millennia-old Chinese worldview embedded in traditional Chinese medicine (TCM) it is assumed that within each of us *ki* has three primary sources. There is "original *ki*" *(yun qi)* that is expressed by an individual's unique qualities of constitution and temperament. There is the *ki* acquired through breathing *(zong qi),* and that obtained from eating *(gu qi)*. In TCM "breath *ki*" and "grain *ki*" are understood to mix to form "nutritive *ki*," which flows through a system of meridians to nourish the various tissues of the body. This is the subtle energy influenced by use of herbs or the stimulus of needles, touch, or heat to promote health and treat disease.

TCM also includes various systems of exercise to cultivate *ki* that are referred to in modern times by the term *qi gong* (breath exercise). In older times, these systems were called *tu gu na xin* (expelling the old energy, drawing in the new), *nei gong* (inner achievement), or *dao-yin* (leading and guiding the energy). Many elements of these systems are incorporated into the schools of Chinese martial arts, especially the "internal systems" of *taiji quan, xing yi quan, bagua zhang.*[8] In the practice of Aikido, elements of *do-in* (the Japanese name for *dao-yin*) have been incorporated along with exercises developed by the Japanese philosopher and yoga teacher Nakamura Tempu, a contemporary of Aikido founder Morihei Ueshiba.[9]

Breath and the Practice of Aikido

The image of martial arts most commonly projected in the media is one reflecting physical power, violence, and control over others. It is true that the objective of past martial training was directed towards the capacity to survive by any means in combat. However, the deeper practice of martial discipline is directed towards cultivating the harmonization of self with others, enabling individuals to act responsibly in a civil society. This deeper image of martial training is expressed in the words of judo founder Jigoro Kano, "Maximum efficient use of power, mutual benefit for oneself and others."[10]

The founder of Aikido, Morihei Ueshiba, was a legendary master of several schools of martial arts and a deeply spiritual man. An early taste of war forged his opposition to the use of martial arts for destructive purposes. His passion to merge spiritual principles with martial training led him to the development of Aikido, a discipline designed to control aggression and violence, as well as help people realize their full potential as individuals: physically, mentally, and spiritually. The importance of *ki* and its close association with breath in the practice of Aikido is expressed in these words of the founder: "The marvelous functioning of *ki* originates in the subtle variations of breath, this is the Generative Principle. It is the essential principle of love that manifests martial valor. In accordance with the marvelous functioning of *ki*, body and mind are unified. When Aikido is practiced, the subtle variations of breath flow through one's being and allow one to manifest techniques in total freedom."[11]

The techniques of Aikido comprise a system of holds, throws, and locks. Through the control of *ki* centered and emanating from the region of the lower abdomen (*hara* or *tanden*) one learns to apply Aikido's various techniques to subdue an opponent. Aikido principles hold that the mind and body are one. Through training we seek to bring ourselves into a state of wholeness, where the rhythms of breath, movement, thought, and action are unified.

Application of Aikido technique also requires that one learn to join with the motion of an opponent's attack, take control of its force, and redirect the power of the attack safely and effectively.[12] The process of forging a unified self and learning to harmonize one's movements with others' is undertaken in tandem through all of the various aspects of Aikido practice. Through the basic forms and etiquette of Aikido practice, we cultivate respect for, and a deeper capacity to listen to, others. While self-defense is an important element of Aikido, it is part of a larger path of self-discovery and a creative connection to life-affirming action.

We begin the practice of Aikido in a kneeling position with the pelvis resting on the feet so that the knees, lower leg, and feet form a triangular base to support the pelvis, spine, and head. This formal way of sitting, called *seiza,* with arms resting at the side of the torso, hands resting on thighs, the back upright and long, neck and head free, shoulders relaxed, the movement of the breath and the feeling of strength centered in the area of the *tanden*, mind quiet and alert, is truly the foundation for Aikido practice. After several minutes of sitting, the class as a whole bows, first towards the front of the dojo (where there is often a photo of the founder and/or some form of shrine (*kamiza*). Then the instructor and students bow to one another.

The act of bowing is accomplished by placing the hands lightly on the floor in front of the knees, lowering the head and torso forward hinging from the hip joints, maintaining an extended spine, with the pelvis in contact with the feet, while executing the movement down and up from one's center (*tanden*). This action is a physical expression of an attitude of respect, gratitude, and humility and represents the physical and spiritual heart of Aikido practice.

After bowing, practice is continued with any number of exercises to warm up, awaken, and condition ourselves. This period of the class often includes specific breathing exercises done both in *seiza* and while standing. For example:

> In a standing position with the feet shoulder-distance apart, draw the breath in through the nose as the hands, with the fingers well stretched, are opened wide to the side with the arms rotating outward so the palms are facing forward, raise the whole body up onto the toes and balls of the feet stretching the spine slightly back pushing the belly forward. When the inhale is complete and the this position of extreme openess is achieved exhale strongly through the mouth, rotating the hands forward bringing them in front of the center so the backs of the hands face each other, fingers still stretched taut, as the heels are lowered the abdominal muscles are activated and the spine bends slightly forward in an action of closing.
>
> The action of breathing is to be synchronized precisely with the movement of the arms and body and with the active participation of the imagination. While inhaling, one imagines that through this action of opening up, nourishment in the form of air and *ki* is drawn into the *tanden*. On the exhalation, one imagines that the breath is released from the tanden extending out through the spine, out through the palms of the

hands in an action of closing that cleanses one of impurities
and generates a feeling of *kokyu-ryoku,* or breath power.

This breathing exercise (*kokyu soren*) is one of many practiced in
Aikido and contains the three classic elements of chigong exercises:
movement, breath, and imagery. It is done to promote an awareness of
one's center and to cultivate breath power (*kokyu-ryoku*) but contains
many other benefits. It conforms to and reinforces the neuromuscular
pattern of a natural breath described earlier in the chapter and affirms
the basic function of breath which is to bring us nourishment with the
inhale and to cleanse with the exhale. The use of imagery focused on
drawing the breath in through the hands and spine to the tanden and
from there releasing the breath outward through the spine and hands,
helps in awakening and stimulating the center and connects the breath
to a whole body action that has the effect of refining the movement so
it is experienced as increasingly effortless.

Moshe Feldenkrais, founder of the Feldenkrais Method˚ of sensory-
motor education and a highly skilled judo teacher, delineated four characteristics of well-coordinated or organized movement: the absence of
effort, the absence of resistance, the presence of reversibility, and easy
breathing.[13] The experience of effortlessness in action arises when the
work is distributed in such a way that a larger proportion of the work
is done by the most powerful muscles, while the smaller muscles work
proportionate to their strength.

All of the most powerful muscles of the body attach to the pelvis,
making the area of the lower abdomen and pelvis the center of power
in the body.[14] The experience of effortlessness comes with action central-
ized in the *hara* and distributed through the whole body. This cannot be
accomplished if the breath is unconsciously held, or if tension or excessive effort is maintained outside of the center.

There are ways to consciously hold the breath to condition oneself
and refine one's action. In executing basic *iaido* (the Japanese martial
art of swordsmanship) forms, the practitioner is sometimes instructed
to hold the breath in the *tanden* from the time one begins to draw the
sword from its scabbard (*saya*) to the time in which the sword is returned
to the *saya,* with several cutting actions conducted in between. The con-
straint on the availability of oxygen to the muscles imposed by holding
the breath requires an efficiency of action. Unnecessary effort, or excess

tension in the muscles burns oxygen needlessly, leaving the inefficient practitioner gasping for breath at the end of the form. The concentration of attention required to hold the breath in the center in the midst of intricately orchestrated action helps galvanize one's awareness of center.

The position of *seiza* provides ideal circumstances for observing and working with the breath. This position facilitates an emptying of tension in the shoulders and chest and an increased access to the movement of breath in the low back, lower abdomen and even the pelvic floor. The frequently overlooked role of the muscles of the pelvic floor (which surround and include the anal sphincter) in support of the viscera and in the action of breathing is critical to the production of powerful action.

Breathing exercises conducted in *seiza* in which one draws up the anus, contracting the pelvic floor and working in strong association with the abdominal muscles in both inhalation and exhalation are important in the cultivation of abdominal breath power (*kokyu-ryoku*). Further elaboration on this topic is beyond the scope of this article but it is worth noting a comment the great jazz trumpeter Dizzy Gillespie made when asked where the breath power for playing his horn came from. His answer was, "From your asshole."[15] This mirrors Tempu Nakamura's saying: "When you face a stressful situation tighten your anus. Center yourself in your lower abdomen and relax your shoulders."[16]

It is important to remember that practices in which we manipulate or control our breathing (and other actions) fall into the broad domain of form as distinguished from technique. When practice takes place in the domain of intentional conscious action it is considered as form (*kata*). When we move into the realm of nonconscious action where judgment, determination and action arise simultaneously and spontaneously, the action can be considered technique (*waza*).[17] Most of what we do in the practice of Aikido is form. Even the vigorous partner exercise where we practice the throws and holds are forms. These forms have developed through the experience and efforts of countless individuals through the many centuries of the Japanese martial tradition.

In Aikido practice there is no sparring or competitive format. When we execute the basic throws, joint locks, etc., we do so within a clearly delineated relationship with our partner. This relationship between partners is comparable to that between the inhalation and exhalation in a single cycle of breath. The person who initiates the attack, be it grab or strike, will receive the technique and is called *uke* ("receiver"). The person being attacked who then executes the technique, be it a throw, lock or pin, is called *nage* ("thrower"). The uke's responsibility is to make a committed attack and then move as necessary to absorb and neutralize the force of the technique applied by the nage, using the whole self, without resisting, trying to escape, collapsing, or flying away from the technique. The skills developed through *ukemi* (the art of receiving) include rolling and falling, the ability to anticipate and follow the movement of the nage and all the methods of attack used in Aikido.

Ukemi requires one to freely give up one's balance while maintaining an acute awareness of one's center. The uke is not a victim of the nage's actions but an active participant in a mutual exchange with the nage, always the subject within their own learning process. Breathing is influenced positively through the practice of *ukemi* in many ways. One obvious way is that in overcoming the fear of falling and learning to remain engaged and alert in the act of falling, the pattern of anxiety normally elicited when one's balance is lost, resulting in the breath being held and perception closed down is countered. We learn through *ukemi* to be able to release our breath at any moment or to be able to draw breath in effortlessly as need dictates. (This is a skill good singers also cultivate). Practicing *ukemi* prepares us for meeting the unexpected.

The responsibility of the nage is to join with the force generated by the uke's attack, unbalancing the uke, and then redirecting the force into a throw or controlling technique. The nage must learn to enter into and capture the center of the movement with the uke and, from there, draw on the circular spiraling movements of whatever Aikido form is being practiced. Practice as the nage develops a strong stable center and the ability to release one's energy (along with the breath) with the movement. The action of throwing, using the connection of our feet to the earth to provide power transmitted through the legs, concentrated and controlled in the center, released through the spine and manifest in the hands, underlies all techniques. The same action is employed in raising and cutting with a sword; to be effective, the breath must be organized such that air is drawn in, in support of raising the sword and released out with the cut.

Many of the basic forms practiced in Aikido are named *kokyu-ho* ("breathing method") or *kokyu-nage* ("breath throws"). These forms utilize breath as rhythm, nourishment and as fuel for power. *Kokyu-ryoku,* the power that is derived from breath unified with body, mind, and *ki,* is manifest when we align with the fundamental force of the earth (gravity), the rhythms of our own inner workings, our partner's movement, and the breath of the world around us. Its expression gives life to every technique. If *kokyu-ryoku* is not present in the execution of a form or technique, then it is empty of its most essential element.

Partners in the practice of Aikido exchange roles as uke and nage and in this reciprocal exchange, outside the concerns of winning and losing, participate in a process of shared learning. Nearly all of the practice in the dojo exists within the context of form and represents the "small" practice of Aikido. Our "big" practice of Aikido exists in the context of our daily life outside the dojo. When conditions arise where there is danger to ourselves or others and we are called to act decisively and immediately, ideally the proper "technique" will emerge, drawn from countless hours practicing "form." The place within us from which true technique can emerge most powerfully is the place free of self-conscious thought (in Japanese, *mushin*).

Every Aikido class ends as it begins, with a bow. We enact and reinforce the attitude of respect, humility, and gratitude, integral to the experience of love. As the poet, William Stafford writes:

> What more can you offer the world
> than the breathing respect that you carry
> where ever you go right now?[18]

Notes

1. Moshe Feldenkrais in his book *The Potent Self* (San Francisco: Harper and Row, 1985) writes, "The ideal standing posture is obtained not by doing something to oneself, but by literally doing nothing, that is, by eliminating all acts of voluntary origin due to motivations other than standing and that have become automatic" (119).

2. This understanding of "martial" being the adaptive capacity of any organism developed from a personal communication with my Aikido teacher, T. K. Chiba Sensei.

3. Frank Wilson,. The Hand: How Its Use Shapes the Brain, Language and Human Culture (New York: Pantheon Books, 1998), 26–30.

4. Moshe Feldenkrais, *The Elusive Obvious*, (Capitola, CA: Meta Publications, 1981), 55–71.

5. Mabel Elsworth Todd, *The Thinking Body* (Brooklyn, NY: Dance Horizon, 1937), 217–246.

6. Kisshomaru Ueshiba, *The Spirit of Aikido* (New York: Kodansha International, 1984), 30–31.

7. Ernst Mayr, *This Is Biology* (Cambridge: Belknap Press, 1997), 8–23.

8. Ken Cohen, *The Way of Qigong* (New York: Ballentine, 1997), 13–20, 32–34.

9. Based on the oral teachings of T. K. Chiba.

10. Ueshiba, Kisshomaru, *The Art of Aikido* (New York: Kodansha International 2004), 71.

11. Ibid., 35.

12. One of the most basic exercises in Aikido is called "tai no henko" in which the action of joining with one's partner is enacted. Readers can see my teacher, T. K. Chiba demonstrate this form in both a turning (tenkan) and an entering (irimi) version on-line at http://www.youtube.com/watch?v=9SIcP Orl-a0.

13. Moshe Feldenkrais, *The Potent Self* (San Francisco: Harper and Row, 1985), 111–15

14. Ibid., 189.

15. From the DVD, "A Night in Havanna: Dizzy Gillespie in Cuba" New Video Group, (2005).

16. John Stevens, *Budo Secrets* (Boston: Shambhalla Press, 2002), 70.

17. Based on the oral teachings of T. K. Chiba.

18. William Stafford, *The Way It Is* (St. Paul, MN: Graywolf Press, 1992), 45.

Part II

Western Breathing Practices

My place is placeless,
A trace of the traceless.
Neither body or soul.
I belong to the beloved,
have seen the two worlds as one
and that one call to and know,
First, last, outer, inner, only that
Breath breathing human being.[1]

—Rumi quoted in C. Barks, and J. Moine.
The Essential Rumi (Edison, NJ: Castle Books, 1995), 32

Introduction to Western Breathing Practices

While Eastern traditions have been more concerned with breathing practices enabling the journey to enlightenment, Western traditions of the breath tend to focus on psychological and physical healing. In the early 1990s, Bill Moyers hosted a PBS series titled *Healing and the Mind*. This program explored research on Eastern healing, meditation. and breathing practices taking place in innovative hospitals and medical clinics in the United States and China. In one such clinic, Doctor Jon Kabat-Zinn was teaching patients in chronic pain to breathe with an atmosphere of compassion and mindful presence. Very often the sensations of pain would diminish, and even disappear, as a result of the practice.

Psychologists Zindel Segal, J. Mark Williams, and John Teasdale broke new ground in their research on mindfulness-based cognitive therapy (MBCT) as they demonstrated its positive results in persons suffering from depression. The initial structure of the client training includes and prioritizes,

> learning how to pay attention, on purpose, in each moment, and without judgment.... First, participants become aware of how little attention is usually paid to daily life. They are taught to become aware of how quickly the mind shifts from one topic to another. Second, they learn how, having noticed that the mind is wandering, to bring it back to a single focus. This is taught, first, with reference to parts of the body and, second, with reference to breathing. Third, the participants learn to become aware of how this mind wandering can allow negative thoughts and feelings to occur ... [and] use MBCT to be vigilant for mood shifts, and then move on to handle them (at the time) or deal with them later.[2]

This Westernized breath training has proven to both increase relaxation and metacognition. In many instances, it is also proving to be more successful than medication, for control and change are taking place within the client in a naturalistic way. Also, client practitioners realize that they are responsible for their own healing, as opposed to crediting a drug.

Likewise, psychologist Jeffrey Schwartz has been conducting research with patients suffering from obsessive-compulsive disorder (OCD). He has shown that mindfulness breath training and the shift of attention away from obsessive-compulsive behavior not only reduces the symptoms, but actually changes the brain patterning previously related to OCD.[3] In short, breathing practices are being used in a variety of ways in the West, from simple five- to fifteen-minute breathing exercises for stress reduction in the workplace to intense, hour(s)-long breathing sessions utilized for emotional release.

Part II will explore somatic psychology (body-focused healing) and the varieties of breathwork practices that have specifically developed in the Western world, including Reichian, Neo-Reichian, Rebirthing,

Holotropic Breathwork, Free-Diving, the Buteyko Institute, and the Middendorf "Breathexperience" school.

Wilhelm Reich, the originator of somatic psychology, was one of the first Westerners to give academic attention to the breath as a healing force. He recognized the healing power of pranic energy, but being unfamiliar with Eastern traditions, called it "orgone." In identifying this field of universal energy and its possibilities for greater human experience, Reich also noted that many people were emotionally armored. He developed breathing, gagging and movement practices to loosen this defensive muscular armoring and to free the restrained life energy. Vincentia Schroader's chapter, "Character Armoring: Walls Between Oneself and the World," discusses this process and the use of the breath in Neo-Reichian traditions.

Rebirthing and Holotropic Breathwork allow for the release of traumatic memories associated with pre- and peri-natal birth experiences. Michael Sky's chapter, "Birth, Rebirthing, and Learning to Breathe," discusses ways to both reexperience and transform this initial journey into life. "The Healing Potential of Holotropic Breathwork," by Stanislav Grof and Kylea Taylor, provides a glimpse into transformational experiences that can occur with Holotropic Breathwork. The practice recognizes four specific stages of birth and their impact upon one's personal mythology, and uses breath, music, and art to encourage a deep process of healing, wherein the breather becomes the healer.

Orion Garland's chapter, "Freediving: Learning Not to Breathe," describes a unique twist on breath training. Freediving focuses on disciplining the breath by retention, a process of "breath holding" used in both recreational and competitive swimming. It seems appropriate to include a chapter on "not breathing" in this exploration of the miraculous power of the breath.

The research and healing work done at the Butcyko Institute in Australia is helping many people suffering from diseases associated with the breath. Jennifer and Russell Stark's chapter, "Buteyko: A Method for Healing with the Breath," demonstrates breath training for reducing the number of asthma attacks while decreasing the need for medications. It represents a naturalistic method of healing that doesn't include the side effects of drugs and is gaining recognition. In response to research on breath training and its influence on dysfunctional breathing patterns of asthmatic patients in Australia, New Zealand and Glascow, the *British*

Medical Journal noted, "If dysfunctional breathing is as common as our data show, facilities for breathing retraining need to be available as part of the overall management of asthmatic patients."[4]

The last chapter in this section focuses on the natural breath. Finding the natural breath and discovering one's innate somatic intelligence takes the breather to a place whereupon the breath becomes the teacher in both one's inner and outer life. Juerg Roffler and Ilse Middendorf's chapter, "Breathexperience: A Somatic Science and Art of Living," describes how the breath allows us to "gain direct access to a knowledge and power that is greater than a simply intellectual understanding."

The following essays continue our journey. They explore and illuminate Western breathing practices for healing and wholeness.

Notes

1. C. Barks and J. Moine, *The Essential Rumi* (Edison, NJ: Castle Books, 1995), 32.

2. V. Zindel, J. Segal, Mark G. Williams, and John D. Teasdale, *Mindfulness-Based Cognitive Therapy* (New York: Guilford Press, 2002), 87.

3. Jeffrey M. Schwartz, Elizabeth Z. Gulliford, Jessica Stier, and Margo Thienemann, "Mindful awareness and self-directed neuroplasticity: Integrating psychospiritual and biological approaches to mental health with a focus on OCD," in *The Psychospiritual Clinician's Handbook: Alternative Methods for Understanding and Treating Mental Disorders,* ed. Sharon G. Mijares and Gurucharan Singh Khalsa (Binghamton, NY: Haworth Press, 2005).

4. M. Thomas, R. K. McKinley, E. Freeman, and C. Foy, "Prevalence of dysfunctional breathing in patients for patients treated for asthma in primary care: Cross sectional survey," *British Medical Journal* 322 (May 5, 2001):: 1098–1100.

5

Character Armoring

A Wall Between Oneself and the World

VINCENTIA SCHROETER

Introduction

This book now moves from Eastern to Western traditions, including the major physical, psychological, and spiritual systems that work with the breath. This chapter introduces you to a Western tradition that views restrictions in the full natural breath, as an indicator of physical restrictions in the body as well as in the psyche of the person. It will supply the tenants of somatic psychology, in the story of the psychosomatic work established by Wilhelm Reich and his students, Alexander Lowen and John Pierrakos.

Rather than just discussing the tenants of somatic psychology in these Reichian and neo-Reichian traditions, I have provided some exercises for the reader to go through in experiencing the breath from this tradition as well as provided a clinical case vignette.

Wilhelm Reich was the first psychoanalyst to create a form of psychotherapy that involved working with the body as well as the mind. This was in the early 1930s, making Reich a forerunner in mind-body work. He developed a method he called "character analysis," which combined direct work with the body along with the psychoanalytic work he had learned from Freud. Two of his students, Alexander Lowen and John Pierrakos, went on to start their own methods for somatic healing, combining Reich's original work with other techniques for healing. Alexander Lowen initiated Bioenergetics, and John Pierrakos created Core Energetics. Reichian Therapy, Bioenergetics, and Core Energetics, were among the first to acknowledge the mind-body relationship and the body's role in emotional healing.

These groundbreakers focused on the way the breath can be used to heal body and soul. Their understanding of the interplay between the physical, energetic and psychological dynamics of breath, including defensive breathing patterns was revolutionary. The exercises and stories within this chapter illustrate the healing power of the breath from both Reichian and neo-Reichian perspectives.

The Founding of Somatic Psychology

Wilhelm Reich was part of Sigmund Freud's inner circle of psychoanalysts in Vienna in the 1920s until he separated from Freud over the issue of mind-body dualism. Reich believed the body and mind were functionally the same, and the body needed to be addressed in therapy. Freud strongly disagreed, and their disagreement led to Reich's expulsion from Freud's inner circle of colleagues. Whereas Freud's emphasis was on the client's mental processes, Wilhelm Reich chose to include the body. He is particularly important in the development of Somatic Psychology as he was the first Westerner to pay attention to the relationship between body tension, rigidity, and psychological problems.

Reich was also unwilling to sit behind a couch in the traditional Freudian style, and chose instead to sit face to face with his clients. This enabled him to better observe their physical movements. For example, during one session he observed an angry client having trouble expressing anger. Reich noticed that the client had developed a redness that moved up from his chest, stopping at his neck. His throat was tight, and his voice was strained, for the man was unable to express his anger clearly. The client was unaware of what was happening within his own body! This unconscious, yet clearly physiological, block in the natural flow of energy caught Reich's attention. Following his intuition, he began to use physical pressure in the area of the neck to release this block. Buoyed by his success with this case, he created many physical techniques, including working with the breath.

Because Reich believed the body and mind were functionally the same, he always included the body in therapy. He observed the body holds tension in the muscles which protect us from unwelcome emotions. For example, in order to avoid being overwhelmed by one's own sadness, someone might tighten the throat, to hold back their tears, resulting in the familiar "lump in the throat." This lump in the throat occurs when the impulse to cry meets the equally strong impulse to restrict those tears. Reich would invite the person with this condition to relax the neck and jaw, and breathe more deeply through an open mouth. The impulse to hold back the tears will be countered by the rising need to cry. Deeper breathing always encourages the release of the held-back emotion. As the person relaxes the tension in the throat the impulse to cry gets stronger. Once the person lets go and cries, the response is one of relief.

Reich found that a client's *breathing style* always reflected this inner tension. Reich came to believe that the way a client handled his energy served to bind repressed anxieties. If someone was afraid that they might be overwhelmed by their own fear, for example, they could find ways in the body, such as shallow chest breathing, to avoid the anxiety of being overwhelmed by their own fear.

This is true of many people. Although we may want to change, we are threatened by change at the same time. Adults carry around suppression of feeling because some feelings were not acceptable when they were children. This suppression, originally a good adaptation to family constraints, is now on a body level—and unconscious. People might go into therapy to become less depressed, or less anxious, but be unconscious that they carry the burden of suppressed feelings in their bodies. Reich called this physical manifestation of psychological protection from childhood wounds "character armor."

This character armor, which helped us cope with our world as children, limits our expressiveness in adulthood, providing an unconscious, and unneeded, protection. The breath is restrained as muscles contract. It keeps us from fully enjoying our lives. This fortress once necessary in the childhood home becomes a wall between oneself and the world. Reich believed that, in order to feel better, we must return to these blocked feelings, make them conscious, understand what purpose they served, and free their expression.

These blocked feelings are held in seven areas of the body called segments:

> The ocular segment includes tension related to sight, hearing, and smell.
>
> The oral segment includes the muscles controlling the chin, throat, mouth, and jaw. Contractions are related to issues of suppressed crying or sucking.
>
> The cervical segment comprises deep muscles of the neck and tongue. The emotional function of armoring in the neck is to hold back the expression of anger or crying.
>
> The thoracic segment involves the chest, including the heart and lungs, as well as the arms and hands. It is the first segment to be blocked, by holding in inspiration to reduce anxiety. The emotions held in the chest are heartbreak, bitter sobbing, rage, reaching, and longing.
>
> The next segment is the diaphragmatic, which includes the diaphragm, stomach, solar plexus, pancreas, liver, gall bladder, duodenum, kidneys, and lower back muscles. This segment holds deep rage.
>
> The abdominal segment is the sixth armor ring and includes the large abdominal muscles and also the lumbar muscles of the back. Spite and fear of attack are bound there.
>
> The seventh and final segment is the pelvic, which holds all the muscles of the pelvis and lower limbs. The tense pelvis and anus contain unexpressed anxiety and rage.

Reich designed two ways of working with each segment. He used techniques that worked directly on muscular tensions by some means of pressure, such as massaging a tense area, or by increasing the breathing or both.

Reich's work changed from working with the psychology of the individual, according to his views of various personality types in his psychoanalytic book, *Character Analysis* (1945), to experiments extending his work to the broader world. Reichian scholar Edward Mann explains that

At first Reich believed that this energy, orgone, was specific to living organisms, but later he defined it as a universal preatomic energy. He later worked with the concepts of energy and was able to develop physical methods to open up the blocks and allow the energy to flow through the body. He wanted to be known as the discoverer of this specific "preatomic universal energy," that he named orgone, a name derived from organism and orgasm. His work from the individual extended to the environment and the cosmos.[1]

Reich's theory of orgone equates to the discussions on prana, ch'i (or qi or ki) in part I of this book. Although Reich may have been unfamiliar with Eastern teachings, he was able to discover this available energy in his own research.

After Reich moved from Vienna to New York in the 1930s he established a reputation in the United States. His work attracted Alexander Lowen and John Pierrakos during the 1940s. They spent years training in Reichian work, and then, building on Reich's concepts, they went on to develop their own styles of somatic psychotherapy. In unison, they developed Bioenergetics in the 1950s. Pierrakos and Lowen created many techniques. At first, they practiced these techniques on each other, and then worked on other interested colleagues. They were also less directive and authoritarian as therapists. They saw the client as a partner in the healing process. Unlike Reich whose later work had expanded beyond the psychology of the individual to the cosmos, Pierrakos and Lowen remained focused in restoring the individual patient to health.

A Bioenergetics practitioner notices where the breathing tends to be the most restricted. The practitioner can see there is minimal movement in that area of the body and helps increase the movement by mobilizing the breath in a structured way. The client also provides feedback, and is totally engaged in the process. The following is an example of a Bioenergetic exercise to assess breathing tension. Please feel free to explore in order to determine where you might have restricted respiration.

Put your hand on your chest and inhale and exhale naturally, noticing how your chest feels. Next, remove your hand from your chest, and put your little finger on your navel, resting the rest of your hand on your midriff area, below your chest.

Inhale and exhale, noticing how your midriff area feels. Finally, put your thumb on your navel, resting your hand on your belly. Inhale and exhale, noticing how your belly feels. Notice your breath and see if you can tell which of these three above areas moves the least upon inhaling. The area with the least movement suggests an area of restricted energy. Place your hand on the area that is the most restricted and increase or deepen your breathing in that part of your body. If that is difficult for you to do, it is an indication of chronic tension in the area.

The Bioenergetics therapist uses a variety of processes to release and heal this chronic tension. The above is one example of its focus in psychosomatic work.

In chapter 14, Neil Douglas-Klotz discusses the meeting points of Western somatic and Eastern spiritual traditions, noting that Reich was the most thorough and influential in understanding small proprioceptive differences in tension and armoring around the body. Douglas-Klotz tells us that Reich as well as Gindler and Alexander were both interested in the relationship of breath awareness to neuroticism. An exercise like the one above gives indications about where the breath is held and indicates techniques for the somatic psychotherapist to apply in order to help increase the breath and break through the "blocked armor." How this relates to neuroticism is that Reich believed that held breath and body tensions serve to bind some anxiety in the person. Once the person opens the blocks, through some technique that deepens the breath, they will feel that anxiety, and then if they keep breathing, they will feel the blocked affect (usually sadness, anger, fear, or longing). The theory is that when they allow the expression of the affect, they will feel relief and the natural breath will be restored. Under stress the persons will return to their own pattern of restricted breathing and holding patterns, but having broken through once, they are now conscious of their tension patterns and can more easily access their feelings that will make them feel better.

In the 1960s, Pierrakos added a spiritual dimension to his work, which was influenced by his wife Eva, the founder of Pathwork, a spiritual guidance program. Her ideas became instrumental in the development of what Pierrakos called his work: Core-Energetics. Pierrakos specifically used processes and beliefs from various spiritual traditions in his treatment of each client.

Pierrakos uses meditation in his fourth phase of therapy, which has two inner and two outer focuses to help the person uncover his or her life plan. I invite you to read them over and then take a few minutes to relax, slow your breathing down, and meditate a few minutes on each of the four and see what you experience.

> Visualize yourself as developed, fulfilled, and integrated.
> Allow the warmth and gentleness of love to stream through you as a developed, fulfilled, and integrated person.
> Concentrate on where you want to go in life. Ask, "What is my task in being?"
> Focus on trusting the environment, including the whole universe as a setting for your individual growth.

Pierrakos believes strongly that the core (of the person) reaches for infinity. As he states, "I believe the testimony of my own development, of the people who have been or are in treatment with me, of soaring minds from every culture and age, that there is a unifying, creative principle toward which living things strive. Many venerate it as God. I venerate it as the god who is every human being."[2]

He also felt that once a person had become healthier through analysis they naturally wanted to become more evolved creatively or spiritually. His style incorporated the character analytic theory of Reich; the Bioenergetic techniques created with Lowen; and incorporated beliefs and processes from various spiritual traditions.

Even though they each moved on in different directions, Reich, Lowen, and Pierrakos had one thing in common as the basis of their life's work: the importance of breathwork in the treatment. They recognized that breath played an important role in understanding and healing their clients' problems.

Somatic Psychology and Breath

Before you read any further, take a moment to,

Focus on your inhalation and fill the lungs with air. Notice your lungs expanding the ribs toward the outside of your body. You may also feel your chest rising in the front and a pressure downward, where the diaphragm descends. The diaphragm is the chief muscle of respiration. Hold your breath at the end of the next inhalation in order to feel the expansions in your body. Sometimes tension in our bodies keep us from taking in enough air, which lowers our energy level. Inhaling deeply is like putting more logs on the fire. The fire will burn hotter and longer and we will have more energy. Now exhale and relax and notice how you feel.

After a few minutes you may be aware that your normal pattern of breathing returns. Most of us do not breathe in the optimum way.

In healthy respiration, which is seen mostly in animals and babies, the chest and abdomen are integrated, with the abdomen becoming distended on inhalation and relaxing on the exhalation. Adults often pull in their abdomens on the inhale, reducing the amount of air they take in. The diaphragm contracts and descends in healthy respiration, allowing the lungs to expand downward as they inflate. This is the direction of least resistance for expansion of the lungs. The chest also expands outward in this process, but relaxed breathing is predominately abdominal rather than thoracic (chest) breathing. In such breathing, one takes in a maximum amount of air for the minimum effort.[3]

Experimenting, I let my terrier dog jump on my lap as I typed this paper. I put my hand on his abdomen and chest to check his breathing. His breathing was shallow as he looked around, surveying his new view of the world from my lap. Neither his chest nor belly moved much. Within a few seconds, as he relaxed, I felt his belly distend. His chest was softer to the touch. As he curled up, falling asleep on my lap, his breathing slowed, and both belly and chest began moving in relaxed rhythm. The puppy has exhibited the belly distended on inhalation, and relaxed on exhalation, a pattern of healthy breathing.

The purpose of reviewing the normal function of respiration is to set the stage for what happens from an energetic point of view when respiration is restricted in some way. Reich believed that healthy living includes the ability to discharge excess energy in order to maintain a stabilized energy level. This process of energy metabolism takes place in a four beat rhythm of: TENSION–CHARGE–DISCHARGE–RELAXATION.

Each normal breath also holds the same pattern: TENSION—if you force yourself not to inhale immediately at the end of your last exhalation, you will feel tension. CHARGE—is inhaling to the peak of the inhalation. DISCHARGE—is your exhalation. RELAXATION—is the momentary rest before the tension causes you to inhale again. The following exercise will help you assess whether your inhalation or exhalation are restricted.

> As you sit and read, arch your back over your chair and stretch your arms above your head by your ears. Holding the stretch, breathe in and out five or six times. See if you can detect which has more strain, your inhale or your exhale. If you can't tell, you may try a few more breaths. Stop when the exercise is too stressful for you. Under the stress of the long stretch, restrictions can be more easily noticed.

Any restriction in the natural full breathing pattern diminishes the capacity of our energetic flow. When we have a cold, it can be accompanied by a stuffed up nose, a sore throat, and a cough, each one of which inhibits normal breathing. The nasal cavity can't efficiently warm, moisten, and filter the air; the sore throat and cough create stress, interfering with the smooth downward progression of the breath to the lungs. This strain on our natural resources for respiration contributes to our feeling of exhaustion when we are sick.

We also have (largely unconscious) restrictions, that serve a psychological purpose. Through breathing we get the oxygen to keep our metabolic fires burning, and these provide us with the energy we need. More oxygen creates hotter fires, and produces more energy. This chemical analogy helps us grasp the importance of good breathing in preparation for the concept of problems inherent in psychologically based restricted breathing.

Adults tend to have disturbed breathing patterns because of chronic muscular tensions that distort and limit their breathing. Somatic psychotherapists see these tensions as a result of emotional conflicts developed while growing into adulthood. When I was a child, I used to tighten my stomach and thereby restrict my breathing, which served to block the impulse to express my fear or anger.

Try the following exercise to experience the effect of restricted breathing on energy:

1. Lift shoulders up into neck and roll shoulders forward.
2. Pull arms tightly into sides.
3. Pull in belly and tighten your waist.
4. Now, inhale and exhale.
5. Notice any constraints.

This tension or pain from this exercise may make you wonder why anyone would choose to breathe less than fully. Perhaps you noticed that it hurts to restrict the breath. Yet, some of us walk around with some version of a restricted breathing pattern, without recognizing that our breath is restricted, and without realizing that freeing that restriction will help restore more pleasure in life.

What does breathing have to do with pleasure? Inhaling is literally intake of air, and exhaling is expelling air. To expand from the literal to the figurative, we take in life as we inhale, and produce or put ourselves out into life as we exhale. Therefore, Reichian breathing theory holds that the deeper we breathe, the more life, the more pleasure we are capable of experiencing. It is only in inhaling fully that we take in all the beauty the earth has to offer, and it is in exhaling fully that we can put out all the love and talent we have to offer back to our world.

We have days of illness or tiredness, when we sense the world at a distance and need to withdraw our resources. We neither inhale nor exhale fully. We have other days when we feel radiantly alive, and the world seems brighter, closer and more real. On these days our breathing is full.

Sometimes, people come into therapy simply because they do not feel the sense of being radiantly alive. They may not know the source of their depression, and they are most likely unaware of the relationship between their restricted breathing and their unhappiness. People restrict their breathing in many ways, and somatic therapists recognize that the unconscious purpose is to constrict some aspect of self-expression.

According to Alexander Lowen, "A person who doesn't breathe deeply reduces the life of his body. If he doesn't move freely, he restricts the life of his body. If he doesn't feel fully, he narrows the life of his body. And if his self-expression is constricted, he limits the life of his body."[4]

An Illustration

Although these restrictions are not voluntarily self-imposed, sometimes people need outside help in order to regain a more vibrant life. In this final section, I will use an example from my Bioenergetic psychotherapy practice that illustrates work with the breath, a physical symptom, and a psychological discovery.

A client complained about a painful dollar sized wound in the center of her chest above her breasts. The infected wound was so painful that it hurt her to walk, and she had to have it treated by medical doctors. During our session, I had her place her hand gently over her wound, close her eyes and focus her attention as she breathed into her chest area. Deeper breathing increased movement in the thoracic region allowing more energy into the area. She reported that with her eyes closed she saw an image of things being pushed off her chest. Then she spontaneously moved her hand off her chest and made a gesture with her hand of pushing something away firmly. She opened her eyes, which looked alert and determined. As she repeated the pushing away gesture, now with both hands, she shared this insight, "There are things I need to get off my chest." She has a history of being accommodating and this work revealed to her that she had been holding in things she needed to say assertively to certain people. After that, she cheerfully practiced how she would assert herself in specific situations.

The unconscious nature of her struggle between being accommodating and being assertive was made conscious by sending the breath to energize and create movement in the injured area. While not all body illnesses or injuries have psychological components, in this case the physical wound was partly a manifestation of the unconscious conflict between accommodation and assertiveness. Her over-accommodating nature was wounding her and made its presence known by creating a physical symptom that she was forced to attend to.

Her story is an illustration of the simple poignant beauty of the body speaking its pain and the healing power of the breath to help the body find its way back to pleasure.

Conclusions

Within Wilhelm Reich's revolutionary mind-body concepts and their development in Bioenergetics and Core Energetics, a specific model is presented that explains how breath contributes to aliveness. The theory is that aliveness involves the capacity to experience a full range of emotions. When that full range of emotions is restored we are capable of deeper sorrow and greater joy, more assertive anger and appropriate levels of fear. Unconscious constrictions in any area of the body related to breath narrows our world and reduces our capacity to feel difficult as well as pleasurable feelings. The function of the narrowed breath is to bind the anxiety associated with expanding the breath. Restoring natural breathing through specific techniques or interventions, as illustrated in the case vignette expands our world and often leads to deeper cognitive understanding or insight. This tradition looks at the restoration of natural breath as a means to more satisfaction in life. The belief is that by inhaling deeply, we can better take in the love and support we need from others, and by exhaling fully, we can produce the gifts we have to give back to our world. This breath consciousness from Reichian and neo-Reichian traditions contain one form of viewing and working with the dynamics of the breath that can contribute to a fuller and richer life.

Notes

1. Edward W. Mann, *Orgone, Reich, and Eros* (New York: Simon and Shuster, 1978), 13.
2. John Pierrakos, *Core Energetics* (Mendocino, CA: Core Evolution Publishing, 2005), 226.
3. Alexander Lowen and Leslie Lowen, *The Way to Vibrant Health* (New York: Harper and Row, 1977), 24.
4. Alexander Lowen, *Bioenergetics* (New York: Coward, McCann & Geoghegan, 1975), 43.

6

Birth, Rebirthing, and Learning to Breathe

MICHAEL SKY

Introduction

In 1975, Dr. Frederick Leboyer published *Birth Without Violence*, his paean to the process of natural birth. The French obstetrician begins with a long, difficult cataloguing of the horrors (there is no other word) of what then passed for a typical hospital delivery. The rushed and oddly impersonal atmosphere, the bright lights, cold temperatures, and loud sounds, the many chemical and mechanical interventions, all assault the birthing child, creating a most unpleasant introduction to human life. "This is birth," writes Leboyer, "the torture of an innocent. What futility to believe that so great a cataclysm will not leave its mark."[1]

The worst torment of all, according to Leboyer, is the premature cutting of the umbilical cord. The doctor explains that nature assures that the birthing child has a constant supply of vital *oxygen*. The umbilicus, which has provided oxygen from the mother throughout the pregnancy, continues to pulse while the infant journeys from the womb and for an average of four to five minutes after delivery. During this interval, the newborn opens her (or his) lungs for the first time, beginning a lifelong process of respiration. "[Nature] has arranged it so that during the dangerous passage of birth, the child is receiving oxygen from two sources rather than one: from the lungs *and* from the umbilicus.... [T]he newborn infant straddles two worlds. Drawing oxygen from two sources, it switches gradually from the one to the other, without a brutal transition. One scarcely hears a cry."[2]

Once the baby has established her breathing, the umbilicus stops pulsing. Fully prepared to breathe on her own, the baby in effect cuts her own cord. The whole process is marked by a sense of innate intelligence, of ancient and eternal rhythms, and of a profound peace that does indeed surpass all understanding.

When, for whatever reasons, the cord is cut just after the baby is born and before the functioning of independent breathing, then a terrible crisis ensues. The infant brain is deprived of oxygen to its most serious detriment. The baby is *dying*, and nowhere in her DNA are instructions for how to effectively respond to this threat.

Having turned the birth into a dire medical emergency, the doctors feel compelled to do whatever is necessary to shock respiration into action. So one unnatural intervention leads to the next: the baby is grabbed by the ankles, swung upside down, and struck on the buttocks. This gross act of violence does indeed get the baby breathing, but her terrified screams bear zero resemblance to the deeply peaceful first breaths of the naturally born baby. "For the baby," writes Leboyer, "it makes an enormous difference. Whether we cut the umbilical cord immediately or not changes everything about the way respiration comes to the baby, even conditions the baby's taste for life."[3]

This is the crux of Leboyer's message: we learn to breathe at birth, and so much more. The process of birth conditions everything that follows. How we feel about our bodies, how we manage our emotions, how we relate to others, how we deal with challenging circumstances as fundamental patterns are established at birth, for good or ill, depending on *how* we are born.

This is, admittedly, a radical notion for many in Western culture. Western science gives a rather different understanding of birth. It thinks of the fetus/newborn as *pre*conscious and therefore unaffected, in any lasting way, by the circumstances of birth. Because an infant's brain has not yet fully developed, many scientists reason that the human faculties of consciousness, emotion, memory, understanding, and learning have likewise yet to develop. In a profound misunderstanding, they have looked at the newborn and concluded that *there is no one there*!

The human infant: body, but not a person; pain, but not emotion; experience, but not memory; and awareness, but not learning. Tragically, it follows that it does not really matter how you treat such a creature, so long as you tend to her bodily survival. Since she has not yet developed into a fully conscious being, she will not take offense nor draw any conclusions from your behavior.

However, a body of research has begun to substantiate what any mother already knows: that the newborn is conscious, intelligent, responsive, and impressionable. Indeed, if anything, we should view the newborn as *hyper*conscious; she has greater conscious awareness of the world in the first few hours of life than she shall likely have at any later time. While she will gradually develop unconscious mechanisms for screening out the vast quantities of sensory input that life imposes, as a baby she remains wide open, totally receptive, and taking the whole world in through all of her senses.

Consequently, the newborn *will* suffer, as surely and meaningfully as any adult will suffer; she will respond to her suffering, like any adult, with the best of her capabilities; and she will learn and grow from such painful (and pleasurable) events as past experiences will influence her present responses and future behavior.

Under the best of conditions birth will involve a fair measure of such suffering/learning, which will in turn contribute to the psychophysical development of the new person. The attending adults have the responsibility to ease the way for the birthing infant as much as possible, and then to provide an environment that emanates warmth, safety, support, nurturance, and love. Ideally, the newborn's early lessons will be of monumental challenges well met, of painful contraction giving way to ecstatic release, and of the absolute presence of "motherlove," the baby's experience of unconditional human and environmental support.

Such ideal conditions rarely obtain, however, and we all carry the unresolved pains of birth forward as we grow. Moreover, when a culture fails to recognize the connection between birth and human development, newborns will take on some especially destructive primal memories. Twentieth-century Western obstetrics, "techno-birthing" as I call it, dictates a particularly traumatic birth experience, with its own load of unnecessary pains. Though somewhat unpleasant, it helps to examine this approach to birth, as it has contributed so greatly to life as we currently know it.

The interventions of techno-birthing often begin at the beginning: rather than wait for the infant/mother to initiate labor, doctors may induce contractions through chemical means. Many births happen according to doctor and hospital schedules, as if the organic timing of the mother/fetus/body has no relevance. Hospitals continuously monitor the fetus (for reasons that have more to do with doctor liability than the process of birth), in ways that often interfere with the mother's labor. Should the fetus's vital signs in any way fall outside of statistical norms, the attendants typically assume the worse and undertake further interventions. Unfortunately, each intervention tends to subvert the natural process, directly causing the need for further interventions.

The use of forceps, caesarean section, and/or anesthetics have all become fairly standard procedures of techno-birthing to help the woman deliver, and each has its own often serious lasting effects for the infant. However she makes it out the womb, the infant generally arrives into a world of chaotic sensory assaults inundated with bright lights, loud voices, cold temperatures, harsh surfaces, masked faces—the perfect environment for surgery, but a foolishly inhuman greeting for one who has spent nine months in the womb.

Techno-birthers may visit other horrors upon this tiny new person, mostly in the name of sanitation and efficiency, such as the immediate separation of the newborn from her mother. (How can we do this?) But nothing causes as much long-term damage as the greatest folly of all—the premature cutting of the umbilical cord.

A lifetime of continuous breathing all begins with, and patterns upon, the first breath out of the womb. This marks a critical first step toward independence: to breathe separately from the mother establishes oneself, in the most fundamental of terms, as an autonomous being. Breathing for oneself is the beginning of truly living free.

For this first breath to occur spontaneously, those attending the birth must have patience and trust. When, for whatever reasons, the attendants abort the process an extreme emergency can result for the infant. Suddenly, with her oxygen cut off and her life acutely threatened, the infant has no innate capacity for responding to this event. Moments from death and totally helpless, she explodes with panic!

Birth, at this point, has indeed devolved into a serious medical emergency, calling for radical emergency procedures. The doctor grabs the infant by the heels, swings her upside down, and slaps—hard. We can only shake our heads and wonder. Birth has been turned into a brutal and irrational torture and an initiation into violence. Learning to breathe has become the most traumatizing event of a person's life.

The newborn's first breath contains all of the terror of the moment. All of the infant's intensely contracted energy, her profound emotional pain, and all of her screaming, "I hate this!" condition that first breath and every breath to follow.

Such "breathing lessons" can lead to a lifetime of shallow breathing. A deep cellular connection between stress and breath has been impressed. A host of painful and unresolved memories have been locked into the newborn's body—the relevant data for the decisions, attitudes, patterns, and beliefs out of which she will create her life.

Imagine for a moment that you have just stepped off an airplane into some new and exotic country. The natives assault you with glaring light and deafening noise, and then they roughly manhandle and abuse your body. They seem calm, happy, even celebratory as they do all this. It would seem the height of rationality to get back on the plane and fly away, firmly resolved to have nothing to do with such inhuman people.

Though we all chose to remain in *this* new and exotic place, if we arrived via techno-birthing then we cannot avoid certain negative patterns and tendencies. If our natural intuitive responses get subverted from the very beginning, doesn't it make sense to grow distrustful of ourselves and irresponsible in our behavior? If the environment attacks us from the very beginning, doesn't it make sense to view the world as a hostile and unfeeling place? If the first person we ever meet inflicts violence upon us, doesn't it make sense to fear humanity and carry deep feelings of unsafety forward into future relationships? And if learning to breathe was a terrifying and panic-stricken event, then doesn't it make sense that we will instinctively avoid fully breathing for the rest of our lives?

The Baptism of Water and Air

In the early 1970s, as Leboyer was publishing *Birth Without Violence*, Californian Leonard Orr was making startling discoveries about his own birth. Orr had stayed in a hot sauna long beyond the recommended time when he began to have physical, mental, and emotional memories of the process of being techno-birthed. Through a series of saunas, he remembered the bright light and the cold room, he remembered the long, arduous struggle, and he remembered the masked doctor, the choking, the sudden vertigo, the pain and anguish, and the unbearable separation and isolation.

In the midst of this deeply unsettling process, Orr had some powerful insights. First, he realized that his introduction to breathing—which he already knew to be vital to human health and happiness—had been terribly mishandled, with dire consequences. Second, he intuited that he could correct any damage done at birth by reliving the event and then "reframing" it—creating and ingraining a more positive set of experiences, memories, and lessons learned. Finally, he understood that he would not be able to undergo this reliving and reframing on his own. Just as birth was essentially a social experience, involving at the very least one's relationship to one's mother, so this approach to healing birth would necessarily unfold in intimate relationship to others.

Thus began both the process of rebirthing and the wider rebirthing movement. Because of the emphasis on reliving birth, early rebirthing took place in sensory-stimulating hot tubs. Small groups would gather for an introductory talk that often included readings from Leboyer's book. When ready, participants would disrobe and head for the tub. The rebirthee, or "breather," would lie face down in the water, breathing through a snorkel. One rebirther would sit toward the head and hold the snorkel so it never went underwater. Another would support the hips so the breather had an experience of being suspended weightless.[4]

The breather was encouraged to breathe deeper and faster than normal, and to breathe without stopping. Typically, after a few minutes of this, the breather experienced any of a wide range of effects, including: a warm tingling sensation in the hands, face, or feet, that could spread quite wonderfully throughout the body, or that might intensify into a tight and extremely painful cramping of muscles; feelings of faintness and difficulty remaining focused, followed by long periods when one barely breathed at all and when all breathing seemed an enormous effort; experiences of nausea, choking, muscle tremors, or sudden extremes of hot and/or cold temperatures; memories of one's birth that came with extraordinary clarity, as visual images, or as the actual movements and expressions of the breather's present-time body; intense feelings of sadness, shame, rage, and fear, of losing control, of vulnerability, of helplessness, or of stark terror; more encouragingly, a body tingling that excited into ecstatic joy; waves of sexual pleasure surging everywhere; a profoundly deep relaxation; powerful insights into the nature of life; visions of deep, mystical content; or an unforgettable spiritual rebirth.

As amazingly transformational as the experience could be, the use of hot tubs was problematic. In part, because finding spaces that were logistically safe and suitable for the whole experience was difficult. Moreover, bringing small groups of naked bodies together for common journeys into vulnerability, intimacy, deep affection, and rushes of ecstatic energy led unsurprisingly to instances of inappropriate sexual play.

In any case, some breathers, while waiting for their turns in the tub, spontaneously began breathing deeper and faster, thus igniting the rebirthing process. As rebirthers attended to these "dry" rebirths, they discovered that not only was the experience every bit as rich and full as in the hot tub, it was in many ways superior. So rebirthing moved to normal therapeutic environments, with the hot tubs reserved for advance work and for the training of professional rebirthers.

Even as the rebirthing process detached from its hot tub origins, the rebirthing movement underwent major changes. Orr had always taken a nonauthoritarian approach to his teaching, encouraging those who had only been rebirthed a few times to begin sharing it with others. He would eventually shift to a more traditional certification process for rebirthers, but too late to prevent the rebirthing movement from splintering into dozens of different styles and approaches as self-appointed experts (the author included) took Orr's insights and techniques in different directions.

By 1977, there were countless variations of the basic breathing process that Orr had developed, many with their own names and defining language. Some eschewed the term "rebirthing" and took firm positions regarding the importance (or lack thereof) of one's birth to the present work. Some made significant changes in the philosophical and psychological underpinnings of Orr's approach. The one thing they all had in common, and would likely still agree upon thirty years later: if we were not properly taught to breathe as children, we can benefit enormously from effective breathing lessons as adults.

Rebirthing Lessons

Learning to breathe requires an understanding of the subtle aspects of the human organism. The strictly material explanations of living things that have so dominated the past three hundred years of Western thought have generated much good, certainly. But they have also steered around, or flatly discounted, a fundamental characteristic of all living systems.

Amoebas, whales, worms, and human beings all share, with all living creatures, one vital attribute: their physical forms pulse with a subtle vibratory essence, called *energy*. This energy flows in regular currents within the physical body, and extends as radiant fields throughout the body and into the surrounding environment. While similar in ways to electricity, magnetism, gravity, and nuclear force, it differs from all of these. Though difficult to scientifically grasp, we can easily experience this energy. With continued experience, one eventually comes to view energy as the essence of the body, mind, and spirit, and the key to the healthy integration of human life.

Even without scientific substantiation, most people are well aware of the flow of energy in their lives. We talk of "having a lot of energy" or of "feeling low on energy"; of "moving forward with a full head of steam" or of "feeling like the fires have gone out." We know what it means to have sexual energy and mental energy. We can feel when a moment has a strong emotional "charge." We easily recognize the radiant glow of love and the powerful aura of good health. We know that energy animates everything that moves in our world.

Furthermore, we understand that energy constitutes all of the matter in the universe, as expressed in Einstein's equation $E = mc^2$. Energy and matter are interconvertible—essentially frozen or crystallized energy manifests as matter, which proceeds slowly or rapidly to transform back into energy. We have spent a great deal of time and intellectual effort developing ways to more efficiently and usefully control this movement of matter into energy—beginning with our first wood fires and culminating in our more recent nuclear reactions.

We understand little, however, about the other half of the equation: the transformation of energy into mass. We do know that plants, for instance, take the energy of light (along with the more material aspects of earth, water, and air) and, through the process called photosynthesis, convert that energy into material form.

We still think of the creation of human bodies, though, strictly in terms of "building blocks": we presume that our material forms grow entirely out of the material constituents of food, water, air, and the genetic gifts of our parents. While we have begun to see that certain "bad energies"—radiation, unfiltered sunlight, radon, and excessive electromagnetism—can create pathological flesh, we have been slow to the study of ways to consciously direct positive energies into the manifestation of healthy bodies.

Every cell of the human body functions, at its core, like an atomic reactor of the most exquisite design, continuously engaged in the conversion of matter into energy and energy into matter. The material constituents of this dual conversion process move through the heart of each cell via physical systems well understood by Western science; universal energy flows through the heart of each of cell along a subtle circulatory system that Western science has yet to describe.

Our daily breath drives this subtle circulatory system. *We convert energy into physical form primarily through the breath.* With every breath we take, we gather and transform the raw material of our bodies and minds.

Breathing energy into flesh begins in purely quantitative terms: the air that we breathe pulses with the energy of life, and provides our most direct and abundant source of "energy becoming mass." The more deeply and continuously we breathe, the more energy we gather, and the more possibilities for physical and mental transformation we enable.

The breath also has vital qualitative aspects: the degree of consciousness that we bring to our breathing determines the nature of our physical and mental manifestations. As we breathe, energy gathers, circulates, and radiates throughout the many aspects of our being. The rate, rhythm, depth, intensity, physical manner, and mental attention of each breath contribute precisely to the movement and embodiment of energy within our lives.

This is the essence of the rebirthing process, in all its many variations: to consciously attend to the rate, rhythm, depth, and intensity of each breath, thereby bringing conscious awareness to the flow (or lack thereof) of the universal creative force that manifests as body and mind, as external reality, and as all our relations. Through any of a number of techniques, breathers learn to pay attention, via the breath, to the essential movements of life. In doing so, they make a profound discovery: intentional human awareness enhances and encourages the creative processes of our world.

As we breathe, so our essential energies flow. As energy flows, so our lives unfold—so we grow, expand, create, learn, love.

When, for reasons typically rooted in childhood and often at birth, we habitually stifle and constrict our breathing, then our creative energies contract and stagnate, and our minds, bodies, and relationships become prone to dysfunction and disease. Chronically contracted breathing begets chronically contracted lives. The botched breathing lessons of techno-births and misguided childhoods compound over time, taking us ever further from the power and promise of our "original breath," until our constant dys-breathing casts a subtle yet corrupting pall on everything.

Fortunately, just as the breath specifically locks in the negative experiences of birth and early childhood, so the breath can free us in this present moment. All of the contracted and unresolved patterns of our past manifest now, in present time, and we can learn to touch, feel, and transform them now, in present time, through simple conscious breathing. While a continuing habit of shallow and contracted breathing will sustain our continuing habits of negatively contracted energy, we can contact and encourage the release of any contracted energy through a single, conscious moment of deep and flowing breath.

Through such conscious breathing we stimulate an increase in quantity and flow/radiance of energy throughout the body and mind. This increase in *moving* energy leads to a direct experience of any stuck and *unmoving* energy. The individual breather thus becomes immediately aware of how she or he most critically blocks the free movement of energy. The person senses it now, in present time. Typically, the present-time awareness of such a block feels unpleasant. It hurts—physically, emotionally, and/or mentally.

The free movement of energy, in contrast with the painful awareness of contracted energy, becomes a growing edge of transformation. This is the rebirthing process: the individual directly experiences habits of the past *and* the capacity for change in the present moment.

In consciously breathing for the space of a minute or so, a person increases the free movement of living energy throughout the many levels of self, which allows him or her to tangibly feel, in present time, specific patterns of contracted energy. While such patterns usually originate in early events, and while awareness of such patterns will often trigger vivid memories, the breather's immediate experience of contracted energy—how does it feel, right now—carries, and turns, the key to positive transformation.

Breath—breathing, breathing, breathing—*is* the key.

Notes

1. Frederick Leboyer, *Birth Without Violence* (New York: Knopf, 1976), 30.

2. Ibid., 50.

3. Ibid., 51.

4. For readers who are interested in learning more of this history and process, consult the following text: Leonard Orr, Sondra Ray. *Rebirthing in the New Age*. Berkeley: Celestial Arts, 1977, and/or Sondra Ray's *Celebration of Breath*. Also, published by Celestial Arts, 1984.

7

The Healing Potential of Holotropic Breathwork

STANISLAV GROF AND KYLEA TAYLOR

Introduction

The use of various breathing techniques for religious and healing purposes can be traced back to the dawn of human history. In ancient and preindustrial cultures, breath and breathing have played a very important role in cosmology, mythology, and philosophy, as well as being an important tool in ritual and spiritual practices. Since earliest history, virtually every major psychospiritual system seeking to comprehend human nature has viewed breath as a crucial link between the body, mind, and spirit.

Most breathing techniques induce a nonordinary state of consciousness. The research into holotropic states of consciousness (those nonordinary states' experiences which occur during Holotropic Breathwork and other transpersonal healing techniques) shows us that these nonordinary states of consciousness have the capacity to touch core places in the psyche that want healing. *Holotropic* is a word that means *moving toward wholeness,* and the practice of holotropic methods has revolutionized the understanding of emotional and psychosomatic disorders. It has shown that psychopathological symptoms and syndromes of psychogenic origin cannot be adequately explained by traumatic events that happen in one's life after birth. Observations from deep experiential psychotherapy have revealed that these conditions have a multilevel, dynamic structure, which regularly includes, in addition to the biography (postnatal), significant elements from the birth experience of the individual (perinatal) and from the parts of the psyche that make connections with the transpersonal realms of consciousness—those that lie beyond the individual's biography and personal psychology.

Holotropic Breathwork as Holotropic Therapy

During the last twenty-five years, Christina and Stanislav Grof have developed "Holotropic Breathwork." It is an approach to therapy and self-exploration that induces very powerful holotropic states by a combination of very simple techniques; accelerated breathing, evocative music, and a particular style of bodywork help amplify and release residual bioenergetic and emotional blocks. In its theory and practice, this method brings together and integrates various elements from ancient and aboriginal traditions, Eastern spiritual philosophies, and Western depth psychology. Holotropic Breathwork differs from traditional Western psychotherapy in two significant ways:

1. The "expert" change agent in Holotropic Breathwork is not an external therapist as in traditional psychotherapy but is the participant's own "inner healer." Holotropic Breathwork theory trusts the inner healer; the structure of the technique assists the inner healer.

2. Symptoms in Holotropic Breathwork, as in homeopathy, are viewed as guideposts to healing fundamental core issues, rather than as pathology or as a focus of treatment in and of themselves.

Trusting the Inner Healer

In Holotropic Breathwork, the breathing, the safety of the proscribed setting and the expanded concept facilitators and breathers share (about what kinds of phenomena may happen in the course of healing) all combine to give permission and provide protection[1] conducive to healing. The fundamental principle of Holotropic Breathwork is that, just as one's body usually heals a wound without the conscious participation of the mind, the same healing mechanism is at work, often below the level of consciousness in the mind, body, and spirit of the psyche. The Principles of Holotropic Breathwork state: "As the process is unfolding, this *inner healer* manifests therapeutic wisdom which transcends the knowledge that can be derived from the cognitive understanding of an individual practitioner or from any specific school of psychotherapy or body work."[2] In other words, the inner healer has much more exact information about what the particular individual needs at that particular moment in order to move toward wholeness and healing, than does any outside expert, however well-trained within the limiting framework of some particular theory of psychology.

The holotropic therapeutic technique of Holotropic Breathwork represents an important alternative to the techniques of various schools of depth psychology which emphasize verbal exchange between the therapist and the client. It even differs significantly from the experiential therapies developed by humanistic psychologists, which encourage direct emotional expression and engage the body but are conducted in the ordinary state of consciousness.

What all schools of psychotherapy have in common is the effort to understand how the psyche functions, why the symptoms develop, and what they mean. This theoretical knowledge is then used in developing a technique that the therapist employs in his or her interaction with the client to correct the deviant psychodynamic processes (symptoms). This approach, although seldom seriously questioned by theoreticians and practitioners, is fraught with some major problems:

1. *Most traditional therapies disagree about what expert approach to apply.* The world of psychotherapy is fragmented into many schools that show a remarkable lack of agreement

concerning the most fundamental theoretical issues, as well as the appropriate therapeutic measures. They disagree considerably in regard to the motivating forces of the psyche and to the factors that are responsible for the development of psychopathology. Consequently, they differ in their views concerning the strategy of psychotherapy and the nature of therapeutic interventions.

2. *The therapist is considered the active change agent and the expert source of knowledge necessary for successful outcome,* although the client's cooperation is an essential part of the therapeutic process, in spite of the disagreements between different theories about what works. The job of the Holotropic Breathwork practitioner, on the other hand, is one of a skilled midwife facilitating a natural process and trusting its timing and direction, rather than that of an "expert" imposing some external idea of how this natural process should go and what to do when.

Verbal psychotherapy often extends over a period of years, and major exciting breakthroughs are rare exceptions, rather than commonplace events. When changes in symptoms occur, they happen over a broad time span, and it is difficult to prove their causal connection with specific events in therapy or with the therapeutic process in general. By comparison, in a Holotropic Breathwork session, powerful changes can occur in the course of a few hours, and these can be convincingly linked to a specific experience.

Physical Healing As Well As Emotional Healing

Moreover, the changes observed in holotropic approaches are not limited to conditions traditionally considered emotional or psychosomatic. In many cases, Holotropic Breathwork sessions have led to dramatic improvement in physical conditions that in medical handbooks are described as organic diseases. We have seen:

Clearing of chronic infections (sinusitis, pharyngitis, bronchitis, and cystitis) after bioenergetic unblocking opened the blood circulation in the corresponding areas.

More solidification of her bones in a woman with osteoporosis, during the course of training to be a Holotropic Breathwork facilitator.

Restitution of full peripheral circulation in several people suffering from Raynaud's disease, a disorder that involves coldness of hands and feet accompanied by dystrophic changes in the skin.

Striking improvement of arthritis in several instances, which seemed linked to a series of Holotropic Breathwork sessions.

In all these cases, the critical factor conducive to healing seemed to be the release of excessive bioenergetic blockage in the afflicted parts of the body, followed by dilation of the blood vessels and improved circulation. The most astonishing observation in this category was a case of dramatic remission of advanced symptoms of Takayasu's arteritis, a disease of unknown etiology, characterized by progressive occlusion of arteries in the upper part of the body. It is a condition that is usually considered progressive, incurable, and potentially lethal.

In a few instances, the therapeutic potential of Holotropic Breathwork was confirmed in clinical studies conducted by practitioners who had been trained by us and independently use this method in their work. We have had also, on many occasions, the opportunity to receive informal feedback from people years after their emotional, psychosomatic, and physical symptoms improved or disappeared after Holotropic Breathwork sessions in our facilitator training or in our workshops. This has shown us that the improvements achieved in Holotropic Breathwork sessions are often lasting. We anticipate that the efficacy of this interesting method of self-exploration and therapy will be confirmed in the future by well-designed clinical research.

Embracing the Symptom as an Ally

In one of his lectures in the 1970s, Fritjof Capra used an interesting parable to illustrate the fallacy of focusing on the symptoms rather than on the underlying problem. Imagine that you are driving a car and suddenly a red light appears on the dash board. It happens to be the light indicating that your oil is dangerously low. You do not understand the functioning of the car, but you know that a red light on the dashboard means trouble. You take your car to the garage and present the problem to the mechanic. The mechanic takes a look and says: "Red light? Piece of cake!" He reaches for the wire and pulls it out. The red light disappears, and he sends you back on the road.

We would not have a very high opinion of a mechanic who would offer this type of "solution." We expected an intervention that would fix the problem and leave the signaling system intact, not the elimination of the mechanism that would warn us if there were a problem. Similarly, the goal of holotropic therapy for emotional disorders is that symptoms do not manifest because there is no reason for them to manifest. It is not the intention to decommission the signaling system so symptoms cannot appear. The holotropic strategy of therapy aims for a solution of full and healthy functioning.

A Homeopathic State of Consciousness

The basic tenet of holotropic therapy is that symptoms of emotional and psychosomatic disorders represent an attempt of the organism to free itself from old traumatic imprints, heal itself, and simplify its functioning. The symptom is considered not only a nuisance and complication of life but also a major opportunity. With this philosophy, effective therapy consists of temporary activation, intensification, and subsequent resolution of the symptoms. The facilitator simply supports and midwives the process that has been spontaneously set in motion by the organism's innate tendency to heal and move toward wholeness.

This is a principle that holotropic therapy shares with homeopathy. A homeopath identifies and applies the remedy that, when given to healthy individuals, has been shown to produce the same symptoms that the client now manifests.[3]

The breath induces the holotropic state of consciousness, which then tends to function as a universal homeopathic remedy in that it activates any existing symptoms and exteriorizes the symptoms that are latent. The inner healer has a kind of "radar" that operates in holotropic states and automatically brings to the surface those unconscious contents that have a strong emotional charge and are most readily available for processing. This is an extremely useful and important mechanism that saves an "expert" therapist from the impossible task of determining what are the truly relevant aspects of the material the client is presenting.

Traditional Therapy Works Toward the Suppression of Symptoms

Under the influence of the medical model that dominates psychiatric thinking, psychiatrists generally tend to see the intensity of symptoms as an indicator of the seriousness of emotional and psychosomatic disorders, despite it being well known that acute and dramatic emotional states, rich in symptoms, usually have a much better clinical prognosis than slowly and insidiously developing conditions with less conspicuous symptoms.

So, paradoxically, Western psychiatry views the intensification of symptoms as a "worsening" of the clinical condition and views amelioration of symptoms as "improvement," even though in systematic psychotherapy, intensification of symptoms suggests emergence of important unconscious material and often heralds major progress in therapy. The confusion of the seriousness of the condition with the intensity of symptoms, together with other factors, such as the workload of most psychiatrists, economic concerns, and the convenience and promotion of pharmacological interventions, is responsible for the fact that much of psychiatric therapy focuses almost exclusively on the suppression of symptoms.

Although this practice reflects the influence of the medical model on psychiatry, in somatic medicine, again paradoxically, such exclusive focus on suppression of symptoms would actually be considered very bad medical practice. In the treatment of physical diseases, symptomatic therapy is applied only if we simultaneously administer causal measures. For example, applying ice and feeding aspirin to a patient with a high fever, without establishing the cause of fever, obviously would not be acceptable medical practice.

When we encourage, facilitate, and support full emergence of the material underlying the symptoms, the process accomplishes what the organism was attempting to achieve: liberation from traumatic imprints and release of pent-up emotional and physical energies associated with them. This understanding of the therapeutic process does not apply only to neuroses and psychosomatic disorders but also to many conditions that mainstream psychiatrists would diagnose as psychotic and see as manifestations of serious mental disease. The inability to recognize the healing potential of such extreme states reflects the narrow conceptual

framework of Western psychiatry that is limited to postnatal biography and the individual unconscious. Experiences for which this narrow
framework does not have a logical explanation are then attributed to
a pathological process of unknown origin. The extended cartography
of the psyche that includes the perinatal and transpersonal domains
provides a natural explanation for the intensity and content of such
extreme states.

Holotropic Therapy Encourages Full Potential

Another important assumption of holotropic therapy is that an average
person of our culture operates in a way that is far below his or her real
potential and capacity. This impoverishment is due to the fact that he or
she identifies with only a small fraction of their being, the physical body
and the ego. This false and incomplete identification leads to an inauthen-
tic, unhealthy, and unfulfilling way of life and contributes to the development of emotional and psychosomatic disorders of psychological origin.

When it becomes clear that the orientation toward the external world
has failed, the individual psychologically withdraws into his or her inner
world and strongly emotionally charged contents of the unconscious start
emerging into consciousness. This invasion of disturbing material tends
to interfere with the individual's ability to function in everyday life. Such
a breakdown can occur in one limited area of life (such as marriage and
sexual life, professional activity, or pursuit of various personal ambitions)
or afflict simultaneously all segments and aspects of the individual's life.

This is clearly reflected in the words many languages use for breath,
and the spiritual and psychological use of the breath is well discussed
by other authors in this book. In materialistic science, breathing lost its
sacred meaning and was stripped of its connection to the psyche and
spirit. Western medicine reduced it to an important physiological function. The physical and psychological manifestations that accompany various respiratory maneuvers have all been pathologized.

The psychosomatic response to faster breathing, the so-called hyperventilation syndrome, is considered a pathological condition, rather than
what it really is, a process that has an enormous healing potential. When
hyperventilation occurs spontaneously, it is routinely suppressed by the
administration of tranquilizers, injections of intravenous calcium, and
breathing into a paper bag over the face to increase the concentration of

carbon dioxide and combat the alkalosis caused by faster breathing. In the last few decades, Western therapists rediscovered the healing potential of breath and developed techniques that utilize it.

There are many breathing exercises from ancient spiritual traditions such as taught by Indian, Sufi, and Tibetan teachers, and there are techniques developed by Western therapists. Each of these approaches has a specific emphasis and uses breath in a different way. The method of Holotropic Breathwork attempts to simplify this process as much as possible. We have concluded that it is sufficient to breathe faster and more effectively than usual and with full concentration on the inner process. Instead of emphasizing a specific technique of breathing, Holotropic Breathwork seeks to trust the intrinsic wisdom of the body and follow the inner clues of each individual's unique process.

The Importance of a Healing Context in Which to Do Breathwork

The breath has the capacity to induce a nonordinary state of consciousness, but we all know from the 1960s that the context determines whether there is the right balance of safety and permission to allow expression and resolution of whatever material surfaces in the psyche during that nonordinary state.

From the very beginning the three stages of ritual (named by and described by anthropologists) were inherent in the structure of Holotropic Breathwork. Holotropic Breathwork offers the same benefits that ritual has offered to groups of individuals for dealing with change, exploration, and healing since the beginning of history. These elements form a crucial, and often overlooked, part of the success of Holotropic Breathwork.[4]

Rituals provide security and structure by repeating expected behaviors. Most of us human beings seem to need to keep one foot in a world that seems stable and familiar, while we launch the other toe (or more) into the ocean of change. Ritual helps us with change in three stages. These three stages of ritual were named by anthropologist, Victor Turner, with the word "liminal," from the Latin *limen*, meaning a threshold.[5]

The first stage of ritual, the *preliminal*, in Holotropic Breathwork is the Introductory Talk, in which the facilitator describes the expansive Grof Cartography,[6] a map of the kinds of experiences of the psyche that tend to arise in nonordinary states of consciousness, whether these occur spontaneously or because of the use of the breath, music, dance, or sacred substances. The facilitator also talks about the Grof Perinatal Matrices,[7] the four stages of birth (and change) and how, as an initial imprint, birth gives us an unconscious blueprint of how to deal with major change. These stages of birth replay again and again in our life passages. The talk also describes the specific structure of the Breathwork day and explains the process and roles which will provide protection and permission for deep work.

The second stage, the *liminal*, is what is commonly considered the ritual itself. This stage includes nonordinary states of consciousness and a special set and setting, so that the ritual and people in it are set apart from ordinary reality together. In the case of Holotropic Breathwork, this is usually a full day of retreat that includes two Breathwork sessions, with each participant having the opportunity to be in the role of breather and sitter in turn.

The third stage is the postritual, *postliminal*, sharing and integration that begins with the Holotropic Breathwork Sharing Group in which all the participants have the opportunity to share their experiences of the day.

In Holotropic Breathwork, facilitators provide this standard model, this ritual, as an anchor. The sameness of the model each time allows participants to relax with what is known and trusted externally, so that at the point of beginning to breathe, they can surrender internally to what will be unknown on the journey.

The Breather/Sitter Relationship

The sitter/breather relationship provides physical support and monitoring for the breather who is in process. But it also gives the opportunity to experience the "giver" and "receiver" roles with greater clarity than that usually available in ordinary life.

In each of those roles, one can experience increased awareness of one's inner and outer relationships. For example, as the breather, a participant has the chance to put him or herself first, and not to be codependent and defer to the sitter's needs. Breathers have the opportunity to have someone pay close attention to them, which is often a corrective experience in a life where inadequate attention resulted in the trauma of omission. Breathers have the permission to express what they need to express, and to have their sitter act as a witness to their process. The external witness of the sitter somehow helps breathers learn a bit more about how to witness themselves internally.

In the role of sitter, a participant has the privilege, not only of staying present for someone's deep process and assisting as necessary, but also of having the opportunity to watch their own impulses and thoughts, without acting on these. In practicing this kind of concentration or meditation with compassion and awareness of their breather's needs, they are strengthening their ability to practice compassion and awareness for their own needs.

Summary

Holotropic Breathwork is a ritual structure that provides permission and protection for individuals to work deeply with the guidance of their own innate healing wisdom. The technique acknowledges that symptoms and expression of energies can be integral to the healing process. Holotropic Breathwork's structure invites the healing benefits of community through the sitter/breather dyad relationship, the group process of Breathwork, and the post-Breathwork sharing group. In Holotropic Breathwork there is the opportunity for corrective experiences in the areas of biographical and perinatal trauma. There is also opportunity for the greater realization of one's full potential as a physical, emotional, mental, and spiritual human being.

Notes

1. Kylea Taylor, "Protection, permission, and connection: Allies on the hero's journey of trauma recovery" (Presentation, International Transpersonal Psychology Association Conference), in *The Holotropic Breathwork Facilitator's Manual*, ed. Kylea Taylor (Santa Cruz, CA: Hanford Mead Publishers, 2008).

2. Stanislav Grof and Christina Grof, "The principles of Holotropic Breathwork," in *The Holotropic Breathwork Workshop: A Manual for Trained Facilitators*, ed. Kylea Taylor (Santa Cruz, CA: Hanford Mead Publishers, 1991).

3. George Vithoulkas, *The Science of Homeopathy* (New York: Grove Press, 1985).

4. Kylea Taylor, *Considering Holotropic Breathwork* (Santa Cruz, CA: Hanford Mead Publishers, 2008), 119–43.

5. Victor Turner, *The Forest of Symbols: Aspects of Ndembu Ritual* (Ithaca, NY: Cornell University Press, 1967).

6. Stanislav Grof, *Psychology of the Future: Lessons from Modern Consciousness Research* (Albany: SUNY Press, 2000), 20–69.

7. Ibid., 29–33.

8

Freediving

Learning Not to Breathe

ORION GARLAND

Introduction

Between inhalation and exhalation is a pause, usually brief, in which we cease to breathe. We do it without noticing, or paying particular attention to it. For thousands of years yoga practitioners have realized the significance of these pauses. They recognize that breathing has four important stages: the inhalation, the pause with full lungs, the exhalation, and the pause with empty lungs. This cessation of breathing is considered to be a moment of complete rest. In daily life, this arrested breath can be quite short, as our cells are in need of oxygen replenishment constantly. However, as we become more relaxed and rested, we can hold our breath for longer periods of time.

Science has shown, through experiments in biofeedback, that the breath affects our whole body. When we consciously breathe quick shallow breaths, our heart beats faster, tension builds up in our bodies, and we tend to feel stressed and anxious. When we consciously breathe slow deep breaths, our heart beat slows down, tension is released from the muscles, and we tend to feel calm and relaxed. What is important here is that we can have conscious control over our breath and, through the breath, have conscious control over many aspects of our bodies and our physiological reactions to the world around us. Freedivers have used this control to create a slowed state of being, in which body functions are intentionally decelerated so that oxygen use is minimal. This allows them to extend the time between breaths for up to ten minutes.

Freediving

Freediving is diving to depth without carrying oxygen. Freedivers have been working for many years on increasing the length of time for which they can swim without breathing. Freediving goes back many centuries as a technique to hunt for fish and mollusks. These skills were even used in naval warfare, with freedivers sneaking up to moored enemy ships at night and cutting their anchor lines so they would drift away. Freedivers were also extensively involved in the pearl trade. This traditional form of diving is kept alive today with the *ama* divers of Japan, who dive for abalone.

Recently, recreational freedivers have approached the practice of breathholding from a scientific angle, studying physiology and adaptation and the reaction of the body to a state of apnea (which literally means without breath). Through this research, they have uncovered techniques to allow almost anybody to hold their breath for more time than they could ever have imagined possible. Expert freediving instructors assure people that, with effort, they can develop their ability to hold their breath for over five minutes within a few months. With training, astonishing world records have been set: one person has held their breath for over ten minutes, and another swam to and from a depth of 113 metres (370.7 feet) on a single breath.[1]

For recreational freedivers, breathholding has more to do with personal challenge and competition than spiritual practice. Traditional freediving began with the pearl divers about a thousand years ago; breathholding was a means of livelihood for these people. Now, many swimmers practice it to improve their snorkeling experience, or for spearfishing. There are also many freedivers around the world who compete in this official sport, under the officiating body of the *Association Internationale pour le Développement de l'Apnée* (AIDA), setting records in a variety of disciplines.

The disciplines include a simple static breathhold, which involves the participant lying face down in the water in a "dead man's float," relaxing all their muscles and letting the water float them softly. Another practice is dynamic apnea, in which competitors swim laps, with or without fins, in a pool underwater without coming up for air. This involves relaxing all of the muscles not needed for the actual swimming process. Lastly, there are the depth disciplines; swimming down into open water with or without fins, or pulling down a line, or riding a weighted sled down to vast depths. These depth dives are the most challenging, psychologically, and yet the most magical. An individual must consciously override the body's survival mechanisms in this treacherous process of swimming away from the surface and life-giving air. Many describe an otherworldly feeling is created by the sensations of weightlessness, the effects of water pressure on the body, and the strange eerie quietness and increasing darkness as the light is filtered out by the particles in the water.

Physiology

The phenomenon of freediving confronts us with the incredible reality that human beings who are not necessarily spiritual practitioners can achieve astonishing feats of breath control and deep physiologic rest. It challenges our concepts of human limitations when we see the human being surviving periods of oxygen deprivation that we have been taught would inevitably lead to irreversible brain damage or death. Research on this is uncovering unexpected human capacities.

There are a number of physiological adaptations that human beings share with aquatic mammals. These instinctive responses remind us that the ocean once was our home, as it is now for dolphins and sea lions. The mammalian diving reflex is an automatic reaction of our bodies, in which the breathing and heart rate automatically slow down when the face is immersed in cold water. This allows for longer and more relaxing dives, optimizing our time underwater. There is also a reflex in which the compression of our chest by water pressure or holding a very full lung of air actually slows down our heart rate.[2] These reflexes are echoes of our aquatic origins.

Additional adaptations occur for freedivers who have been training their bodies over time. These changes demonstrate our body's remarkable adaptive capacities. Blood vessels in the brain, lungs, and heart dilate to allow more efficient oxygen uptake and use, while blood vessels in the skin and muscles not in use constrict to use less oxygen. Lung volume increases, more blood cells are released into the bloodstream, and the muscles shift to alternate metabolic pathways that do not require oxygen. Muscles that are not in use relax, the heart slows, and the brain adapts to longer periods without oxygen. The mind becomes more disciplined and suppresses the urge to breathe through willpower. Basically, the whole human body relaxes and shuts down selectively by our own choice and determination.

When a person first learns to freedive, the "arrested breath" at the top of the breathing cycle can be quite short and uncomfortable. Over time and with effort, however, this discomfort arrives less quickly, as our bodies and minds learn to become more relaxed. One of the greatest challenges the freediver faces in their training is that as times are extended they are in fact hovering closer and closer to that edge between life and death. So much so that freedivers agree never to dive alone, and have elaborate safety protocols by which they need to signal that they are still in conscious control.[3]

What happens if an individual pushes the physiologic boundaries to the extreme? When a person holds their breath, after some time the diaphragm begins to contract, attempting to push the air from the lungs to restart the breathing cycle. If the breath is held through these contractions, they become more forceful and closer together as the person continues to hold their breath. Next, the limbs become heavy, and feel hot or cold or tingly, as the lack of oxygen hinders the action of the muscles and the blood shunts from muscles not in use towards more important tissues. The body goes into conservation mode, centralizing blood flow and the now precious oxygen to the heart and brain. Then it slowly starts to shut down nonessential functioning in the brain—higher thought goes first and the mind goes almost completely blank. Then the hearing starts to fade, and a ringing noise is all that can be heard. Then comes the experience of perceptual narrowing, where peripheral vision is lost, and sometimes the perception of colour is also lost, turning the world black and white. This is followed by the loss of motor control, in which conscious control over the muscles is lost, leading to the shakiness known as "samba" (named after a trance state). Finally, an extended breathhold can lead to a blackout, at which point the person can no longer hold their breath and will automatically start breathing again. No one can choose to hold their breath until the point of death, as when the mind loses control over muscles or loses consciousness altogether, the body begins the breathing process again by itself.

In the world of competitive freediving, success does not look like that of a marathon runner struggling, panting, and collapsing on the finish line. In recognition of the fact that this is a potentially life-threatening practice, the standards of the sport require that there be conscious control at all times. Each participant is required to raise their head out of the water on their own, calmly remove their mask, look directly into the eyes of the judge, and say "I'm OK." These tasks require as much conscious effort and control as the breathhold itself, and demonstrate the athlete's composure. These components give even competitive freediving a graceful quality resembling traditional spiritual breath control practices in yoga and Sufism

In fact, the techniques necessary for freediving are core practices common to a number of spiritual traditions, especially Buddhist, yogic, and Sufi practices of mindful attention and breathing practices similar to those described in the yogic, Buddhist, and Sufi chapters in this book. In addition these practices awaken us to a deep gratitude for the preciousness of human life, and a freedive in itself can symbolically evoke the experience of life, death, and rebirth. There is a saying in freediving: "A freedive is like life: it begins and ends with a breath."

Attending to the Breath

When beginners learn meditation, the first thing they are taught is to pay attention to the breath, rather than the mind (as described in chapter 2). In attempting to attend to the breath in meditation, beginners are constantly distracted and losing focus and may feel frustrated with themselves for losing awareness. Nevertheless, this challenge is incorporated into the practice, as returning to the breath is like returning to the source; even if the mind wanders many times, each of these are opportunities to return to the source. A Centering Prayer teacher has described this as "a thousand opportunities to return to God."[4] In most practices, the focus on the breath is either associated with a mindful presence in a still body or is accompanied by dissociation from the physical body through radically altered states of consciousness.

Freediving is unique in that the breath control and breath cessation are being done while undertaking *physical tasks*, which require extraordinary awareness of the physical world, while being suspended in that infinite space between breaths.

Freediving requires an incredible integration of control and relaxation. The diver must accomplish the remarkable goal of focusing on the breath to prevent automatic breathing, while retaining exquisite awareness of the physical world to complete specific tasks and attending to life-saving survival strategies. And all of this must be achieved while meeting the requirement that at the end they must demonstrate extraordinary equanimity, which is a calm, poised, and fully present state. Freediving is a potentially life-threatening activity. However, excessive activity of the mind, especially worry, is incompatible with freediving. The physiologic demands of worry and the associated tension in the body would not only make it difficult to let go to enter the dive, but the dive would be quickly aborted because the tolerance of apnea would be impossible. Common to many spiritual practices, freediving requires meticulous training, followed by surrender. Before the dive, freedivers focus on relaxing the body and mind and use the breath as a vehicle to calm themselves and prepare for the dive. They also revel in the last few minutes of breathing, knowing that they will soon be without this vital and pleasurable bodily function. They begin the process of conservation of energy to reduce oxygen demand. The slower and deeper they make their breathing, the slower their heart beats, the more relaxed their muscles become, and the calmer their mind becomes.

During the dive, the body must conserve as much oxygen as it can, so it both relaxes every muscle it does not have immediate need of, and also focuses energy on the vital functions—the heart, the brain, and muscles being used for movement, if any. The mind is emptied, except for core survival systems, and the inhibition of breathing. In this extraordinary state, our usual thinking patterns are in a state of shock and awe at what is happening. Into this still and spacious mind, within this otherworldly environment, spiritual experiences may emerge. This is similar to what may be experienced in a sensory deprivation chamber: there is no sound, even of our own breath; there is almost total darkness, weightlessness, and few physical sensations, even of temperature due to the wearing of a wet-suit. This effect is even greater during a static, or floating, breathhold.

At the end of the dive, the diver faces the greatest challenge. The body is screaming to breathe, and yet they must take very measured, controlled breaths, according to a prescribed pattern. In a composed manner they must then undertake the ritual greeting of the judge.[5] While the diver must be outwardly calm for the first twenty seconds, inwardly there is joy at being able to breathe, and at their accomplishment.

Fasting from the Breath

One of the most fundamental spiritual practices in many traditions, including Jewish, Buddhist, yogic, Christian, Islamic, and many others, is fasting. Fasting involves a component of both control and surrender. We are submitting to a discipline, surrendering our physical desires to a higher value. One of the reasons that fasting is so powerful is the realiza-tion that something that we engage in out of necessity and often without awareness can be consciously put aside and done without for a period of time. This is true of fasting both from food and from air. We break from our old habit patterns in a most extreme way and also declare that we are more than our physical body or the "animal" human. We have choice and free will, and our spirit is strong enough to override both our physical and mental needs. Obviously, we can do without food for a much longer time than we can do without air, but if we fast in order to gain greater awareness and greater gratitude for what we have already, then "breath fasting" is a much more efficient way of bringing this about.

More than the physical cravings for food or air, our minds crave these things, and it is our minds we must learn to tame most of all. During a fast, the mind is always questioning us, even when we feel good. It con-stantly wants to know why we are doing this, trying to make some sort of logical sense out of our self-imposed deprivation. But usually there is no logical reason that the mind can accept, because fasting makes no sense to the rational mind. Does it make sense to go without nourish-ment? Even more so, how could you possibly explain to the instinctively self-protective body-mind consciousness that it needs to give up the very breath of life? Sufi teaching emphasizes the need to "die before you die," which involves relinquishing physical desires and attachments to worldly needs, desires, and possessions, even our own lives. Breath fasting takes this to the most fundamental level. How does one explain to the mind that the spirit will be stronger for it, that it will allow the spiritual nourishment that we so often go without? The mind can be convinced of the physical rationale for a food fast, related to purifying the body or improving health, but there is no rationale for a breath fast. Fasting is partly a reminder that the spirit is in control of both the physical and mental aspects of ourselves. On the other hand both the mind and the body are meant as a vehicle for the spirit to experience and express itself, and the beauty of the freediving experience allows this as well.

Often the most beautiful part of fasting is its ending: there is so much joy and gratitude for the food that we eat after we have gone without it, just as there is so much joy and gratitude for each breath taken after we have suspended it for a few minutes. The simplest meal tastes like a heavenly feast, and we can almost feel the food nourishing every cell of our body and energizing us. In the same way, that first breath of air after a breath-hold feels so fresh and pure, and we can feel the air coming into every cell of the body and nourishing it, quickly clearing out the uncomfortable build-up of lactic acid. There is such a joy in just breathing, and a deep gratitude for being alive!

Birthing

Each dive is also a remembrance of the birthing process: we swim in a sea of darkness, noises are faded and dulled, our body feels like it floats in a sensory deprivation chamber, hardly feeling anything at all. We are weightless, rolling in the same primordial sea that life first emerged from. Then, we feel discomfort, contractions in our own bodies. With this is the realization that we are separate from all other beings and matter, we are our own person. There is the desire to breathe, to *live*, and so we turn upwards and head for the surface, traveling faster as the buoyancy takes over and pushes us upwards like an air bubble being pushed up and out of the sea. Moving towards the light, we shoot upwards and with our last arm sweep our face breaks the surface and we breathe out, then in; we feel as if we are taking the first glorious breath of air we ever took.

And then to lie down on our backs and float on the surface, just relaxing and rolling with the waves, and breathing, breathing, breathing. All that matters then is the breath; somehow, it is enough. The following exercise is an example of a preparatory practice for freediving.

> One of the best ways of finding out what it is like to go without air is to try it. Get comfortable somewhere, perhaps leaning back in a chair or lying on your bed. Take a moment to pay attention to your breathing. Slow the breath down, and feel the effects on your body. Can you feel your heart rate slowing, your muscles relaxing, your mind starting to drift pleasantly rather than worrying about your to-do list? Pause briefly after inhaling, and again after exhaling. What effect does that have on you? Now, try inhaling and holding your breath, just until it feels uncomfortable, then breathe again. Take a few more deep, slow breaths. Next, try inhaling and holding your breath, even through the discomfort. You may notice that your heart rate starts to increase somewhat, that your lungs feel like they want to empty themselves. If you continue to hold your breath, you will notice some strange sensations in your lower chest— this is your diaphragm contracting, attempting to force the air out of your lungs in order to restart breathing. At this point, you should breathe the air out of your lungs and take a few quick breaths to rid yourself of the stale air in your lungs and replenish it with oxygen-rich air.

This practice can even be used within a meditation, by simply extending the amount of time the breath is held at the top, and even at the bottom of the breathing cycle. In this case do not forcefully hold your breath, simply allow it to stop and also allow it to start again when it feels like it is time to do so. This strange and beautiful place of rest, in which no breathing takes place, is a wondrous place to visit.

Personal Experience

Having had experience with Buddhist and Sufi meditative practices, I know that it can be challenging to continually attend to breath and not get caught up in the mind. But when I began freediving, this became much simpler. The attention to the breath was a means to an end, a way of experiencing and interacting with the underwater world without cumbersome diving equipment, bringing the feeling that I really belonged underwater. The movement in this other world of weightlessness and breathlessness brings such great joy, both from the stillness and also from the seemingly effortless movement of swimming. A long slow undulation of the body brings relaxed movement. And the holding of the breath, with the accompanying slowing of the heartbeat, is a place of greater stillness and relaxation than a simple sitting meditation, particularly if the body is suspended in the water. Freediving is a spiritual practice even when it is undertaken for sport. The control of the breath, the focus of the mind, and the giving of power to the consciousness or higher aspect of the self, all are fundamentally spiritual practices and can be used as a means to glimpsing the divine. Freediving also has the added quality of maintaining an exquisite sense of composure and awareness, what Buddhists term "equanimity." In freediving, the mind and body must surrender to the spirit. In turn, often the spirit must have a component of trust and faith in something greater than itself.

Conclusion

Cessation of the breath by conscious choice is a very powerful meditative technique. It is a difficult and advanced technique in traditions such as Sufism or yoga. Yet the practice of freediving challenges limiting concepts of our capacities. The process of undoing the habits that we have and the ideas we have about our bodies and the world is actually extraordinarily liberating. Freediving allows experience of the spacious, calm mind in the efficiently functioning body, while relishing the joy of being alive.

Notes

1. Association Internationale pour le Développement de l'Apnée (AIDA), retrieved July 9, 2008, from http://www.aida-international.org.

2. Randall W. Davisa, Lori Polaseka, Rebecca Watsona, Amanda Fusona, Terrie M. Williamsb, and Shane B. Kanatous, "The diving paradox: New insights

into the role of the dive response in air-breathing vertebrates," *Comparative Biochemistry and Physiology, Part A, Molecular and Integrative Physiology* 138 (July 2004): 263–68.

3. Terry Maas and David Sipperly. *Freedive!: A Complete Guide to Breath-hold Diving* (Ventura, CA: BlueWater Freedivers, 1998).

4. Cynthia Bourgeault, personal communication.

5. Deeper Blue, retrieved July 9, 2008, from http://www.deeperblue.net.

9

Buteyko

A Method for Healing with the Breath

RUSSELL AND JENNIFER STARK

Introduction

A young medical intern sat at his desk in a Russian hospital ward one night, rubbing his head in an effort to relieve the throbbing ache. As he reached for an aspirin, he noticed that he was breathing heavily, and so he focused on his breath, making it gentler and slower. Almost immediately his headache eased. Puzzled by this, he began to increase his breathing pattern again, and noted the headache returned. After he had been experimenting in this way for a few minutes, one of the patients in the ward woke up, asking for pain relief. Instead of giving him medication, the intern asked the man to decrease his breathing. This simple act eased the man's pain to such a degree that he was able to sleep.

With youthful enthusiasm, the intern woke each of the patients in turn, asking them to alternatively increase and decrease their breathing pattern. Each of them felt worse when they breathed more deeply and coarsely, having fewer symptoms when their breathing was quiet and gentle. The young doctor was totally shocked, because until this time he had believed that breathing deeply promoted health.

The simple observation that coarse and heavy breathing could be connected to a headache led Dr. Konstantin Pavlovich Buteyko down a path that would engulf his whole life. He spent the following weeks at the medical library researching all he could find on breathing processes. His research led him to read about Dr. Da Costa who first discovered what has since been called the "hyperventilation syndrome" in the American Civil War. Da Costa had noticed many soldiers with strange and varied symptoms that did not appear to have any organic cause. The one thing the soldiers all shared were conditions of extreme stress and chronic, low-grade hyperventilation or breathing more air each minute than the body requires.

Konstantin Buteyko also spent hundreds of hours personally observing the breathing patterns of sick people, noting how each one enacted a noisy, heavy breath. The deeper the breath, the more likely it was that death would occur.[1]

Dr. Buteyko was granted research space at a government-sponsored laboratory in Siberia after obtaining his degree in medicine, and he then devoted his time to researching breathing patterns in more detail. He proved that Da Costa and other scientists in this area had been correct in their theory that hyperventilation caused a disturbance in the body. This disturbance manifested itself in many different ways. The most common of which are:

> *Respiratory system:* Shortness of breath, chest tightness, extra sensitive airways, excessive sneezing and production of mucus, long-term blocked or running sinuses, coughing, and frequent yawning or sighing.
>
> *Nervous system:* Light-headedness, unsteadiness, poor concentration, restless legs, numbness, tingling, and coldness, especially in the hands, feet, and face. In severe cases, loss of memory or loss of consciousness.
>
> *Heart:* Racing, pounding, or skipped beats.
>
> *Psychological:* Degrees of anxiety, depression, tension, irritability, and apprehension.
>
> *General:* Dry mouth, abdominal bloating, belching, flatulence, easily tired, poor sleep patterns, vivid dreams, snoring,

sweaty or cold hands and feet, repeated throat clearing, itchy
skin or rashes, chest pain (not heart-related), headaches, sore
muscles, general weakness, and chronic exhaustion.[2]

Even though many of these symptoms are not directly related to the
process of breathing, Buteyko understood that breathing affects every
cell in the whole body, because each cell requires oxygen and produces
carbon dioxide. His research proved that breathing the correct volume
of air is the key to good health and regulating the breath creates a healing effect. Symptoms begin to disappear as one consciously limits the
volume of air breathed per minute. In short, Dr. Buteyko concluded that
many health conditions are nothing more than chronic over-breathing,
or hyperventilation, that is often so subtle that it is not noticed.[3]

The word "hyperventilation" conjures up images of vigorous breathing
causing extreme reactions in the body, but this type of breathing cannot
be maintained for any length of time. So while it can be frightening, it is
less of a problem in the long term. The type of hyperventilation that Dr.
Buteyko noticed is subtle, but virtually relentless, and can be maintained
for weeks, months, or even years without anyone recognizing that the
breathing is more than required for the level of activity. He called this
type of breathing "hidden hyperventilation" because it is unlikely to be
noticed unless it is specifically looked for. However, it has a powerful
effect on the body as carbon dioxide is constantly being washed out of
the system.

Breathing Patterns

The amount of air breathed per minute automatically changes with the
demands of metabolism by increasing the volume of air breathed when
metabolism rises, such as during exercise, exertion, excitement, and at
stressful times. The volume of air reduces again when metabolism slows,
such as during sleep, or when the person is calm. Because breathing
changes with each new situation, it is normally a subconscious function
like blinking, and most people pay little attention to it until they are
short of breath or want to blow up a balloon.

The average healthy adult breathes approximately twelve times each
minute when resting, with about half a liter of air each time, resulting in

4 to 6 liters of air.[4,5] If a person breathes twenty times a minute with half a liter of air, the volume will have doubled, yet virtually no one detects this because taking a breath every three seconds, instead of every five, is a very subtle change. Not everyone increases the amount of air breathed each minute by speeding up the breathing pattern. Instead, some people find themselves repeatedly sighing or yawning. Others use their strong upper chest muscles instead of diaphragmatic breathing, or they may simply be breathing through their mouth, which is a considerably larger aperture than the nostrils. No matter how it is done, hyperventilation usually goes unnoticed because breathing is such an automatic process.

The Stress Response

The natural response to stress of any kind is to activate what is commonly called the "fight-or-flight response." This enables the person to generate extra strength and speed for short periods of time that can be used to escape from physical danger. Not many people face life-threatening events on a daily basis, and many stressful situations require no physical activity at all, yet we all have the potential for the fight-or-flight response.

Buteyko practitioners take a broad view when they use the term "stress" because to them stress means anything that disturbs homeostasis or the inner balance of the body.[6] It might be a physical stress, associated with pain or illness. It could be environmental, caused by sitting in a hot room, or the inhaling of allergens. It could be mental stress, such as worrying about taking an examination without sufficient preparation. It could be emotional, as when a loved one dies. The stress can also be something that is perceived as good (eustress), such as excitement or anticipation of something fun. The stress does not even have to be logical, because the brain does not differentiate between imagined and real danger. Even the experience of watching an exciting movie can set off the fight-or-flight response.

Dr. Buteyko found that constant low-grade stress, caused by day-to-day events, initiates a constant low-grade increase in breathing. The body adapts to this experience and although the stressors may disappear, an unhealthy breathing pattern will have been established because hidden hyperventilation maintains its own constant stress on the body.

The Lack of Carbon Dioxide

Hidden hyperventilation lowers the volume of carbon dioxide found in the blood stream, creating a situation that is called respiratory alkalosis. When this happens the red blood cells that carry oxygen to the tissues do not release as much oxygen as they do when the carbon dioxide pressure is in the normal range. Christian Bohr, a Danish scientist, discovered this phenomenon a century ago, and called it the Bohr effect. Tissues that do not receive adequate levels of oxygen will not function at an optimum level. They may exhibit fatigue, pain, extra wear and tear, or some form of malfunction. It is therefore a paradox that the person is breathing more air per minute than the body requires, yet less oxygen is being released to organs and other bodily tissues.

A lack of carbon dioxide contributes to other functional changes in the body as well, including:

Smooth or involuntary muscle, which is wrapped around almost every tube in the body, will tighten, which could mean that the passage of blood, air, or food are impeded.

Extra histamine is released into the system, causing an increase in inflammation and mucus production, as well as contraction of smooth muscle, redness, heat, pain, and swelling.

As respiratory alkalosis develops, not only oxygen delivery is affected but also metabolic acidity and a change in mineral retention or elimination.

Using the Buteyko Method for Asthma

Once Dr. Buteyko had established to his satisfaction that the lack of carbon dioxide contributed to ill health, he began developing a series of exercises, techniques, and principles to normalize breathing patterns, increasing the pressure of carbon dioxide in the lungs and bloodstream. Over time these physical techniques and principles were organized into what has become known as the "Buteyko Method." This method is particularly known in the Western world for its ability to treat asthma because clinical trials have shown that the method greatly reduces the need for medications and other treatments.

Asthma presents itself in many different ways, with the typical symptoms of occasional tightness in the chest, wheezing, coughing, and shortness of breath in varying degrees. These same symptoms also occur with other conditions, such as bronchitis or a cold. To add to the dilemma, asthma has no standard definition; instead diagnosis is based on the symptoms of airway narrowing that happen for short periods of time. All of these things make it difficult to accurately diagnose the condition.[7] However, typically, three things occur in an "asthma attack," which is defined for the purposes of this chapter as a situation of difficult breathing that requires a short-acting bronchodilator for relief:

The bands of smooth muscle wrapped around the airways spasm.
The inner lining of the airways swell.
An excessive amount of mucus is produced in the airways.

These factors narrow the airspace in the tiny tubes, leading to increased airway resistance, making it especially difficult to exhale. Being unable to freely exhale causes the lungs to become over-inflated, which then compounds the difficulty because the person wants to breathe in again before they have finished exhaling. As resistance in the airway increases, the person naturally breathes harder to overcome the restriction, and paradoxically this over-breathing increases resistance, making the problem worse.[8]

The Buteyko theory proposes that the reason it is difficult to exhale is because the body is protecting its store of carbon dioxide. Narrowing the airways is a very effective way to retain more of this valuable gas that both regulates body functions and allows oxygen to be released to the tissues. Buteyko practitioners believe that the asthmatic suffers from chronic and low-grade hyperventilation.[9,10] When exposed to an asthma trigger, the person becomes more stressed and increases their breathing pattern even more. For example, the person could be sitting in a chair, yet breathing the same volume of air that a healthy person would breathe if they were jogging.

The first clinical trial of the Buteyko Method in the Western world was conducted in Brisbane, Australia. It confirmed the Buteyko theory that asthmatics hyperventilate and have low carbon dioxide pressure when they are not having an asthma attack. The trial participants were found to be breathing on average more than 14 liters of air each minute. This is far in excess of the normal 4 to 6 litres that a resting healthy adult would normally breathe.

By following the Buteyko program, these people showed an average of a 31 percent reduction in the air breathed each minute, a 71 percent reduction in symptoms, a 96 percent reduction in bronchodilators, and a 49 percent reduction in steroid preventers three months after starting to learn the techniques. The participants also showed marked improvement in their quality of life.[11] Considering that a person who learns the Buteyko Method in a trial situation has not voluntarily made the decision to take on this extra work, the results are outstanding.

Other clinical trials have shown the same type of dramatic results, and what is most interesting about these results is the reduction of both bronchodilators and steroids.[12,13] When conventional treatments are used, the usual way of reducing the need for bronchodilator medications is to increase steroid preventer dosages, and so it is a rarity for both to decline. Buteyko practitioners attribute this to the novel way that Dr. Buteyko considered the condition of asthma. Having difficulty breathing is normally considered the major problem of asthma, but Dr. Buteyko saw it as part of the solution to the real problem of over-breathing.

The perceived trouble with the conventional approach to asthma management is that instead of treating the subtle hyperventilation with breathing exercises, the person with asthma is treated with medications that both mask the symptoms and encourage more breathing. As the breathing pattern increases, the defense against it grows with worsening symptoms, stronger and thicker smooth muscle, mucus cells that are both larger and more numerous, as well as an increase in histamine production.[14]

Airway narrowing also occurs as a protective measure to keep irritants, bacteria, and other foreign materials out of the airways, and to prevent cooling and drying of the airways that is caused by moving too much air in and out of the lungs. Every time foreign particles enter the airways they cause scarring, with the airways losing tone and elasticity. To keep foreign matter out of the airways, or to at least keep it in one place while building a defense, the immune system can create excessive amounts of mucus, airway inflammation, and smooth muscle spasm. By following the Buteyko program, the automatic breathing pattern begins to revert to a more normal level, carbon dioxide rises, less irritants are inhaled, airways narrow less frequently and with less severity, and consequently the need for asthma medication drops enormously.

Breathing Through the Nose

Breathing through the nose instead of the mouth is a major goal for all Buteyko students. Because so many people with breathing problems have a blocked nose, the first exercise that is usually taught in any Buteyko course of instruction is one that unblocks the nose. The nose warms, moistens, and filters the air, while at the same time allowing an appropriate volume of air to enter and leave the lungs. When the mouth is used for breathing, the nose tends to block up. This is the opposite of the common and mistaken thought that the person is breathing through their mouth because their nose is blocked. Try the following exercise to see if you can make your nose a little clearer:

Sit down.
After a normal and gentle breath out, close your mouth if it is open, and softly pinch the nostrils closed.
Gently nod head 10 to 20 times until there is an urge to breathe. Be careful that you do not nod so vigorously as to cause dizziness or damage to your neck.
Remove your hand, keep the mouth closed, and *slowly* inhale through the nose.
Continue to breathe through the nose if possible or repeat if needed.

Buteyko Asthma Case History

The following story is typical of the life style and medication changes occurring with the Buteyko Method. This is the story of Jessica's healing.

Jessica had her first episode of asthma when she was three years old. By the time she was seven, she was caught up in a cycle of ongoing asthmatic attacks that never seemed to go away for more than a week at a time. Virtually every three weeks her nose would start to run. Within a few days she would develop a dry cough and a tight chest. Her mother

Terri would then give her a nebulizer of Ventolin three times a day to relax smooth muscle spasm. Her symptoms then appeared to be more like bronchitis, with an increasing amount of mucus. In fact, her parents wondered how such a little girl could produce that amount. Also, the wheezing and nighttime coughing were particularly disturbing for the family. Jessica also took a nonsteroid preventer medication daily.

Jessica's general practitioner was not in favor of young children taking inhaled steroids unless absolutely necessary. He convinced Terri that daily nebulizers of Ventolin were perfectly safe. Terri was not convinced of this when she saw the effects upon Jessica, for example, they caused trembling. She was reluctant to give Jessica a steroid medication because a homeopathic practitioner had warned her that steroids were dangerous drugs. Finally, Terri reconciled herself to giving the powerful bronchodilators to her daughter.

Jessica lived with what seemed like a continuous cold. Her asthma symptoms were also triggered by such things as excitement, laughter, food reactions, and happy, playful tumbling around on the floor with her brothers. Jessica's bubbly personality also worsened her asthma simply because she was often laughing and caught up in rapid speech. Her mother Terri was a physiotherapist. She had seen plenty of people hospitalized with asthma, so she knew how debilitating this condition could be. But it did not seem possible, or even morally right to stop Jessica from being her natural spontaneous, playful, and happy self. Because the asthma was getting worse, Terri began looking at different ways of managing Jessica's asthma. One of the things that she tried was putting Jessica on a restricted diet that involved no dairy, gluten, or wheat. In the early stages this seemed helpful, but after a time it failed to make a difference in the asthmatic cycle. Having a special diet was a difficult thing for Jessica to handle. Years later she still remembers that when she was invited to other children's parties she had to take her own food as she was unable to eat the goodies typical of a child's party. "Even as an adult I think that this would be hard to do, but as a young child it was really difficult. Instead of making me feel special, I felt left out."

When Jessica was seven years old, Terri read an article about a Russian system of controlling asthma that involved breathing techniques. In absolute desperation, because Jessica was starting on the dry cough part of her asthmatic cycle again, Terri phoned the man who was teaching the method in Sydney. Unfortunately, he could not teach Jessica the special breathing exercises at that time, but he took the time to explain that Buteyko looked at asthma from a different point of view, and that taking nebulizers of Ventolin was worsening the condition. This confirmed Terri's suspicions, and she immediately changed Jessica's medication including an inhaled steroid in her asthma plan. This single step made a huge difference to the management of Jessica's asthma. The condition remained somewhat of a problem until the following March when Jessica was able to travel to Brisbane, Australia, where she began learning the Buteyko breathing techniques for children.

Terri tells us what happened next: "For the first few months after learning the techniques there was the odd occasion that Jessica required a puff of her reliever, but once I understood the concept of Buteyko drug management, I could manage it a lot better. Gradually her phlegm lessoned, and so she stopped coughing at night, which meant that we all got a better night's sleep. Within six months she was weaned off her steroids and she has remained that way ever since."

In the past twelve years, Jessica has not required asthma medication. She is now a healthy twenty-year-old, As she retold her story, she added that "Once I started to get my asthma under control with Buteyko, I could play more sports and athletics, without getting breathless. Everything seems so much easier now because I've got Buteyko to use if I ever get asthma, though it seems to have disappeared. I play eighty minutes of indoor soccer, and I get a bit short of breath sometimes, but so does every one else, and ten minutes after we stop playing, I feel fine once again."

Other Health Conditions

Because breathing affects the entire body, there are other conditions alleviated by the Buteyko Method. For example, allergies, chronic bronchitis, bronchiectasis, emphysema, snoring, sleep apnea, insomnia, panic attacks, hyperventilation syndrome, and stress management all seem to respond well to an improved breathing pattern. There have not been any clinical trials on the effect that the Buteyko Method has on these conditions, but Buteyko practitioners regularly receive comments like the following:

> The improvement in my overall health has been dramatic. I rate my health as pre- and post-Buteyko. Pre-Buteyko meant

colds, coughs, and bronchitis every six weeks. Post-Buteyko means increased energy, lack of dizziness, and coughs and colds only two or three times a year.

During the week of the course alone, the improvement was amazing. I went from waking three to four times a night to sleeping right through, which is much better for day-time energy. This improved sleeping pattern has continued for the past few months even though I do not do as much of the Buteyko exercises now.

My nose was permanently blocked and my skin terribly itchy—my fingers cracked and bled so that I had to wear band aids by day and plastic gloves over ointment by night. By day four of my Buteyko course, my condition had improved as if I had taken a short sharp course of prednisone, only without the health risks. I could smell the grass and my fingers and cheeks felt warm and I have stopped scratching. My doctor advised me to see an ear, nose, and throat specialist in order to be operated on for correction of an alleged deviation in my nasal septum. However, since I began Buteyko six months ago, I have been able to breathe wonderfully easily through both nostrils. Prior to Buteyko, I had not breathed through my nose for 12 years. For me, Buteyko means breathing easily through the nose with consequent vastly reduced symptoms.

The Buteyko Method

When learning the Buteyko Method, the student gains practical tools that begin to normalize the breathing pattern by following a basic program that is uniquely designed for each person. The program reduces chronic symptoms and improves the person's ability to overcome acute symptoms. The Buteyko Method also puts the person more in control of their health because each student is taught how to monitor their own breathing pattern. By knowing how good or bad your breathing is on a daily basis, the person is provided with sufficient information to make good choices about their activities. It also allows the person to predict how much medication or how many symptoms can be expected that day. The exercise that is used to do this is called a "Control Pause." Breathing changes constantly in response to emotions, foods that you eat, and any activity. So do not be surprised if you get different results when you try the Control Pause at different times of the day. To find your own Control Pause, follow these simple instructions:

> Find a watch or clock with a second hand and sit so that you can see the clock face.
>
> Keep the mouth closed the whole time that you are doing this exercise.
>
> Breathe through your nose without any effort for at least 30 seconds.
>
> After a normal and relaxed breath out, softly pinch nostrils closed.
>
> Look at the clock and time how many seconds it is comfortable for you to pause your breathing.
>
> On the first signal you receive from your body that it is no longer comfortable to suspend your breathing, remove your hand and keep your mouth closed.
>
> Breathe in through the nose in a normal, relaxed way. If you need to take a deep breath or open your mouth, then you have paused for too long and need to try again.

Dr. Buteyko found that the average healthy adult is able to pause their breathing for forty-five seconds when the respiratory center is activated by a normal pressure of carbon dioxide. Most people learning the Buteyko Method are able to pause their breathing comfortably for only ten to fifteen seconds, so if you have just tried the Control Pause and your pause is less than twenty seconds, you will have a lot in common with many people starting the Buteyko Method.

The Progress of the Method

Many individuals are grateful to learn the necessary tools to heal their own health problems. Therefore, it is not surprising that Buteyko is rapidly growing. Until the early 1990s, the Buteyko Method was virtually confined to the USSR and almost unheard of in the rest of the world. In just fifteen years the growth of Buteyko practitioners has gone from a mere handful of people teaching the Buteyko techniques in Australia, to hundreds of people teaching or practicing it in almost every country around the world. As a result, thousands of people suffering with health problems associated with hyperventilation have been helped.

Both natural and conventional health professionals find the Buteyko theory meaningful because it is based on sound physiology. By eliminating hyperventilation, the Buteyko Method eradicates the symptoms that hyperventilation causes, and because practitioners do not encourage alteration of prescribed medicine without consultation with a medical doctor, the Buteyko Method is a safe way of providing natural healing. In an effort to control the frightening symptoms of hyperventilation, people very often avoid certain foods, or activities. This causes a shrinking of their enjoyment of life. Buteyko helps to open up the world again so that people feel more confident to try new things, or to reinstate old ones. The words of one student sum up Buteyko perfectly: "I did not expect to have such control of my asthma problem and have been swimming, hiking etc., without asthma. It has almost been too good to be true. No asthma. No drugs. No problems!"

Notes

1. Alexander Stalmatski, *Freedom From Asthma* (London: Kyle Cathie, 1997), 12.

2. William Gardner, "The pathophysiology of hyperventilation disorders," *Chest* 109 (1996): 516–34.

3. Stalmatski, *Freedom from Asthma,* 165–66.

4. Paul Ameisen, *Every Breath You Take* (Sydney: New Holland, 1997), 18.

5. Arthur Guyton, *Human Physiology and Mechanisms of Disease* (Philadelphia: W. B. Saunders, 1982), 298.

6. Jennifer Stark and Russell Stark, *The Carbon Dioxide Syndrome* (Auckland. Buteyko On Line, 2002), 11–14.

7. Anne Tattersfield, Alan Knox, John Britton, and Ian Hall, "Asthma," *Lancet* 260 (2002): 1313–22.

8. Andrew Lumb, *Nunn's Applied Respiratory Physiology* (London: Reed, 2000), 256.

9. Stark and Stark, *The Carbon Dioxide Syndrome*, 96–100.

10. Stalmatski, *Freedom from Asthma,* 36.

11. Simon Bowler, Amanda Green, and Charles Mitchell, "Buteyko breathing techniques in asthma: A blinded randomised controlled trial," *Medical Journal of Australia* 169 (1998): 575–78.

12. Patrick McHugh, Fergus Aitcheson, Bruce Duncan, and Frank Houghton, "Buteyko Breathing Technique for asthma: An effective intervention," *New Zealand Medical Journal* 116 (2003): 1187.

13. Robert Cowie, Diane Conley, Margot Underwood, and Patricia Reader, "A randomised controlled trial of the Buteyko technique as an adjunct to conventional management of asthma," *Respiratory Medicine* 2008 Jan 30: 18249107.

14. Jennifer Stark and Russell Stark, *The Carbon Dioxide Syndrome* (Auckland. Buteyko On Line, 2002), 95–103.

10

Breathexperience

A Somatic Science and Art of Living

JUERG ROFFLER WITH ILSE MIDDENDORF

Allowing my Breath to come on its own
Moving myself throughout.
Yet, I and my Self
are the Contents
of these movements.
I live, I breathe—
I become aware
how big the realm
that I call my Self.
One world I am
when slowly awakening
to conscious being
fulfilling
what I am given.[1]

An Interview on the Nature of Breath

This chapter begins with both a discussion and an acknowledgement of
Ilse Middendorf, the now 96-year-old founder of the Middendorf School

of Breathexperience. During our interview Ilse provided the historical beginnings that led to the creation of the Middendorf tradition. First, it should be acknowledged that Ilse was one of the early pioneers in somatic education and the role of the breath in healing. Our chapter provides the history and the process of an unique approach to breath and its power of healing.

Ilse acknowledged that "Breath is a very special power."[2] She shared her unique experience with the breath, an experience that had begun in her parent's garden when she was around 11 or 12 years old. Something within her had prompted her to stretch out her arms towards the blue sky and looked upward at the sun. As she followed this prompting, a strong inner voice told her: "You need to breathe!" She knew that something was touching her deeply for the words had a certain strength in them, and they were said in a voice that she "hadn't known before." It was a command to truly recognize the power of the breath. This led Ilse to both experience, and later pursue, a strong interest in the breath for she recognized its role in developing a oneness of body, mind, and spirit. From that very early age she had gained the impression that many people fail to acknowledge—the importance of the breath in their lives. Now as an adult she began to experiment and find out more about breath. She began "searching for the essence of a person's Self through body movements and soon found the breath to be a medium for relating to the essence of Self and to creating a connection to it. This led her to meet the right people as the path of her work unfolded before her. For example, she soon met Cornelis Veening, who had worked with C. G. Jung. In Ilse's words,

> This confirmed my understanding of the potential of breath to connect in this way, which meant connecting in depth with the essence of Self and its creative and inspiring nature. Veening became a very important supporter in the search and development of my work. I was not satisfied with just researching and developing with the breath by myself. I knew I had to take it further by making my work available for others.

After many years of research and practice Ilse founded the Institute for the Perceptible Breath in Berlin, Germany, in 1965. She then began training practitioners in this blossoming somatic science—an artistic form of breath education she called *Breathexperience*. This then led to more training institutes being established throughout the 1980's in various parts of Europe. Eventually, together, we decided to further the movement leading to the founding of the Middendoft Institute for Breathexperience in San Francisco in 1989.

As we talked, I felt the deep appreciation for this woman, and her understanding of the breath. Her work had a major impact upon my own life, and the eventual development of the current Institute in Berkeley, its certification programs, and the deep understanding she stimulated in me for the natural breath. In one conversation Ilse went on to share her contentment that her work had received international attention because of its effectiveness as a process leading to therapeutic, artistic, and personal growth. Reflecting on this development, I asked her to explain more about the function of the unconscious or autonomous breath, and its different forms, and she replied as follows:

> There is the unconscious breath, or you can breathe with an inner will, but I had found another form of being with the breath, one which connected with the immediate reality of the physical sensation of the movement of breath. For instance, it is a natural principle that wherever we have a physical sensation and bring our presence, breath movement will follow and develop there, if we allow it to come and go on its own. Consequently we have an experience of the physical sensation of breath movement, which eventually processes through our whole body and being. This breath movement makes the whole body permeable.

The Middendorf school recognizes that breathing is part of the autonomic nervous system for it accompanies every act of the body and being. We may think that we are fully breathing all the time, but actually, if we have worries, fears, struggles (either of an internal or external nature), our muscles become tight and inflexible and disturb the normal function of our organs, joints, and processes in the body, causing cramping and tension and often as a long-term effect, illness. However, we can reverse this process by learning about our breath in focusing, becoming sensorially aware, and experiencing our natural breath movement. Through processing with breath, pain, conflict, or illness can be transformed, absorbed, and integrated as a part of our whole being, and we find that breath can become our teacher within.

Understanding this, I asked Ilse if she could describe the importance of breath movement as she had experienced it. Ilse explained that we open ourselves to the movement of the breath as it travels through our body. The inhalation expands us, "it stretches us." According to Ilse we can follow the movement of the exhalation, and then sense the pause that follows. She pointed out that it is more than a physical phenomenon, for example, "There is a strong connection to psyche, soul and spirit within this experience. We receive the substance from which we live, and we give it back in a new way, after we have integrated it."

We can become more present with ourselves during the pause that follows the exhale as we wait for the impulse to inhale once again. This has a really significant meaning for us all, because breath accesses and encompasses all levels of being. In this process we are more deeply aware of the Self. Ilse ended her description of her experience of the breath by noting that,

> Breath in partnership with the Divine is the next step that can be experienced. When we allow our breath to come and go on its own, we are breathing, but at the same time, there is the "yes" to the higher power, and this is always so, even the smallest breath cycle has it. Once we have sensed it and experienced and accepted it, we continue on that path because it's deeply fulfilling, peaceful.

What is the Experience of Breath?

Breath is more than just the function of breathing. Additionally, breath provides us with the substance to live, and it carries a deeper meaning than simply an exchange of oxygen. As discussed in other chapters of this book, ancient cultures already knew about the potential and wisdom of a much wider experience and understanding of breath. Breath encompasses all levels of being, the physical, emotional, and the spiritual.

Breath comes and goes on its own, and in a peaceful rest we trust that the next breath cycle emerges again on its own. This is the foundation of the experience of breath. The simplicity of this statement is full of richness and wisdom. It is one of nature's basic principles that we can experience in ourselves and learn about in all living creatures.

Breathexperience, also called the Experience of Breath, is an artistic form of somatic education, based on connecting experientially with the natural breath—free from control of the human will. Rather than a series of techniques that help "fix" problems through structural conditioning, Breathexperience is a comprehensive system, a somatic practice, which promotes self-responsibility and in-depth participation in personal growth and development.

Breathing affects our entire being. By focusing and sensing breath movement, we experience our breath, without interfering with its natural rhythm. Through this breath we gain direct access to a knowledge and power that is greater than a simple intellectual understanding. We call this a form of somatic intelligence, which holds our essence, and encompasses the sensation of breath movement in the body as well as the spiritual and mental spheres of thought, feeling, and intuition.

The Power of Allowing the Breath
Come and Go on Its Own

We enter the process of breath awareness by simply allowing our breath to come and go on its own, sensing the breath movement develop throughout our body. The simplicity of sensing and participating in this breath experience connects us through the body to a source within ourselves. This source holds a vast intelligence, our essence, which can help grow and develop our true Self. Through the sensation of breath movement, the access to this intelligence becomes available to us. If we can "listen" well, it will reveal its knowledge, as a guidance that leads us on the path to heal and balance ourselves. The experience of connecting with a part of ourselves that is healthy, intact, and sane becomes stronger than our orientation to aches, pains, and illnesses and gives us a sense of oneness. The breath organizes all the healthy cells in the body, allowing an environment wherein the conflicting parts are invited back into this oneness.

It takes some practice for us to relearn how to allow the breath come and go on its own, without controlling or directing it. Our culture has developed far away from the principle of receiving or allowing, and as a result, we struggle in developing our sense of being. A good balance between the receptive and directive principle is the fertile ground for a healthy growth and development of the Self. We need to give ourselves more time and space to reconnect with our ability to allow the breath to come and go on its own. Opportunities for this to happen are offered to us in each phase of the breath cycle: inhale, exhale, and pause. On inhalation, the opportunity to recognize the principle of allowing is in receiving and surrendering to breath movement. On exhalation we recognize this principle by allowing expression and direction to happen. In the pause, we find the principle of allowing in our trust that the next inhalation comes back on its own. An experience of ease and well-being results when a breath cycle has completed in this way.

Breath as an Experience of Self

The awareness of breath movement encompasses the physical experience as well as the experience of the true nature of Self. It is our natural breath that we allow to come and go on its own, which sustains and reveals the basic rhythms of our life processes. Inhalation, Exhalation, Pause build a breath cycle, a small but very important and meaningful piece in the sum of many breath cycles together. Each individual cycle is different from any of the previous or future ones. The sum of a series of these breath cycles is an artistic composition, like a symphony, a painting, a dance piece, etc. We call this *breath rhythm*. As our practice with the experience of breath expands, we learn to trust that our breath rhythm can develop without being compromised. We experience movements that originate from breath as the source of our creative potential and an outlet for our expression. Simply being aware and present with each of these movements of breath expressed through the body, the meaningful message from our essence unfolds. We enter a self-analytical process of growth and development. Breath becomes our guide and teacher.

Breath not only reaches our inner world and moves us, it also connects us to the world outside. It brings us closer to each other and breaks down our sense of isolation.

How Can We Learn About Breath?

First of all we need to discover and become sensorially aware of our natural breath. We learn how to let the breath come and go on its own and wait until the next breath cycle emerges without manipulation. Breath, creating inward and outward movements in the body, reflects life itself. Breathing is a constant, rhythmic movement, like the eternal dip and swell of the waves of the ocean. With inhalation, emphasis is on allowing the air to come in. We experience expansion, space, openness. With exhalation, we sense breath moving through our body and we experience connection and direction. The acceptance of the end of exhale brings us a peaceful rest, and the trust, to let the next breath cycle emerge on its own. Through the simplicity of being in this physical sensation of movement of breath our orientation changes from a premature and rational interpretation of what we think we are to the immediate experience of an authentic Self.

Our culture still teaches us to treat our bodies as objects, dominated by our will, or what we or others "think" is good for us. We are taught to decide to not trust ourselves, our breath, or to not recognize our own life-giving force. We can relearn how to understand and appreciate our bodies as a collection of forces working together as one, with the breath as both a source and a guide.

The unconscious mode of breathing is part of the autonomic nervous system and accompanies every act of the body, be it physical, spiritual, or emotional. Whereas anxiety restricts our breathing, joy permits it to flow freely. Every activity changes our breath rhythm. When we have worries, fears, and struggles, either of an internal or external nature, our muscles become tight and inflexible and disturb the normal function of our organs, eventually causing illness. We become cramped and tense. These states restrict our natural breathing and are harmful to us. By being sensorially aware and present with the movement of breath and allowing it to come and go on its own, we realize that through the uncompromised allowing we have given over to a higher force within ourselves. In this way the breath rhythm can stay in a free flow to avoid holding, pushing, and pulling on the breath that feed into patterns of restriction, creating conflicts and illness. Instead we find ourselves in a state of well-being, making decisions that bring balance and support a healthy and fulfilled life.

Natural Laws and Principles of Breath

When we enter into Breathexperience, the natural laws and principles of breath become available. The trinity of *Sensation, Presence, Breath* holds an important one of these principles. This can become clear, when we bring our presence and sensory awareness to a particular area of our body. At the same time, we have transposed our Self there. For example, when I place my hands around my ankle, and sense it between my two hands, I *am* there, with full presence, with my whole Self. As I am there, my breath movement starts to develop there as well, if I allow breath to come and go on its own. This is one of the natural principles of breath. Through this process, we incorporate a particular part of our body into the whole, and consequently we sense our breath movement growing, expanding, and moving more than ever before.

Being sensorially aware, being present and allowing breath movement in and through the body, are interrelated processes, which we refer to the principle of Sensation, Presence, Breath. Each one induces the other:

> Wherever we have presence and sensation, breath movement develops
> Wherever we have sensation and presence, breath movement joins in.
> Our focus on breath movement brings sensation and presence.

The awareness and experience of this principle takes us from an unconscious level of breathing to a composed state of being, where breathing is conscious, yet independent of our controlling will. We experience breath awareness as our present state of being with a sense of Self.

Breath principles are natural forces, archetypes, blueprints of our truth. The experience and understanding of more of these breath principles help us to develop and build on a state of breath awareness becoming the source and guide for our daily life.

Somatic Intelligence—Essence

The experience of breath principles such as Sensation, Presence, Breath makes possible our access to an enormous body of knowledge, which we call *Somatic Intelligence*. This Somatic Intelligence, holding our Essence, manifests through a greater presence with the sensation of the movement of breath, coming and going on its own. Somatic Intelligence is not just based on a cognitive or mind-oriented process. It includes the knowledge of each individual cell in our body.

Within each person we can find a core of health, unity, and sanity, our Essence. Each individual cell in our body has the longing to participate in realizing that Essence. Each cell actually holds the essence within itself and knows its rightful place in the dynamic of the whole being.

Somatic Intelligence is the accumulation of essential cellular knowledge, which the breath can uncover, develop and organize throughout the entire being. Cells and parts of the body that have lost this knowledge, be it through injuries, traumatic experiences, or simply a lack of consciousness, are revived through the experience of breath, regrouping into wholeness.

More than just opening the path into our depth, breath also shows us how to evolve from that essence with awareness of Self, in a joyful discovery. We experience our Self as a creative and expressive being, capable of moving our inner world as well as affecting the world around us in our everyday life.

Vowels and Consonants

Part of the practice and training with the breath includes work with vowels and consonants. When we contemplate or receive individual vowels on inhalation, the movement of breath creates specific spaces in the body. Each vowel refers to its own particular breath space or "home." For example,

> As you sit on a stool or chair, contemplate silently the sound of *O* as in "rose," on your inhalation, and then silently sound *O* in yourself on exhalation. Allow the pause after exhalation. You may recognize that the inner part of your middle has become more spacious. You might even say that the *O* occupies that particular place, space, or home in your body. After a few breath cycles, without pushing or pulling on the breath, let the sound of *O* flow out on exhalation. Try this for five to

ten breath cycles. Remember to contemplate the O silently on inhalation. Then sense what part of your body has developed more space for breath movement.

Working with all the vowels, one at a time, provides and stimulates breath movement in different spaces throughout our whole body. When we contemplate the vowel sound as we inhale, and voice the sound as we exhale, sounds then become rooted, substantial, and full of personal meaning. They reach their intended goal and reflect back into our own depth. We can also proceed in a similar way with consonants.

We can discover that while vowels create space for the breath, consonants accentuate, define, center, stimulate, relax, or stroke throughout the body's cavity. Similar practices are found in some Eastern spiritual approaches, for example, the mantra-yoga or the sound meditations of the Tibetan Buddhists.

Hands-on Breath Dialogue

As a complement to breath and movement work, and to deepen a client's understanding through breath, individual appointments are arranged for a hands-on breath dialogue with a Breathexperience practitioner. Together the client and the practitioner develop what we call "breath dialogue," which encourages the client to allow breath movement to develop throughout the whole body. This is important because breath movement supports and reflects the process of a healthy body's capability of self-regulating responses to the shifts that occur in an alive and vibrant body. If breath is allowed to come and go on its own, it can clear through habitual patterns or muscle restrictions, which have interrupted this natural process. Using the same principles as in breath and movement work, the goal of hands-on breath dialogue is for clients to recognize from within, how the power of their own breath movement can initiate possibilities for healing.

The client lies on a low padded table, wearing comfortable clothes. The practitioner asks the client to let him or herself be carried. Letting yourself be carried promotes a state of being that supports the building of trust that we can shift away from controlling to allowing the breath to come and go on its own. The crucial difference is that we are asking to receive the floor/ground we are standing/sitting/laying on, rather than sinking or falling into the ground. The client is also asked to allow the breath to come and go on its own, without trying to control or direct it and to be fully present in sensing the movement of breath as it changes.

Awareness of breath dialogue begins with the practitioner's hands meeting the client's breath movement, until a natural rhythm is established. Both practitioner and client are involved—each one in his or her own breath rhythm, neither merging nor adapting. This nourishes growth and self-responsibility. The practitioner offers presence, easy stretches, or gentle pressure to the client's breath movement. The client's individual response in breath movement shows the possible developments in growth and balancing and guide the practitioner to the next offer, rather than the practitioner making a plan or agenda. This presents a situation in which breath dialogue is determined by the somatic intelligence of the natural breath, respecting the client's capacity for integration. Clients can recognize and sense a new form of growth.

Sequences in Breath Practice

The following sequences are just a few of the many possibilities for developing the practice in Ilse Middendorf's work. In a series of effortless movement sequences, we work with stretching/expansion, pressure points/consolidation, vowel breath-spaces, and movements originating from breath.

Since breath practice is experiential, it is useful to have someone lead you through the first steps to discover your natural breath. Experiences from this practice in the beginning are more internal, helping you to become aware of your breath movement in the body by shifting your presence from thinking, to sensing movement of breath. You ask yourself, "Where do I sense my breath movement?" and "Can I allow the breath to come and go on its own?"

We suggest that you choose a quiet place, sitting upright on a stool or an armless chair, preferably with a firm, flat seat. Sit at the front edge of your seat. Sense your feet on the floor, and rest your hands on your upper thighs. Let yourself be carried. This means to receive the floor and the chair or stool as a support, rather than falling or sinking into the seat or the ground. Letting yourself be carried creates a particular state of being that facilitates trust that we can allow breath to come and go on its own. This breath opens the gate into an enormous body of knowledge.

Begin your exploration by closing your eyes. Focus inside, bringing your full presence to your breath movement. Without controlling it, let your breath come and go on its own. With neither expectation nor plan, sense where your breath is moving you. For the next few minutes, continue to simply sense this movement that breath creates, following its rhythmic coming and going—as it naturally happens.

Practice Sequence: Spinal Roll

Keep connected with the sensation of the movement of breath and come into a standing position. As your breath is coming and going on its own, begin to roll down, one vertebra after another. Start with your head; continue with the seven cervical, then the twelve thoracic, the five lumbar vertebrae, and finally the sacrum with the pelvis, until your torso hangs from your hips, securely supported by your legs, with knees slightly bent, the weight on the front part of your feet. Let your shoulders and arms hang loosely.

Bring your full presence and sensation to each vertebra as you bend forward and down. Even though you may not be sensorially aware of every individual vertebra when you start practicing, you can maintain your presence on the area where you expect it to be. Go down in this spinal roll as far as it feels comfortable for you—preferably all the way down—until your spine is hanging down, from your pelvis, and your hands or arms touch the ground. After a while, begin to grow up, sensing how one vertebra moves on top of the other, until the head tops this growth like a crown.

Do not worry if it is not possible for you to roll all the way down. It is more important to keep allowing your breath rhythm as you roll down just as far as your breath will allow your spine to move without forcing or effort. When you meet a conflict or pain, wait there and sense your movement of breath. Come up a few vertebrae and try rolling down again. Perhaps this time your breath will help you move through, and you can go deeper. If not, then grow up again, vertebra by vertebra. You will be satisfied with what you can do and be with breath, rather than wanting more. The key for this exercise is to allow the breath to come and go on its own, at all times, without holding, pulling or pushing it.

If you allow the breath to come and go naturally, you will experience the effect of a strong transformation. Your inner structure is reorganized, with an understanding that is free from the influence of your mind and ego.

Practice Sequence: Sensation of the Movement of Breath n the Inner Spaces

Orient to the sensation of the movement of breath as your guide and become aware of your "lower space," which includes your feet, legs, and pelvis. With a simple circling with the pelvis, as you allow the breath to come and go on its own, you promote the development of breath movement in the lower space. This space can be experienced as your base, containing instinct, earth force, and holding your vital power. As you become more aware of your inner space, you will recognize a differentiation of this inner space into a lower, middle, and upper space and the specific experience of powers that connect through these spaces. Here is an example:

Expanding upward, you become aware of your breath movement in your "middle space," which reaches from your navel to the middle of your sternum (breastbone). As in the lower space, circling in the middle space helps to develop the breath movement in this space. The middle space holds the center of ourselves, a place where everything that we are comes together, the experience that I am. You can become aware of this by placing your hands on the breath movement in the middle space between your sternum and navel.

Continuing with the process, sense the urge to conclude it by entering the "upper space," reaching from the middle of your sternum all the way up, including your head. The experience of breath movement in the upper space, refines, completes, shapes, and expresses the forces of the lower and middle spaces. All three spaces together form the Inner Space.

A whole new world of experience opens up as you sense your breath moving through the inner space. For example, when you are aware of your breath movement on inhalation in the lower space, your exhale consequently wants to move up, rise up, from the lower through the middle into the upper space. An experience of empowerment is possible. Or if you receive your inhalation over the upper space, your exhale movement wants to flow from the upper space through the middle down into the lower. An experience of release and relaxation is possible. These are just two of many breath principles, showing in this case how breath can develop connection and direction through your body, your being, and thereby bring more understanding and clarity in experiencing the Self.

Movement Originating from Breath—into Expression

As breath awareness develops, the experience of other breath principles can help build a state that expands our interest to grow from the inner out. The space around ourselves becomes important, and we realize the possibilities that it holds for us to express and unfold our creative potential. The result is dialogue, the need to connect, to interact. We recognize that we are not the only "one." We are inspired by answers from the other and find ourselves answering to what touches us. The kind of dialogue we are describing here encompasses a physical, emotional, and spiritual reality. This experience is far greater than words can describe. The experience of breath reaches into all levels of being. In communicating, not only the words hold substantial information, but every little movement in the body, every expression in the face, every gesture and posture delivers the truth of our answer. This shows in our practice of the so-called *Movement from Breath*. Breath movement in the body initiates and determines all movements and actions. Through breath awareness we learn to develop a multidimensional understanding of ourselves and others. We find ourselves not only listening to words, but we also acknowledge the somatic reality in the dialogue through the sensation of the movement of breath.

We can learn that breath moves us, rather than us moving our body around unconsciously, with breath having to adapt to our conscious movements. Our breath is able to move us in a way that our soul, spirit, body, and our whole Self wants to participate, because we are allowing our breath to come and go on its own.

As a result of growing breath awareness, our embodied Self gives in to the movement of breath that now develops into what we call our individual Movement from Breath. This is a practice, in which the source of our movements is not a fixed idea or plan but the essence of what we truly are. The movements are not controlled but initiated and supported by the breath. We remember that the crucial key for this to happen is in the allowing of the breath to come and go on its own. Through this we participate in what is inside of us, calling for expression; a passion or vision looking for fulfillment, sadness, joy, an insight, an inspiration, and such. We experience and see ourselves in this movement from breath. As breath moves us, we are able to recognize and foster changes within. Rooted in the essence of our Self, breath now reveals the intelligence that it is connected with and we can participate in the development of its healing and reorganizing process. We recognize our Self, our life, our destiny, in the experience of our breath movement. The being and the becoming are realized, together with possibilities and challenges. We now take the next step and embrace our breath in a way, where it becomes a voice within, that we are capable of listening to, serving as a guide in living our life.

Movement that originates from breath is simply the continuation of our inner breath movement being realized in the world. The body is being moved by the breath, and in this the Self participates. The result is a deeper connection and a more authentic communication on all levels. This leads to breath dialogue in partnership and groups.

Supporting and Clarifying Breathexperience in Relationships

We discover that breath not only moves in and through our body but also from our inner being, through our expression into the outer world, connecting us with others. The experience of breath expands into partnerships and interactions with others. We come to an understanding of the importance of our unique breath rhythm in ourselves and in our relationships.

Even the smallest incidents in our life are reflected in the breath rhythm. When we are happy, our breath rhythm is different from when we are sad or angry. When we are physically active, again our breath rhythm is different from when we rest or sleep, etc. Our own individual breath rhythm shows our individuality.

The breath rhythm emerges as an important indicator of all conscious and unconscious events within and around us. Breath becomes both the basis of our orientation, and the opening that shows us what the next step can be in our personal process, and with our partner(s).

As we receive the breath in our body, it becomes more and more substantial. Inhalation, exhalation, and pause create movements in the body that can be physically sensed. When we sense these movements, we not only have a sensation of breath in the body but also an emotional and spiritual experience of ourselves that comes with this sensation. It is through sensation in the body that enables our feelings and thoughts to become real. Once feelings and thoughts have reference through the body, together they support a process of identification of Self. Breath encompasses sensation, feelings, and thoughts. A sense of oneness and a sense of Self can then be experienced.

When entering partnerships, the recognition of one's own Self through breath awareness can develop the potential for a true meeting of another's Self. This meeting can happen when both persons understand the importance of not compromising each one's allowing of the breath to come and go on its own, so that individual breath rhythms stay authentic. The result is an authentic meeting. Conflicting parts in the relationship are replaced by an understanding and acceptance of each other's truth. More tolerance and flexibility result. Old patterns drop away as possibilities emerge for new ways of being.

Through its connection to the intelligence of the healthy inner core, which is our essence, breath stimulates the whole being to participate in the spreading of this intelligence throughout our whole body and being. We can then outgrow our conflicts and shed them, as the dead leaves of a tree in autumn release for the sake of the next year's growth. Life forces that were fragmented and isolated by physical and mental conflicts become available once again for processes of restoring, creating, unfolding, and growth.

The balancing and self-regulating forces and principles of breath become the source of movements as couples or small groups interact through Movement originating from Breath. A practitioner/facilitator is supervising this process by making offers to help them stay with these principles and help them maintain their allowed breath rhythm. Integration can happen because each person involved maintains presence and participates in the process of the experience of breath.

In the movements that originate from breath, qualities of being can be expressed and seen within each individual. Qualities of being that include complements, such as receptive/directive, inner/outer, stability/flexibility, instinct/spirit. Recognizing these complements in the movements that originate from breath become important tools in developing balance. Allowing the breath to come and go on its own and following the natural principles of breath, brings all complementary forces into balance. The result is a deeper connection and a more authentic communication on all levels.

We end our chapter with further tributes to the breath. Ilse explains that, "On my inhale, I receive matter, when I exhale I give back what I received as a creation. Then I come into the pause where I am protected within creation." And I, Juerg, likewise understand that, "With the completion of a breath cycle I release myself, I have completed my creation, a cycle. I'm empty, and ready, fully receptive for the new, the next breath cycle. In this state of being, I am open, I fully trust, without worries and fears. This immediate reality heals and allows for my Self to come through—with authenticity, realizing both its importance and its unimportance."

Notes

1. Excerpt of poem from Ilse Middendorf, *The Experience of Breath in Its Substance,* (Paderborn, Germany: Junferman Verlag, 1998). English translation by Juerg Roffler, Middendorf Institute for Breathexperience, Berkeley, CA 2005.

2. This interview is composed of excerpts from a video program, filmed by Kevin Braband, Samuel Merritt College, Oakland, and produced by Margot Biestman, Faith Hornbacher, and Juerg Roffler, Middendorf Institute for Breathexperience, San Francisco, 1997, as well as private conversations between Ilse Middendorf and Juerg Roffler between 1996 and 2006.

Part III

Middle Eastern Breathing Practices

There is no mystical cult in which the breath is not given the greatest importance in spiritual progress. Once a man has touched the depths of his own being by the help of the breath, then it becomes easy for him to become at one with all that exists on earth and in heaven.

—Sufi master Hazrat Inayat Khan[1]

Introduction

The sacred breath has always been a fundamental element of Middle Eastern mystery schools. Even the Ancient Egyptian mythologies acknowledged the breath. The Egyptian word *hetau* refers to the process of sailing into and through the afterlife on the breath itself. Legends relate that the Egyptian god *Hu* was birthed from the sun god *Ra*.[2] He represented the ultimate sound, the voice of authority. As Hu drew his first breath, the sound *Hu* was heard within it. In fact, creation began with this breath, and its first manifestation was the soul of the god Osiris (the sun itself). Hu represented the first and last (Hu Hu) breath itself. The sacred intoning of Hu on the breath is part of the rich history within Sufi practice(s), and is used by most, if not all, Sufis in this modern era.

The reverence for divine breath emphasized in ancient Egyptian mystery teachings is also seen throughout the Middle East. In particular, breathing practices are given special emphasis in the mystical schools of Jewish Kabbalism, esoteric and Aramaic Christianity, and Sufism.

References to divine breath are found in the Hebrew book of Genesis, which relates, "And the Lord God formed man of the dust of the ground [from matter], and breathed into his nostrils the breath of life; and man became a living soul" (Genesis 2:7). Another Jewish creation story, found in the Haggadah, is slightly different than the one chosen for inclusion in the Bible. In this version, Adam's birth and life were only possible because a divine feminine soul was crafted and breathed into Adam. She was also referred to as the *breath of life*.[3] The story explains that as the ideal human, Adam, was being created, the soul was also prepared. It was the soul's entrance into the physical realm that awakened life. These Jewish stories related both life and spirituality to the presence of breath.

Both Eastern and Middle Eastern traditions convey the message that feminine and masculine poles are inherent in creation itself. For example, the feminine soul *breathed into* Adam has similarities to the yogic description of Shakti (the feminine principle) rising up the central spinal nerve to meet Shiva (the masculine principle), resulting in the illumination. This process of illumination is the alchemical transformation sought by the medieval alchemists, influenced by Middle Eastern Kabbalists and Sufis. It is the transmutation of base metal into gold, the personality into the soul—facilitated by the power of the breath.

Kabbalists, practitioners of Jewish mysticism, intone and breathe sacred phrases in order to open the inner gates to mystical unity. The *Sefer Yetzirah*, attributed to the Jewish patriarch Abraham, defines the ten *Sefirot*, paths to experiencing the divine. The first is the acknowledgement of the breath of the living God, and the knowledge of *Ruah Hakodesh* (Holy Spirit), as the voice of breath and speech. In his chapter on Jewish mysticism, Sheldon Kramer discusses the receptivity inherent in the inhale and notes how this opens the gates to *Ruach Hakodesh*.

An examination of Semitic languages reveals that the term "Holy Spirit" is related to "Holy Breath." Neil Douglas-Klotz, a Sufi mystic and translator of the Aramaic teachings of Jesus, explains that, "In both Hebrew and Aramaic, the same word—*ruha* in Aramaic, and *ruach* in Hebrew—[stands] for several English words: spirit, wind, air, and breath."[4]

This emphasis on breath is supported in the Christian story of Jesus' resurrection, when Jesus stood before his disciples following his initial appearance to Mary Magdalene:

> Peace be unto you. And when he had so said, he shewed unto them his hands and his side. Then were the disciples glad, when they saw the Lord. Then said Jesus to them again, Peace *be* unto you: as my Father hath sent me, even so send I you. And when he had said this, *he breathed on them, and saith unto them, Receive ye the Holy Ghost.* (John 20:17–22, KJV, emphasis added)

Christians alternately use the terms Holy Ghost and Holy Spirit to refer to the same divine emanation, but few consider its relationship to breath itself. Thus, Dr. Klotz's chapter provides a significant message on breath from a Christian perspective.

Sufism is believed to be the mystical path of Islam. In 1910, the late Sufi master Hazrat Inayat Khan (1887–1927) brought the Sufi message of the universality of all religious teachings to the Western world. Inayat Khan believed that the breath contained the secret of life. Its power was both visible, in that it gave life, and invisible. He taught that the breath could enable one to direct his thought to any place or plane, and thereby experience the mysteries of inner and outer life. Hence, Sufis use numerous breathing practices in order to awaken to full potential. Sonia Gilbert, a member of the Bawa Muhaiyaddeen Fellowship, is the author of the chapter focusing on the importance and training of breath, sound and vibration in all stages of a Sufi student's development. She describes her own rituals and intention to remain in this inner attunement "until there is nothing but the breath and the vibration within it."

The chapters included in part III guide the reader into the deep wisdom of sound, breath and vibration as practiced and expressed in Middle Eastern traditions.

Notes

1. Hazrat Inayat Khan, *The Heart of Sufism: Essential writings of Hazrat Inayat Khan* (Boston: Shambhala, 1999), 164.

2. April McDevitt, *Ancient Egypt: The Mythology,* 1997–2005, available at http://www.egyptianmyths.net/sail.htm.

3. Willis Barnstone (ed.), *The Other Bible* (New York: Harper Collins, 1984).

4. Neil Douglas-Klotz, *The Hidden Gospel* (Wheaton, IL: Quest Books, 1999), 41–42.

11

Jewish Mysticism

Kabbalah and the Breath

SHELDON Z. KRAMER AND MAURA RICHMAN

Introduction

The Jewish mystics sought to discover the mystery of existence in the hidden meanings of the Hebrew Bible (Old Testament). Their scope ranged from the cosmology of the universe—how we got from nothing-ness to somethingness—to the energetic DNA of the universe, levels of consciousness and to the ultimate reality of the human relationship to the Source.

These mystics are known as Kabbalists from the Hebrew word *le Kebbel*, which means to receive. They used meditation, including breath meditation to receive divine inspiration. In fact, the word "inspire" embedded in *inspiration* means to take in as a breath.

The human inspiration begins in the second chapter of Genesis in the Torah (the five books of Moses): "And G-d blew into his nostrils a soul of life" (Genesis 2:7). G-d's breath into Adam, primordial man, represents the soul connection between G-d and man; the divine manifestation. One of the Kabbalists' texts called *The Zohar* states that when G-d exhaled,

He did so from His innermost being. In addition, when the breath is placed into the body, the human being is never severed from Him.[1] The breath then, becomes a channel for unity. Therefore, we can consider that when we are in contact with our full breathing process and commune with this aspect of ourselves, then we are moving closer to the living G-d within ourselves.

> AND HE BREATHED INTO HIS NOSTRILS THE BREATH OF LIFE. The breath of life was enclosed in the earth, which was made pregnant with it like a female impregnated by the male. So the dust and the breath were joined, and the dust became full of spirits and souls. AND THE MAN BECAME A LIVING SOUL. At this point he attained his proper form, and became a man to support and nourish the living soul.[2]

This passage from *The* Zohar, illustrates the poetic Zoharic understanding that man is man only because of his soul. The body exists to nourish and support the soul. The *breath* of life is "enclosed" in the earth.

You will note that in these translations breath and soul are used interchangeably. This is because the Hebrew word for both has the same root letters (*nshm*). The Hebrew word *neshama* means soul and the word *neshimah* means breath which expands on the connection between the soul and breath

The Kabbalists conceived of the soul as having five levels. We can think of them as levels of consciousness or awareness. Breath meditation and refinement of the lower levels of the soul are avenues for humankind to bridge the levels of consciousness. In so doing, personal transformation affects universal transformation and repairs the brokenness of the world. The levels of the soul are connected with the process of creation itself. The highest level called *yechida* means unity. As its name implies, it is beyond duality. The next highest level is called *chayah,* or living essence. It is also beyond our ability to internalize and be influenced by us directly. The next three levels—*neshama, ruach,* and *nefesh*—are where breath practices are centered. These three lower soul levels are creatively utilized in the teaching called "the three strands of the soul."

The symbol for these three strands is depicted in the flame of a candle. According to the Kabbalists, the three parts of the flame consist of:

1. The black and blue flame, which is connected to the wick and material substance of the wax itself. This part of the flame is called in Hebrew *nefesh*, which is considered the lowest part of the soul and connected to the physical body. It is the densest part of the soul and is sometimes called the animal soul. It is the foundation of all the soul levels. This is the level where the body gains awareness that it is a receptacle for something more than itself. It is also connected to our always changing desires and our thoughts that are in constant flux which can lead us to distraction. In order to experience the next level of consciousness, all static must be tuned out.

2. The second strand of the soul is depicted in the yellow glow in the center of the candle flame, which represents the divine wind called *ruach* that stands above the always changing animal soul with all its desires and thoughts that flicker here and there. As *netzach* is correlated to physicality, *ruach* is correlated to emotional awareness. When the air around us is in spiritual motion, we become more aware of its effect on us. It is in this state of consciousness that information can be communicated; one can hear things and become conscious of higher levels of spirituality.

3. The third strand of the soul is represented by the topmost part of the candle flame, which is the filmy piece of light, called the *neshamah*, which is considered the Higher Self. It is where the higher qualities of soul are stored, including such states of mind as compassion, love, forgiveness, patience, humility, strength, faith, and unity. In fact, by focusing on this divine breath, we can facilitate the contact with G-d's breath and therefore be indirectly connected to His mouth and a level of very close intimacy. Just as *ruach* is supported by *nefesh*, *neshamah* is supported by both *nefesh* and *ruach*.

Ruach serves as a spiritual transmitter between *nefesh* and *neshama*. When one is able to focus attention on the *ruach*, one can reach a *neshama* level of consciousness, which is connected to the breath. The use of *ruach* to bridge the gap between *nefesh* and *neshamah* can be compared to the use of a copper wire as a conduit to make electricity flow from the generator to the outlet. In Jewish meditation, there are different conduits to aid in this endeavor. For example, the Jewish mystics or Kabbalists would utilize the Hebrew letters, which are considered a secret language that resonate within *Neshamah*. Each Hebrew letter is a symbol of different aspects of the soul and as one gazes on each letter, it is stated that one can understand the mysteries of each shape and the differential aspects of the divine. Permeating the breath with the Hebrew letters then becomes another conduit to *Neshama*. Additionally, since the Hebrew letters also have numerical value, counting the length of breaths also has mystical properties.[3] Four examples, two from a thirteenth-century Kabbalist, one from commentaries to the ancient *Sefer Yitzirah*, and one from a contemporary Kabbalist, will be discussed below.

Breath and Name of G-d Practice:

There is clear evidence in the early writings of Kabbalah that Jewish mystics traditionally used breathing practices but they were not put into writing until the thirteenth-century by Rabbi Abraham Abulafia. Many of these methods involved working with a variety of sacred names and permeating the breath with the various letters of the different names of G-d.

All meditation techniques are to refine one's attention or concentration called *Kavvanah* in Hebrew which means intention. In this center of meditation, the intention is to unify ourselves with the name of G-d through cleaving to the four letter name of G-d known as the *tetragrammaton*. The *tetragrammaton* is composed of four Hebrew letters transliterated as *Yud, Hey, Vav, Hey,* an amalgam of the words *hayah, hoveh,* and *yihyeh*—was, is and will be. This cleaving process is occurring between the *ruach* and the *neshamah* and if we are totally at one with our breath as we focus on the letters, we can have what is called in *Hasidism*, the state of *devekut*, which means merging with G-d or becoming unified with His highest principle.

The first two meditation practices below focus on the *tetragrammaton* (Hebrew is written from right to left).

He   Vav   He   Yod

Sit in a chair or on the ground cross-legged with your spine erect. Allow your eyes to close and begin to slowly inhale and exhale consciously through your nostrils. Allow yourself to focus on the inhalation and exhalation of your breathing through the nostrils. As you begin to let go of any tension in your body and allow yourself to deeply relax, begin to visualize the letters of the *Yud-Hey-Vav-Hey*. It is proper to sometimes be able to look at these letters externally as well.

When your mind is fully attended to the letters, as well as your breathing process, allow yourself to inhale the *Yud*, exhaling the *Hey*, inhaling the *Vav* and exhaling the *Hey*. It is instructed in Kabbalistic writings never to say the four letters out loud, but to permeate the letters within the meditator's breath in a subtle manner internally.

This particular meditation is a good beginning tool to slow one's mind and body down and can be the beginning of a transformation process in bridging *ruach* with *Neshamah*.[4]

Breathing techniques in Kabbalah, as seen in Abulafia's writings, contain hints at techniques of how to pronounce the name of G-d. The most significant passage regarding these are found in a document called *Mafteah Ha-Semot* where it states:

One must take each one of the letters of the Tetragrammaton and wave it with the movements of his long breath so that one does not breathe between two letters, but rather one long breath for however long he can stand it and afterwards rest for the length of one breath. He shall do the same with each and every letter until there will be two breaths in each letter, one for pausing when he enunciates the vowel of each letter and one for resting between each letter. It is known to all that every single breath of one's nostrils is compared to taking in of the air from the outside to the inside.[5]

Abulafia would integrate sounding out vowels sounds and put these sounds in different permutations under the letters of the tetragrammaton. For example, he would repetitively use as a mantra either *Yo-Ho-Vo-Ho* or *Yay-Hay-Vay-Hay* or *Yeh-Heh-Veh-Heh* or *Yooh-Hooh-Vooh-Hooh* or *Yah-Hah-Vah-Hah*.

Abulafia also gave attention to the following passage from the Old
Testament, namely, to "Remember, G-d at all times" (Psalms 16:8) or
to "Put G-d before you at all times. . . . All that has breath shall praise
Yah, halleluyah." (*Yah* is one of the names of G-d in Hebrew.) With each
and every breath that mantra is within your praise of G-d. It is interesting to note that the last sound of hallelujah is *Yah,* and *Yah* is reflec-
tive of the quality of wisdom. We are praising the divine gift of wisdom
as we utter halluluyah. He additionally promoted the idea of using the
Tetragrammaton with putting the variety of Hebrew vowel sounds under-
neath the letters, combining breathing, vowel sounds, and head motions
into a holistic approach.

The Gates of Vowels Practice

The Abulafia meditation called the "Gates of Vowels" uses the vowel
sounds as a gate or portal to higher consciousness. "It is useful for going
deeper into integrating the mind, emotions, and body. It involves the
conscious use of visualizing, sounding and moving to the shape of the
Hebrew vowel sounds with head motions. It also entails imagining the
shape of each vowel sound in the chest area" (4).[6]

In Hebrew, the vowels are not letters but rather notations at the bottom of a letter or after it. The five vowels used in this meditation, their
names and notations and the directions they represent are:

Name	Notation	Sound	Direction
Holam	וֹ	*oh,* as in bone	upper worlds
Kamatz	ָ	*ah,* as in calm	north to south
Tzere	ֵ	*ay,* as in say	south to north
Hirik	ִ	*ee,* as in see	lower worlds
Shuruk	ֻ	*oo,* as in too	east to west

The five vowels are associated with five directions based on the shapes of
the notation as indicated above. These directions in turn determine the

head movements. We suggest that as you practice this meditation, you work with one vowel sound until you are comfortable and familiar with it and then each of the others.

1. *Holam:* Sit in a chair or on the ground with your spine erect facing East toward Jerusalem. At the beginning of the meditation, create an inner intention by stating, "I praise G-d as creator of the *upper worlds.*" With a deep breath, sound out the *oh* sound of the Hebrew vowel of *Holam.* As you begin to sound out the vowel, your head, starting in a balanced position on top of your shoulders, begins to rise slowly upward, integrating the movements with breath and sound. Continue the head, position slightly moving the head up and towards the ceiling and then down. It is important to integrate the breath and the sound with the movement so that when the sound stops, the movement and breath stop too. Visualize the *Holam* in the center of your chest as you do this.

2. *Kamatz:* The second part of this meditation, once again begins with an inner intention: praising G-d as creator of the direction of *North to South.* Begin to take a deep breath and sound out the Hebrew vowel *kamatz,* an *ah* sound. Your head movement begins centered, balanced on top of the shoulders and moves to the left, then to the center, to the right, back to the center, the chin moving down toward the chest and then back to an upward position with the head balanced on the shoulders. Once again, coordination of the sound and the movement with the breath is important. Visualize the kamatz in your chest as you do this.

3. *Tzere:* Next, focus on the Hebrew vowel *tzere,* an *ay* sound. Begin with the following inner intention praising G-d as creator of the direction of *South to North.* With a deep breath, begin to sound out the *ay* as you move the head in 45-degree angles, first to the right, back to the center, then to the left and back to the center. Remember to integrate the breathing and sound with the movement, as well as visualizing the *tzere* in your chest.

4. *Hirik:* The next section in the meditation is focused on the Hebrew vowel *hirik*, which makes an *ee* sound. Begin with the following inner intention of praising G-d as creator of the direction of the *lower worlds.* Take a deep breath and sound out the vowel *ee* while moving the head in a downward position, chin moving towards the chest. Be sure the breath, sound and movement are integrated as you also visualize the *hirik* in your chest.

5. The last major vowel sound is the *shuruk, oo* sound. Begin with the following intention to praise G-d as creator of the direction of East to West. Then take a deep breath and make the *oo* sound as you move the head forward slightly and then return to the center with the head balanced on top of the shoulders. It is important to continue the breath, sound, and movement as you visualize the *shuruk* in your chest.

Sound and Breath: The Shema

The power of the Hebrew letters, both visually and with sound, is also experienced with a meditation using letters from the most important Jewish prayer, the *Shema. Shema* is the first Hebrew word of the declaration of faith as follows: It means listen or hear: "Listen Israel, YHVH is our G-d. YHVH is one" (Deuteronomy 6:4).

The Torah prescribes that the *Shema* be said twice daily. It is both a call to prayer reminding us of the principle of universal unity and reminding us to be quiet and listen. It is said that the spelling of the *Shema* is itself very important. The two consonant sounds that we hear are the *sh'* and the *mm*. If you say these letters to yourself—*sssssss* or *shshshshsh* and *mmmmmmm* you will notice that the *s* or *sh* have a hissing sound like fire and a sense of chaos like white noise. The *mmmm-mmm* sound, on the other hand, has a humming, peaceful, tranquil, and harmonic sound reminiscent of water. The contrast of the two sounds allows us to experience the difference between everyday consciousness and the meditative state.

The following exercise can be used as an effective practice to entering the meditative state quickly:

Inhale.

On the exhale, pronounce *sssssssss*.

Inhale.

Exhale for the same length of time *mmmmmm*.

Continue by alternating the two sounds until the *mmmmmm* sounds draws you deeper and deeper into a meditative state.

With practice this meditation has the potential to draw you into the meditative state using only the *mmmmmm* sound.[7]

Breath and Joy

The use of breath to praise G-d comes from the last line of the book of Psalms. Psalm 150 ends with "Let all souls praise G-d, Halleluyah." A contemporary Jewish mystic, Rabbi Yitzchak Ginsburgh, translates this as: "Every breath shall praise G-d, Halleluyah" and explains that to experience life is to experience the joy of feeling my Creator blowing into my nostrils the breath of life. Therefore, I praise Him with every breath, Halleluyah![8] His meditation combines the Hebrew word for joy, *chedva*, with a breath practice. *Chedva* is composed of four Hebrew letters: *chet, daled, vav, and hey*. Their numerical value respectively is 8, 4, 6, and 5.

The following practice can be used to bring more joy into your life:

Breathe deeply and praise G-d with every breath.

With every breath, I feel your presence.

With every breath I express my infinite gratitude to You and Your gift of life.

Now breathe joy (*chedva*) into your life.

Each breath has four stages:

Inhale 8—count in your head from one to eight while inhaling.

Hold 4—hold for a count of four.

Exhale 6—count to six while exhaling.

Rest 5—finally, rest for a count of five before repeating the process

It is important to breathe deeply and maintain the 8, 4, 6, 5 ratio. Since each individual has his or her own rhythm, the length of the count is not important as long as the rhythm is maintained.[9]

Conclusions

The connection between G-d's breath and man's soul/breath as expressed in the earliest chapters of the Hebrew Bible 2,500 to 3,000 years ago, give testimony to the power of the breath to reach higher levels of awareness and connection to the Source.

There were breathing practices being utilized as part of the Kabbalistic methods of the early Jewish mystics and these same breathing practices are used today by contemporary Jewish mystics. Their techniques were connected to the idea that one could directly experience G-d and attain higher states of joy and ecstasy through the use of these meditation tools. The Old Testament mystics were practitioners of methods that led to experiencing unification with a Higher Power. They utilized breath, Hebrew letters, vowel sounds, and motions to achieve this kind of unity. It is interesting to note that the Jewish mystics seemed to be holistic practitioners, trying to utilize different aspects of the body to achieve their aims. They would also use, simultaneous techniques of attention and concentration, using different senses and even the thought process itself to create the powerful connection with their object of meditation in order to reach enlightenment.

Notes

1. Rabbi Aryeh Kaplan, *Inner Space: Introduction to Kabbalah, Meditation and Prophecy* (New York: Moznaim Publishing, 1990).

2. *The Zohar*, vol. 1, trans. Harry Sperling and Maurice Simon (London: Soncino Press, 1984), 156.

3. Sheldon Z. Kramer, "Jewish spiritual pathways for growth and healing," in *Modern Psychology and Ancient Wisdom: Psychological Healing Practices from the World's Religious Traditions*, ed. Sharon G. Mijares (Binghamton, NY: Haworth Press, 2003), 99–122.

4. Sheldon Z. Kramer, "Opening the inner gates: New paths in Kabbalah and psychology," in *Jewish Meditation: Healing Ourselves and Our Relationships*, ed. Edward Hoffman (Boston: Shambhala Publications, 1995), 224–49.

5. Moishe Idel, *The Mystical Experience in Abraham Abulafia* (Albany: SUNY Press, 1988).

6. David R. Blumenthal, *Understanding Jewish Mysticism: A Source Reader,* vol. 2 (New York: KTAV Publishing House, 1982), 54–59.

7. Rabbi Aryeh Kaplan, *Jewish Meditation* (New York: Shocken Books, 1985).

8. From direct conversations between Rabbi Yitzchak Ginsburgh and Dr. Sheldon Z. Kramer, Ph.D., as well as workshops given at the San Diego Jewish Meditation Institute at San Diego during the1990s, available at www.inner.org.

9. Ibid.

12

The Holy Breath

Breath in the Cosmology and Spiritual Practice of the Aramaic Jesus[1]

NEIL DOUGLAS-KLOTZ

Introduction

Over the past twenty-five years millions of people around the globe have joined in interspiritual circles to chant and breathe the sacred phrases spoken by Jesus in his native Aramaic language. Pursuing spiritual goals, as people learn and breathe Aramaic sacred phrases, they feel that they are also experiencing Middle Eastern teachings—building bridges of healing in a time of war and conflict based upon centuries of misunderstanding.[2]

On the secular side, many Western scientists have admired the prophetic figure of Jesus and his reported sayings. Yet they have presumed that the actual wisdom and mysticism of the prophet is buried under centuries of acculturation as well as the editing of the Christian scriptures themselves. Some scientists have felt that when some Christian churches rule out scientific theories like evolution and relativity in the name of Jesus, they set up an impassable barrier between science and religion.

Attempts to create windows in this barrier have been pursued by both theologians and scientists.[3]

The differences may, however, have less to do with science and religion than with two different ways to view the relationship between God, humanity, and nature—the Middle Eastern and the Western. As the Western Christian church began to emphasize faith in Jesus as the definition of salvation, it excluded nature from this definition. Nature and wilderness became defined as arenas of conflict rather than contemplation. This led to the desire, almost the imperative, to conquer and control nature. In the Eastern Church, nature remained a support for the spiritual life and was seen to participate in "salvation."[4]

I believe that Western culture subconsciously carries an understanding of spirit, and the spiritual, which is an overmaterialization of Jesus' very profound and symbolic worldview. He shared this view with the Jewish prophets before him, and used it in unique sayings and stories to evoke a radical change of heart in his listeners. Many of his sayings on breath and breathing reveal a "native" wisdom that has been rediscovered only in this century by various body researchers.

Breath and Spirit

In both Hebrew and Aramaic, the same word—*ruha* in Aramaic, *ruach* in Hebrew—must stand for several English words: spirit, wind, air, and breath. Translations that arise out of European Christianity assume that only one of these possibilities is appropriate for each passage. However, when we meditate on the words of a prophet or mystic in the Middle Eastern way, we must consider all possibilities simultaneously. This is the Middle Eastern tradition of *midrash*, translation-interpretation that includes the reader's or practitioner's own spirititual experience.[5] So "spirit" must also include or be equivalent to "breath" in all of the cases attributed to Jesus in the Gospels. Here are some examples, heard with "Aramaic ears."

Here is an alternate reading of John 4:24 from the Aramaic. (The King James Bible reads, "God is a spirit.")

> God is breath.
> All that breathes resides in the Only Being.

> From my breath
> to the air we share
> to the wind that blows around the planet:
> Sacred Unity inspires all.

And here is an alternate reading of Matthew 5:3 from the Aramaic. (The King James version reads, "Blessed are the poor in spirit: for theirs is the kingdom of heaven.")

> Ripe are those who reside in breath;
> to them belongs the reign of unity.
> Blessed are those who realize that breath is
> their first and last possession;
> theirs is the "I Can" of the cosmos.

Jesus uses the word *ruha* in expressions like those above as well as in the statement that to speak against the Holy Spirit is an unforgivable sin (KJV): "whosoever speaketh against the Holy Ghost, it shall not be forgiven him, neither in this world, neither in the world to come" (Matthew 12:32). Understanding these sayings transcends word play and requires us to shift our consciousness. The separations between spirit and body, between humanity and nature, which we often take for granted in the English language, begin to fall away.

Spirit and Truth are Breath and Harmony

In the four canonical Gospels Jesus refers to "spirit" more than one hundred times. If we consider that spirit is synonymous with breath, than our understanding of his message can embrace other, alternate meanings. Let's look, for example, at the full statement from John 4:24, rendered in part above, which is translated in the King James Bible as, "God is a Spirit: and they that worship him must worship him in spirit and in truth."

We have already seen how the first half of the statement differs in the Aramaic version: From the perspective of Sacred Unity, my breath is connected to the air we all breathe. It participates in the wind and atmosphere that surrounds the whole planet. This atmosphere then connects to the ineffable spirit-breath that pervades the seen and unseen worlds.

The Aramaic word for worship (*seged*) in this passage can also mean to bow oneself or surrender. The word *sherara*, translated as "truth," has several meanings in Aramaic and Hebrew: that which liberates and opens possibilities, that which is strong and vigorous, and that which acts in keeping with universal harmony. It is the sense of a right direction at a particular time that enlivens one's personal purpose and at the same time harmonizes with all. Drawing on these additional meanings, the second half of John 4:24 can also read:

> Those who surrender to Unity,
> bowing to it in utmost adoration,
> must do so
> in breath and harmony,
> like the sense of right direction
> that drives the universal winds.

In a very expansive way, this statement unites us with all other breathing beings in a melody of unity. In a very practical, here-and-now way, it connects us to the most diverse voices of our inner and outer worlds.

Breath Entering Body

The idea of breath coming into a body, progressively and with various effects, goes back to the Jewish scriptures in Genesis, and perhaps to the formation of the Hebrew language itself.[6] According to an interpretation of Jewish mysticism, Hebrew's four different *h* sounds, which are four different letters, represent the degrees of interpenetration of matter and breath, as well as its consequences:

> The letter *hey*, a very refined sound, like the *h* in the English "hear," refers to the breath that is free and unencumbered, not yet attracted by an individual body.
> The letter *heth*, like the *ch* in Scottish *loch* (no English equivalent), refers to the breath as it begins to enter a body and enliven it.
> The letter *kaph*, like *ch* in German "Bach," an even rougher sound than *heth*, refers to the breath as it is fully embodied.

The letter *eh* has no precise English equivalent, but is guttural like an emphasized *e* in "they," though without the *y* sound. It represents the breath that has become overly involved in a body and trapped there. It cannot feel its connection to other expressions of breath.

In the final condition, one not only falls out of contact with the sacred, but also with other living beings. This sound, for instance, is the central root of the word for enemy in Aramaic, (*be'eldebaba*) which could also be translated, "one who falls out of rhythm" in relation to someone or something else. To breathe with an exclusive focus on one's small self—the individual "I" disconnected from the sacred "I," the only being—is the definition of egotism.

"Sin against the Holy Spirit"

The notion of an "egocentric breath" also makes sense of the saying about the "unforgivable sin" in Matthew 12:31,[7] which has Jesus saying (KJV): "Wherefore I say unto you, All manner of sin and blasphemy shall be forgiven unto men: but the blasphemy against the Holy Ghost shall not be forgiven unto men."

The Aramaic word translated as "sin" (*hataha*) could also mean that which misses the mark or falls into error, as well as a failure or mistake. Its root points figuratively both to frustrated hopes and to threads that have become tangled. The same root can also mean to dig out a well or furrow, or to sew, patch, or mend something. So the seeds of restoration are, so to speak, implied in what has been broken.

The Aramaic word for "blasphemy" (*gudapa*) can also mean a reviling, or more literally, from the roots, a cutting off, incision, irruption, or furrow. To blaspheme would be to cut oneself off from the object of blasphemy.

"To forgive" (*shebaq*) can also mean to set free, let go, loosen, leave out, omit, or from the roots, to restore something to its original state.

So from these possibilities, we could compose the following expanded rendering of Matthew 12:31, which attempts to give some of the nuances that Jesus' listeners may have heard:

All types of tangled behavior,
the missing and falling,
the rips and tears—
all the ways you cut yourself off,
break your connection, or
disrupt the pattern—
can and will be mended.
Sooner or later, you will be freed from error,
your mistakes embraced with emptiness,
your arrhythmic action returned to the original beat.
But your state cannot be mended or repaired,
when you cut yourself off from the Source of all rhythm—
the inhaling, the exhaling
of all air, wind, and atmosphere, seen and unseen—
the Holy Breath.

When we "sin against the Holy Spirit," we can only be healed by an involuntary action of surrender that places one back in the sacred communion of Unity. We cannot, of course, actually forget to breathe. We can, however, fail to breathe with a sense of connection to other people and our surroundings. Our current Western culture does not, in fact, encourage us to be aware of our breathing communion with our surroundings. If it did, we would probably have quite a different world than we have today. Yet we can learn to heal our relationships through a deeper experience of breathing.

Honoring the Sacred Breath

As Jesus says, "where your treasure is, there will your heart be also" (Matthew 6:21). We can begin by devoting some time to finding the unique gifts of our own breathing, which is like that of no other human being. We each have our own rhythm, our own way to sense the wave of our breathing as it rises and falls.

Interspersed with the commentary and renderings here, I have also added examples of simple "body prayers" or meditations inspired by the themes. These meditations use traditional Middle Eastern prayer methods such as sounded words, contemplation, breathing awareness, and body awareness. I have done this not to be "New Age" in any sense but to underline the fact that in a Middle Eastern way of sacred interpretation, translation *is* spiritual practice and usually accompanied by prayer and meditation. In this tradition, the words of a prophet or mystic are not a dead text, an object existing outside of oneself, but rather a living, breathing reality that one embodies as one hears, remembers, repeats, and meditates upon them.

> Lie or sit comfortably for a few minutes, and again place one hand lightly over the heart. Without trying to change anything, simply notice the breath. There are many different moments in the breath's journey: the feeling of it as it begins to come in, when it approaches fullness, as it briefly turns over, and then when it begins to go out, when it approaches emptiness, and when it turns over again. At each twist and turn of the breath's journey, our bodies respond in a particular way. We may also notice a presence or absence of sensation, thought, or emotion at a particular stage. We may feel that we want to stay longer in one part of the journey than another—the beginning, the middle, or the end.
>
> Simply notice all of these sensations without judgment for a few minutes. If you wish, gradually come back into everyday awareness by drawing freely on paper the feeling of your own breathing wave. This is not a clinical assessment or an art project, but a kind of intuitive snapshot of your feeling of breathing at one moment in time. Perhaps some words and images will also arise.
>
> This type of practice is best done regularly over a period of a month or more. Your drawings and words become a sort of "breath journal," and at the end of the month, they may tell you more about your relationship to breath than any book can. Like a dream journal, as you begin to recognize your own signs and symbols—in this case the signposts on your own breath journey—you can begin to interpret them in light of your own experience. Breathing can become a sort of oracle or barometer that tells us what emotional "weather" will enter our lives.

Such exploration, and the wisdom implied in the words of Jesus, relates directly to the insights of several body-oriented therapists and psychologists of this century. A primary tenet of all the new therapies, as well as the so-called New Physiology can be stated simply: the degree of flexibility of breath in the body not only indicates internal psychic or emotional health but also the degree of healthy connection to others.[8] From this standpoint, many of the problems of our world today may simply be due to a failure to breathe properly. Or as Jesus said, to a sin against the Holy Breath.

Finding Our Home in the Breath

To allow oneself to breathe with a simple, unencumbered connection to the Sacred is not so simple, however. As soon as we begin to breathe consciously, we encounter all of the subtle ways in which we hold our breath.

For instance, in Matthew's version of the Beatitudes (5:3ff), Jesus affirms various conditions in which one finds oneself and shows how they lead to a condition of harmony with the Universe. As we shall see in a later chapter, the word for *blessed* that begins each saying can also be translated *ripe*. An Aramaic reading of the first three Beatitudes reveals their message as intimately concerned with breathing and with what happens when we begin to breathe more deeply and consciously.

For instance, the translation of the first Beatitude at the beginning of this chapter points to the first step in any deep healing process: the realization that we ultimately have no home or possession except our breathing. When we say that a particular event in our lives has "knocked the wind" out of us, we experience this state. When it occurs, then at least for a period of time, we begin to breathe more deeply. Deeper breathing can also make us aware of sensations and emotions that we have not been feeling. In fact, we may have been subtly holding our breath in order to avoid feeling them. With this in mind, we can take another look at the second Beatitude, translated in the King James version as, "Blessed are they that mourn: for they shall be comforted."

"To mourn" (*ebal*) in Aramaic can also mean to be in confusion or turmoil, to wander literally or figuratively. Certainly many of us have discovered this confusion when we begin to breathe more deeply, for

instance when we have faced our own mortality. "To be comforted"
(*baya*) in Aramaic can also mean to be united inside, to return from
wandering, or to see the face of what one hopes for.

With these additional meanings, we could do open translations of the
second Beatitude like this:

> Ripe are those who feel at loose ends,
> coming apart at the seams;
> they shall be knit back together within.

> Blessed are those in turmoil and confusion;
> they shall be united inside.

As this follows the saying about breath in the first Beatitude, I believe
it suggests a necessary state of confusion that we can "breathe through"
and realize as an opportunity to grow more conscious of Sacred Unity.

The third Beatitude takes this theme a step further. Here the Aramaic
sense of the words is startling compared to the King James translation:
"Blessed are the meek: for they shall inherit the earth."

In Aramaic, the word translated as "meek" (*makike*) means literally
those who have softened what is rigid. This softening implies a condition
both inside and outside us. The phrase "inherit the earth" in Aramaic
does not mean to acquire a piece of property. The word for "inherit"
(*yiret*) also means to receive strength, power, and sustenance. The word
for "earth" (*ar`ah*) can also refer to all of nature, as well as to the natural
power that manifests through the diversity of beings in the universe.

So a very plausible open translation of this saying, with the Aramaic
nuances added, might sound like this: "Ripe are those who soften what
is rigid, inside and out; they shall be open to receive strength and power—their natural inheritance—from nature."

The first three Beatitudes tell us that the natural result of conscious
breathing is, first, some confusion and turmoil. Then we soften and can
begin to absorb universal energy from everywhere around us.

We can again compare these insights to those of various body
researchers of this century who have demonstrated conclusively that the
idea of the body as a machine is completely inappropriate. The body's
movement is not an automatic system of levers and pulleys, but rather
a living flow of a whole organism in which awareness plays a very large

part. For instance, one can become aware of the sensation of the position in space of joints, muscles, tissues, and organs on a very minute level. These sensations can be sensed and influenced by fine-tuning one's awareness. In this context, the awareness of breathing and the breathing wave can have a powerful therapeutic effect.[9]

Born Again—Revisited

In Jesus' conversation with Nicodemus in the Gospel of John, we find another beautiful expression of the spiritual life as a life of conscious breathing. Here Jesus advocates that one be reborn from the breath by following one's sensation of it inside, into the seeming darkness and back out again. This is the foundation of many Western breathing therapies today (for instance, Reichian therapy) in which one uses the proprioceptive sensation of the breath to enter the seeming darkness of one's inner emotional life. With perseverance, one can emerge with new understanding and a new state of being in the world.

The last part of Jesus' advice to Nicodemus, which is phrased beautifully (if translated misleadingly) in the King James version, seems to point to such a spiritual awakening. This awakening takes us beyond a world of duality into a communion with all that is: "The wind bloweth where it listeth, and thou hearest the sound thereof, but canst not tell whence it cometh, and whither it goeth; so is every one that is born of the Spirit" (John 3:8). With many of the nuances of breath and spirit that we have explored so far, we can expand this to:

> The breath, the wind, and the spirit
> obey their own mysterious moods,
> their own harmonious laws.
> When you hear their voices
> and feel their touch,
> you know they exist without a doubt.
> But you do not understand
> how they come together,
> how they rise and fall as they
> pass over and through the earth.

> Just as mysterious seems
> the movement and purpose
> of every human being
> who has returned to the Source
> and been reborn from the Great Dark
> through the power of breath and spirit.

One of the earliest Jewish mystical practices saw the practitioner try to reexperience the descent of the spirit and breath into form, then experience resurrection and ascension in a journey of return to the "throne" of the Holy One. This practice related to both the mystery of creation as well as the vision of various prophets.[10] An Aramaic view of Jesus shows us clear links to this tradition. Jesus consistently tried to connect Semitic concepts of holiness, light, kingdom, earth, and heaven with his listeners' personal, often mystical, experience of the sacred, rather than with the conditions of their class, wealth, or ritual purity as defined by the political and religious structures of his day.[11] To take such a stance was both revolutionary and dangerous.

The Breath in Action

Each time we feel the wind pass over our skin, we can remember a time when we were only breath. We can also remember when the whole planet was still the germ of an idea in the mind of the Holy One. In the normal business of our everyday lives, this may be too much to ask. In nature, at ease, we are sometimes inspired to such profound contemplation. Even in the city, however, we can learn to breathe in rhythm. By so doing, we can begin to free ourselves from patterns of held breathing that prevent us from uncovering the perfection of our humanity. Here is a final body prayer in the spirit of the Aramaic Jesus:

> While you walk down the street, bring the rhythm of your footsteps into alignment with the rhythm of your breathing. At first, try inhaling to a count of four and exhaling to a count of four, and use this balanced rhythm to harmonize breathing and walking.

As you proceed, sense the breath more and more in the middle of the chest, in the area near the heart. Feel as though the breath leads you and helps you along, preparing you for what is ahead. At the same time, the awareness of breathing allows you to be more present to the needs of the moment. To help focus, you could also say to yourself the Aramaic words *Ala-ha Ru-hau* (Unity is Breath) in a rhythm of four. After five to ten minutes, or when you reach your destination, allow yourself to come to standing. Sense your breathing as it returns to whatever its natural rhythm wants to be. In the space of one or two breaths, celebrate the connection of your breath to all that breathes, and to the Sacred Breath itself.

To affirm Jesus as a native Middle Eastern person not only opens up the insights I have here. It can enable Christians to understand that the mind and message of the prophet they revere arise from the same earth as have the traditions of their Jewish and Muslim sisters and brothers. In the recognition of this fact lies the power to overcome centuries of mistrust and tragedy. How far back this tragic divide began is not the subject of this article. My purpose is to build bridges of meaning that can help connect the lovers and devotees of Jesus of all traditions, as well as all who have been inspired by his words and example.

If these efforts have some merit, they go to my teachers. If there is benefit, let it be toward the next two thousand years, when—by the will of the One—the wisdom of a native Middle Eastern Jesus takes its rightful place in the discussions and actions that determine the future of our planet.

Notes

1. An early version of this chapter, entitled "Holy Spirit and Holy Breath in the Aramaic Words of Jesus," was delivered as one of the keynote papers at Mystics and Scientists 21, sponsored by the Scientific and Medical Network at the University of Warwick, Coventry, England, April 1998. Subsequently, another version of this chapter was published in my third book, *The Hidden Gospel: Decoding the Spiritual Message of the Aramaic Jesus* (Quest Books, 1999). This book contains the formal academic transliterations of the Aramaic words cited in this chapter.

2. Elizabeth Reed, *Abwoon Circles: Starting a Local Group* (Worthington, OH: Open Heart Publishing, 2007). For the work of the Abwoon Circles worldwide, see the website of the Abwoon Resource Center, www.abwoon.com

3. For instance, in an encyclopedic summary of the last half century of this dialogue, Ian Barbour (1990) wends his way toward a conclusion that both domains, science and religion, find their most fruitful meeting place in the process philosophy of Alfred North Whitehead. As it developed in process theology and many trends in deconstruction postmodernist thought, this approach is, according to Barbour, based on an "ecological metaphysics."

4. For this line of argument, I am indebted to Sufi scholar Seyyed Hossain Nasr's early work on spiritual ecology (1968), pp. 99–100.

5. For more on the tradition of midrash (in the Jewish tradition) and ta'wil (in the Islamic tradition) in relation to this work, see my "Midrash and Post-Modern Inquiry: Suggestions Toward a Hermeneutics of Indeterminacy." Paper presented at the International Meeting of the Society of Biblical Literature, Krakow, Poland, July 1998. Published in *Currents in Research: Biblical Studies*, vol. 7. (Sheffield: Sheffield Academic Press, 1999), and "Re-hearing Quran in Open Translation: Ta'wil, Postmodern Inquiry and a Hermeneutics of Indeterminacy." Paper presented in the Arts, Literature and Religion Section of the American Academy of Religion Annual Meeting, Toronto, Ontario, Canada, November 23, 2002 on the theme of Hermeneutics. The latter was subsequently published as part of "Ordinary and Extraordinary Ways of Knowing in Islamic Mysticism" in the anthology *Ways of Knowing: Science and Mysticism Today,* ed. Chris Clark (Exeter: Imprint Academic, 2005).

6. For more on this, see Fabre D'Olivet's extensive discussion in *The Hebraic Language Restored* (1815), especially pp. 3–60.

7. Also Mark 3:28–29, Luke 12:10, and Thomas, Saying 44.

8. For instance, Wilhelm Reich, an early student of Freud, broke with his mentor over the issue of the importance of the body in therapy. Reich wrote that holding the breath,which he saw as an attempt to suppress feeling the divine and erotic life-force flowing through one, not only created disharmony in the individual, but also in society at large. See his pivotal work, *Function of the Orgasm* (1948), pp. 333ff, 360.

9. This is the so-called proprioceptive awareness. For instance, see E. Gindler (1926), F. Alexander (1932), G. Alexander (1985) and Brooks (1982). The most famous story of this in somatic therapy concerns Elsa Gindler, a teacher of physical exercise in Germany in the 1920s. Gindler was diagnosed with fatal tuberculosis in one lung. By fine-tuning her body awareness, however, she taught herself to breathe solely in her healthy lung, thereby giving the diseased side a chance to heal. The fact that this was not simply labeled "spontaneous healing" by the medical establishment of the time was due to the fact that she thereafter taught many others the same techniques, and started several schools of somatic therapy that still exist today. Brooks, (1982), pp. 229ff.

10. These practices, sometimes called merkabah mysticism, had many different elements, including attaining a vision of the divine "throne-chariot" similar to the visions of Ezekiel and Isaiah. For more on this, see first Gershom Scholem (1954). In relation to possible influences on the Gospels of John and Thomas, see, respectively, Kanagaraj (1998) and Patterson and Robinson (1998).

11. For more on these and other themes found in the Aramaic Jesus, see my other work in *Prayers of the Cosmos* (Harper SanFrancisco,1990), *Desert Wisdom* (Harper SanFrancisco, 1995), *The Hidden Gospel* (Quest Books, 1999), *The Genesis Meditations* (Quest Books, 2003) and *Blessings of the Cosmos* (Sounds True, 2006).

13

The Divine Vibration in the Breath— A Song of Life

SONIA GILBERT

Introduction

There were mystics of ancient days who were called Sufis. They contemplated life in its essence. To a Sufi, the supreme value of breath is that within it lies our connection to God. A Sufi is one who lives with a constantly compelling need to know God, and to become integrated with God. He recognizes that the entire manifest creation relies absolutely on God. The Sufis knew how to teach the subconscious to emerge from its animal stage to a fully realized state of Divine consciousness.[1]

Though they had wandered about for centuries before, it was in the ninth century of the common era that Sufism was brought to full recognition as the mysticism within Islam. We have their Wisdom and their poetry in writing. There were saints who walked from village to village and town to town, giving solace and knowledge to others while keeping nothing material for themselves. They were the ones of renown who lived then and thereafter and even now.

My teacher, Sheikh Mohammed Raheem Bawa Muhaiyaddeen, once said, "Everything which is conveyed through your eyes, your teeth, your nose, your mouth, your sound, must be conveyed as the Resonance of God. All your smiles must be those which come from the Light of God. All the sounds that you hear must be the beautiful sounds which come from God. Your vision must be the vision of God's Love and your speech must be as the honey of Grace. If your bodies are seen they should exist in the form of the Light of Divine Wisdom. Every breath must end in Him."[2]

When Bawa taught us the first Kalimah, the strong affirmation of faith, "There is nothing but You. You alone are God," he explained, "This sound must come from within the movement of the breath. It is like a song played by a flute. The music comes from the flute, not from the flutist's voice. This sound must come forth from every one of the 4,448 blood vessels in the body, from the 248 bones, from the ligaments, the nerves, the muscles, and even from the blood. It must emanate from the 105 million hair follicles and pores of the skin. The sound of *la ilaha, illallahu*[3] must come forth from every single part of the body. It must come forth without your actually making a sound. This should go on continually, just as the heart does."[4] What he also said is that when we take in the breath on the right side saying, *"Illallahu,"* the sixth level of wisdom makes contact with that which is the Wisdom within wisdom. Then all the inner aspects of the senses must come together to focus on this breath, monitoring it. While they are doing this, Divine Analytic Wisdom checks out the current of the breath as it pulls it along. It goes from the nostril to the eye of wisdom in the center of the forehead, halts there, and then spreads out through the brain to reach the crown of the head. From there it goes to the tongue with the vibration which brings forth *Illallahu* and that becomes seated in the mystical heart as the sound *"hu."* Be aware of all this when making that sound from that instrument. There is a particular sound that comes from anything a person recites, in whatever language he uses. So the sound produced when a true man prays has the resonance of *hu, hu, hu,* the sound of God. This resonance comes from God to man and from man to God. It is man's inner heart, his *qalb,* which speaks to God and God's *qalb,* the Sacred Heart that speaks to man.

We have to give ourselves permission to believe that there really is another dimension to our senses. With courage and steadfastness and Grace and a good teacher, the inner ear opens and that becomes the way we really want to hear. The entire universe is filled with sound. It comes in waves of vibrations and they come as a continuous resonance with tiny musical notes. Our bodies, too, are naturally made with tiny musical notes. A bonus for our musical breath is what are called overtones. In every perfect musical sound there are tones of a higher pitch which are present in a regular series. These sympathetic vibrations released are not accidental. They follow a law that causes them to occur in a regular and orderly succession. The human voice is probably the richest of all instruments in overtones. Once more we see that in this life things tend to the upward. Still, we understand that the tone emitted should be perfect in order for this to happen. The breath carrying the tone must be produced by the use of all the tools given to us by the Grand Designer.

When the full concentration of the remembrance of God (what the Sufis call *Dhikr*) is activated by the conscious use of a correct way of breathing, we become the supreme musical instrument. Through the Light of Divine Luminous Wisdom a true human being realizes a state where the explanations of the subtle world are known. All the inner senses are working, and there can be communication with events far away. Grace, itself, has awakened us to know that breathing is a mystical experience.

At the age of eleven I went to my first singing lesson and my teacher said, "Before I can teach you to sing you must learn how to breathe." She was speaking about diaphragmatic breathing. From then on whenever I was walking, I was taking in breath by extending outward the diaphragm and chest, practicing and practicing. This actually pulls on the lungs to become longer and larger. A surprised doctor once told me after an examination that my lungs were two inches longer than that of the average person. If a singer does not breathe correctly she cannot produce a beautiful tone. It was a good beginning for what was to happen thirty years later. It was then, in 1972, that I came into the presence of a guru, Sheikh Mohammed Raheem Bawa Muhaiyaddeen, a Sufi saint from Sri Lanka. No words are adequate to describe this experience. For years, all I wanted was the wisdom to know God. Then, for the second time in my life, I was told that I had to first learn how to breathe. This time it was to be the special inhalation and exhalation through the nasal passages while reciting, with fixed intention and concentration totally towards God. The following is an example of this practice:

> Draw the remembrance up through the left side of the body, breathe out through the left nostril, as you say: "La 'ilaha, there is nothing other than You, O God."
> Taking the breath in through the right nostril, realizing and focusing on the Essence of God within your own heart say: "Illallahu. You Alone are God."

The practice of the remembrance of God should then be performed silently. The breathing should be natural, your intention focused only on Him. All seven states of consciousness—feeling, awareness, intellect, discernment, wisdom, Divine Analytic Wisdom and Divine Luminous Wisdom—should operate together in unison to perform this kind of remembrance the Sufis call *Dhikr*:[5] "First, one must sit properly, and start with laaaah as you send the breath out the left nostril. As the breath reaches the back of the tongue, the laaaah continues as laaa-il-laa-ha."

While awareness is carrying this along, Divine Analytic Wisdom is saying, "Other than You there is nothing," and pushes the impure breath out in its exhalation. The other levels of consciousness should know whether the sound has moved along. The Master Musician, God, will know it. When the nerves are being strummed like the strings on a vina, the sound of the *Dhikr* vibrates in the hair and in all the follicles of the body. "The One Who is the expert in that music, The Master Musician, will recognize the beat, the tune, and what instrument is being played."

There are so many practical benefits to knowing about rhythmic breath. One of the best for me is what I came to understand when trying to put a very reluctant baby to sleep. It worked whether it was my little brother, a friend's child, or my own child. I found that if I joined my breathing to the child's breathing rhythm and continued doing that for a while, I could ultimately gain control of the rhythm of the child's breathing. I could then slow it down and breathe the child to sleep. Imagine how powerful this knowledge can be. It is another success story for the power of the vibration within rhythmic breathing. It may be the secret hidden in all lullabies.

The value of willingness to serve the Universal Soul lies in the common breath. One Friday when I went to our mosque to participate in the special communal prayers[6] of Islam something unusual took place. As I stood with the other ladies in silence focusing on my intention for prayer, I heard myself breathing but there was also someone else breathing with me. This had never happened before. It was so identical that it sounded like I was being heard on a microphone. I opened my eyes to see and there, hunched over in a crippled way at the wall across from me, was a small nicely dressed Black lady, taking in the same breaths as I. I quickly got a chair for her. While the imam, who is the leader of the congregation and prayers in the mosque, was reciting from the Qur'an, I quietly asked her what had happened to her. She said that after her son died in November, she had a stroke. She said it was so bad that she was hospitalized for fifty-two days. She was still dragging one side of her body. She had come to get food and money from our mosque that day. Unbelievably, she had come on the bus. When I asked how that was possible, she said it was easy. Some people carried her onto the bus and when she arrived at our street others carried her off. Two Fellowship sisters helped carried her downstairs, and there, she told us the rest of her sad story. Everything she had placed in storage during her hospitalization had vanished. There was nothing left to start over with, not even a bed. She slept on the floor of a low-income housing unit. Well, we all collected money from our pocketbooks; brought food for some days from our kitchen. I called Dial-a-Mattress, which will deliver a mattress of your choice within hours and bought a bed to be delivered to her the next morning. Then my dear sisters drove her to her house in North Philadelphia. The next morning we found our way to her little house with linens and some furniture and kitchenware and found her sitting on a stool looking at the new bed, which had already come. In less than a day, a life was changed. Was it because she breathed with me that I took her plight as my own? That breath knows no boundaries. That breath is made to hold vibrations from the Source of all Compassion. I only know that her breath was at one with mine in both rhythm and sound. There was no difference.

Revelation on Pilgrimage to Mecca

How does a message like the one brought by Mohammed [Peace be upon Him[7]]. a small human being in a tiny desert place in far off Arabia, become the focal point of millions in an earlier time and by more than a billion people in our time?

There is a chapter in the Qur'an called "Help," in which a prophesy that came through Mohammed [Peace be upon Him], foretold that believers would one day come in droves to pray in Mecca, Saudi Arabia. This was the place of the Messenger's birth and later his home. Certainly, this is extraordinary. To overcome a world of idols with the message of an all powerful, formless God had to go against all the odds of success. What is not often seen in the media is that it is Abraham's message that is embraced there. The Ka'aba is the focal point for that message. It is in circling the Ka'aba that breathing is of primary importance. The circling is not walked at a slow pace. The movement is rather swift and unites the walkers with one another.

I believe it was somewhere after or during the fifth circling, saying prayers all the while, that the very Soul of me went spinning off like a kite while God held the string. O the beauty of the confidence that my Soul is in That Hand! Because Wisdom showed me that the same Soul life was also within my body, the experience was complete.

Second Pilgrimage

The second revelation came a year later, when the overwhelming love in my heart gave its gratitude at the station of Abraham after circling the Ka'aba. A response came that sang out from my heart. It revealed that the Power we call God has a Heart. From that Heart come radiating resonances. These resonances have within them the Source of Wisdom and all Life. These become the world of souls. It is the Love in the Sacred Heart that produces manifest creations. Human souls take with them a tiny part of the Sacred Heart and that connects them eternally with their Creator.

Now comes the hard part. It is one thing to leave God but quite another to leave a mother, laboring mightily, to bring forth a baby who will suddenly be called upon to breathe! It is astonishing how many are capable of doing this in each and every birth. It must be Divine Intention. The obligation to breathe well during pregnancy and the delivery process is vitally important, both for the mother and child. When the baby's cry is heard it is always welcomed with joy. That first breath establishes us in our new realm, a place destined for us and which we call Earth.

If ever there was a sacred thing it is this planet Earth. Cast out into the heavenly sphere, it contains all the riches in the Universe. It breathes! It makes music! And there is even harmony. When you get to know how harmony works, you will understand why it is the ideal for human beings. To be in harmony we need to agree to the key and the pitch of our universe. In an orchestra no one ever argues with the oboist or concertmaster when he draws his bow across the string to produces an A440 pitch. [Pitch is the sound determined by the number of vibrations and oscillations a note creates while it is sounding. 'Concert pitch' is the directing note sounded so all the instruments will match each other in sound and pitch during a performance.] When the conductor picks up the baton or holds his hands high, all the players are at attention. They all know which is to be the opening music and which instruments will be playing. Other melodies may join, and though their notes are differ- ent, they must agree with each other harmonically. We, as harmonious human beings are striving to find a way to combine our efforts for the good of all. The more we feel the subtle Resonance of God the stronger we can vibrate because the sound is in the *true key*.

In 1972, when I first came to hear Bawa he used to sing very long songs; sometimes forty minutes or more. The room was not very wide. I sat opposite to him leaning against a wall of cabinets. In those years though he had some emphysema, his use of the breath would impress any singer. Between his breathing and my breathing something unusual happened. It seemed as though his sound was playing the molecules of my body. First, it was felt to be horizontal, and then it played in me vertically. After that the song went faster and that caused both horizon- tal and vertical to combine to form an elliptical movement within me. All sense of body orientation left me. It seemed my energy was leaving through my head. I was in a transcendent state, marvelously pleasant. It happened whenever Bawa sang those long songs. I had no explana- tion regarding this for thirty-two years. Then, by chance, I heard a lec- ture at the University of Pennsylvania given by Dr. Andrew Newberg on brain science and the biology of belief. He and Dr. Eugene D'Aquili were exploring the field of neurotheology, dedicated to understanding the complex relationship between spirituality and the brain. The book is titled *Why God Won't Go Away*.[8] In it, a certain brain scanning machine

was used in a very remarkable way to see what was happening in the
brains of Tibetan meditators when in deep meditation and Franciscan
nuns when in deep prayer. They were all known to be very credible
people in these rituals. No one was allowed in the room of these individuals as they went into their deepest states of meditation or prayer. A
length of string tied to a finger alerted those in another room to start
the machine. What was revealed is pretty much what I was experiencing in 1972. At last, there was visual evidence of the neurological secret
behind the power of ritual.

Another important aspect of the Divine breath is its ability to breathe
in fragrances that may only be known to one in a special state of meditation. Once, after one of Bawa's very long songs I began to smell a glorious
scent of a perfume I had never smelled before. Later, I walked around
the room trying to find out who was wearing it. It did not come from
any brothers or sisters in the room, but it emanated from the area where
Bawa sat. When I was asked to describe it, all I could liken it to was a
kind of rose I had never smelled before. It was entrancing. Someone suggested musk but I was not familiar with musk, so it remained a mystery.
However, there is a musk rose. What I do know is that in breathing the
aroma my entire body accepted its beauty. The experience was repeated
once more soon after that as if to affirm the reality of the earlier happening. There is a breath within the breath. It is a mysterious gift, sometimes
spoken of by poets.

My personal ritual is to move towards and stay with "inner" until
there is nothing but the breath and the vibration within it. My personal
understanding is that a special breathing practice can take one quickly
from being a bodily oriented person to a totally different transcendent
state. It is the relaxation or a melting away of *self* to a point where it
has no value. Now breath moves through me, animating my dust but not
disturbing it. This is, after all, the duty of the breath.

Notes

1. M. R. Bawa Muhaiyaddeen, *The Golden Words of a Sufi Sheikh*
(Philadelphia: Fellowship Press, 1982), 3.
2. Ibid.
3. (a) Qur'an, chapter 20, verse 98; Mohammed (sal.) is actually quoting
Moses as this chapter retells the story of the golden calf. Moses says "Your

God is the only God. There is no other God but He. His knowledge extends over everything." In chapter 21, verse 108: "This is what has been revealed to me: 'Your God is one and only God.' So will you bow in homage to Him?" (b) Asma-ul Husna: these pages explain the Power and Dominion of That One God in every way.

4. Quote from M. R. Bawa Muhaiyaddeen in his book, *Dhikr: The Remembrance of God* (Philadelphia: Fellowship Press, 1999), 73.

5. *Dhikr* (Arabic) a common name given to recitation of certain words in remembrance of God and in praise of God; a practice for all Sufi lineages. See M. R. Bawa Muhaiyaddeen, *Dhikr: The Remembrance of God, an Explanation* by (Philadelphia: Fellowship Press, 1999).

6. *Salat*—Islamic prayers practiced five times daily.

7. Muslims traditionally say "Peace and Blessings be upon him" following a mentioning of the name of the Prophet. This honoring exists in many traditions as a natural expression of love and respect for the soul of one whose life was and is praiseworthy. For example, a Muslim would use this same expression when mentioning the name of Jesus or the name of any of the major Prophets.

8. Andrew Newberg, Eugene D'Aquili, and Vince Rause, *Why God Won't Go Away* (New York: Ballantine Books, 2002).

Part IV

Further Explorations of the Healing Power of the Breath

A Goat Kneels

The inner being of a human being
Is a jungle. Sometimes wolves dominate,
Sometimes wild hogs. Be wary when you breathe!

At one moment gentle, generous qualities,
like Joseph's pass from one nature to another.
The next moment vicious qualities move in hidden ways.

Wisdom slips for a while into an ox!
A restless, recalcitrant horse suddenly
becomes obedient and smooth-gaited.

A bear begins to dance.
A goat kneels! . . .

At every moment a new species arises in the chest—
now a demon, now an angel, now a wild animal.

There are also those in this amazing jungle
Who can absorb you into their own surrender.
If you have to stalk and steal something,
steal from them.[1]

                                        —Rumi

Thus far we have examined Eastern, Western, and Middle Eastern perspectives on the breath. Is there a point at which they overlap? How does the breath unite East and West?

In the first chapter of this section, Neil Douglas-Klotz emphasizes the connections among Eastern breathing philosophies, Western somatic traditions, and Sufi beliefs and practices. Dr. Klotz examines the work of Elsa Gindler, Gerda Alexander, Wilhelm Reich, and F. M. Alexander, all pioneers in somatic breath work; while discussing their relationship to the Vijnana Bhairava Sutra of the Yoga tradition and the Chishti Sufi lineage. His chapter also explores the varying degrees of breath awareness often associated with neuroticism, schizophrenia, and visionary states of awareness.

The spiritual journey of awakening includes the healing of early life developmental problems and integration of various archetypal energies. Conscious breathing practices utilized as part of this journey stimulate mental, emotional, and somatic responses, and encourage an inner porosity; opening the practitioner to increasingly sensitive fields of nonordinary experience. Therefore, the practitioner should be carefully guided by a seasoned teacher, for unexpected physiological, psychological, and spiritual experience may well arise at various stages. My chapter, "Be Wary of the Breath," addresses some of these phenomena. I also share the healing and balancing *Element Breaths*, purifying breaths related to the energies of Earth, Water, Fire, Air, and Ether. All of these practices enable the deeper, experiential fields of life to enter into our physical existence. As Quantum physicists have verified, there is no such thing as empty space. Everything around and within us is alive with activity. We live in a sea of energy. We breathe it in, and it also breathes us.

As we recover our natural spontaneity and creative power, we regain the innocence and innate pleasure so often observed in young children. This is our birthright! Waldorf teacher Ken Friedman points out the importance of the natural breath in children, noting how this breath is cultivated in the Waldorf education model developed by the late Rudolf Steiner. The Waldorf exercises encourage a breath that moves with the natural rhythms and spaces in life. Friedman's chapter emphasizes the task of creating a better life for our children, a most important endeavor, for they also represent humanity's future.

In our final chapter, Breathing for a Better World, Puran Bair discusses the underlying theme running through this book. We all share the same breath. And all of nature is engaged. Bair demonstrates how "the act of breathing is our most fundamental interaction with life. Not only does breath give us life, the way we breathe determines the way we live."

Notes

1. *Delicious Laughter: Rambunctious Teaching Stories from the Mathnawi,* trans. C. Barks (Barnesville, GA: Maypop Books, 1990), 113.

14

The Natural Breath

A Dialogue between Western Somatic and Eastern Spiritual Approaches to the Body Awareness of Breathing

NEIL DOUGLAS-KLOTZ

The nature of breathing and the use of breath practices have, over the past seventy-five years, raised a great deal of controversy in the various schools of somatic psychology as well as in various lineages of spiritual training. There is a common stereotype in Western psychology that all Eastern breathing practices are *disembodied*, and that all Western therapies are therefore *embodied*. This is largely a language problem. It is time to reopen a dialogue that has been limited by stereotypical views held on both sides in order to see and appreciate both the differences, and the similarities of the practices involved.

The term *somatic* was originally created to avoid an aspect of Western dualism, which refers to the body as being separate from anything else, failing to consider that this body affects all areas of human life.[1] The term *soma* refers to a nexus of mind, emotions, body awareness, and spiritual concerns. Somatic traditions include Reichian and Neo-Reichian breathwork, Eutony, Feldenkrais, Alexander Technique, and Sensory Awareness, among others. They represent *experiential, body-based* methods for healing psychological problems.

Spirituality differs from religious dogma in its emphasis on personal *experience*, and includes such practices as those used in Yogic breathing, Buddhist meditation, and Sufi breathing processes. For example, the chapters describing these traditions within this book clearly reveal a difference between religion and spirituality.

This chapter explores the meeting points of Western and Eastern traditions of the breath. It examines the main somatic psychology pioneers Elsa Gindler, Wilhelm Reich, Gerda Alexander, and F. M. Alexander, with regard to the relationship of breath awareness to neuroticism, schizophrenia, and visionary states of awareness. It also suggests a more appreciative conversation between these voices and selected ones from the Vipassana Buddhist, Yoga, and Sufi traditions.

There are many bridges between the various somatic and spiritual approaches regarding breath. In fact, the very nature of this book is to explore the differences in the way varying traditions use the awareness of breathing.

Why Is Breathing Important?

All somatic schools begin with a more or less commonsense approach, which equates breathing with one's ability to function in life in a healthy way. This is well expressed by the German pioneer of somatic education Elsa Gindler who noted in 1926 that successful people often revealed healthy breath responses when changing from a resting state to an active one. Their breathing patterns were in harmony with this flexibility of movement. She recognized this ability was not easily earned. In comparing it with the inflexibility and associated rigid breathing patterns of many of her students, she noted how this lack of ease impeded their own flexibility and adaptability to life's changing conditions.[2]

The failure to breathe in a flexible fashion was also noted by another founder of somatic therapy, Wilhelm Reich. Reich, an early student of Freud, broke with his mentor over the issue of the importance of the body in therapy. In *The Function of the Orgasm* (1948) Reich noted how holding the breath not only created disharmony in the individual, but also in society at large and expressed the belief that "There [was] not a single neurotic person who is capable of breathing out deeply and evenly in one breath."[3] He recognized that breath-holding began in childhood, and evidenced itself in muscular blocks, the rigid postures expressed in the military and those manipulated by social controls.[4] For Reich, respiration was intimately tied up with the natural human impulse to expand in pleasure and contract in anxiety.

In the spiritual practices mentioned above, breathing is cited as a means to enlightenment, realization, or full awareness. In his commentary on the *Sutra on the Full Awareness of Breathing,* one of the earliest texts on Buddhist breathing practices, the Vietnamese Zen master Thich Nhat Hanh describes sixteen different ways of inhaling and exhaling. In discussing the relationship of these patterns with Buddhism's Four Foundations of Mindfulness, he explains that these are "the essence of the Full Awareness of Breathing Sutra. Breathing is a means of awakening and maintaining full attention in order to look carefully, long and deeply, to see the nature of all things and arrive at liberation."[5]

Various texts in the Yoga tradition also affirm that the awareness of breathing is a doorway to enlightenment. One of the oldest of these, the *Vijnana Bhairava Sutra* possibly predates the composition of the Vedas (c. 2000–1000 BCE).[6] The *Vijnana Bhairava Sutra* takes the form of a dialogue between Shiva and his consort Devi. Devi begins by asking several questions. To these questions, Shiva replies with 112 suggested methods. The following quote opens their dialogue:

> Devi says: O Shiva, what is your reality? What is this wonder-filled universe? What constitutes seed? Who centers the universal wheel? What is this life beyond form pervading forms? How may we enter it fully, above space and time, names and descriptions? Let my doubts be cleared.

> Shiva replies: Radiant one, this experience may dawn between two breaths. After breath comes in (down) and just before turning up (out)—*the beneficence.*[7]

Likewise, the ninth-century Persian Sufi mystic al-Qushayri cites traditional sayings that relate the awareness of breathing to the remembrance of divine Unity (*tawhid*):

> They said: "The best act of worship is to count your breaths with Allah, Most Praised and Most High". . . . Every breath that arrives upon the carpet of need without the guidance of recognition and the sign of *tawhid* is dead, and its master will be called to account for it."[8]

Similarly, the early twentieth-century Indian Sufi teacher and interpreter, Hazrat Inayat Khan describes how the awareness of breathing can unify the various essences (*lata'if*) of the body and link these to the divine. His metaphors unite psychology with cosmology:

> Breath is the very life in beings, and what holds all the particles of the body together is the power of the breath, and when this power becomes less then the will loses its control over the body. As the power of the sun holds all the planets so the power of the breath holds every organ. . . . Breath is a channel through which all the expression of the innermost life can be given. Breath is an electric current that runs between the everlasting life and the mortal frame.[9]

As one can see the differences between the states of health and flexibility mentioned by Gindler and Reich may not differ that much from the more grandiose goals of spiritual practitioners. For example, many somatic schools also have the goal of bringing the client or student to some ideal standard of "health." The idealized somatic breath expressing full human flexibility and natural individuality may not differ significantly from the breath of a person who sees the "nature of all things" in Buddhist terms. The difference may simply be in the use of language. For instance, a Buddhist teacher guides students in the mindful awareness of the breath, recognizing that this stills the mind from its endless chatter. This becomes a means to peaceful thoughts and feelings.

Likewise, the Australian educator F. M. Alexander, considered another major founder of the somatic field, equated unhealthy breathing habits with an overly active tendency to think, especially about one's self. During one of his sessions with students in the 1920s he was recorded as saying: "That isn't breathing: it's lifting your chest and collapsing. . . . If I breathe as I understand breathing, I am doing something wrong. . . . I see at last that if *I* don't breathe, I *breathe*."[10]

On the other hand, many somatic and spiritual schools may differ on the way each uses the word "breath" itself. Somatic practitioners criticize expressions like "breathing in the heart" or "breathing in the feet" because, from a physiological standpoint neither the heart nor the feet are involved in the exchange of gases that constitute breathing. Nonetheless, somatic practitioners also speak of feeling the breath in various parts of the body. In fact, the phrase "awareness of breathing" makes a direct bridge to most of the terms used by the spiritual practitioners.

In much of the Chinese Taoist literature, the word translated as "breath" is often interchangeable with ch'i (as described by Dr. Tong in chapter 3). There are also many similarities with the yogic term *prana* to Wilhelm Reich's orgone (discussed in chapter 5). Each describes the breath, its energy, and pulsation.

In the Middle Eastern traditions, especially those where Hebrew, Aramaic, or Arabic texts are concerned, the same word *(ruach,* Hebrew; *ruha,* Aramaic; *ruh,* Arabic) can be translated as "breath," "wind," "air," or "spirit" and indicates a connection between soul and divine Unity. A different term in these languages *(nephesh,* Hebrew; *naphsha;* Aramaic; *nafs,* Arabic) can also be translated as "breath" but implies the personal self or subconscious that has not fully realized its connection with the divine.

To Intervene Directly or Not?

Gerda Alexander, the founder of the European somatic therapy Eutony and a teacher of Moshe Feldenkrais, makes a very clear summary of some of the difficulties in working directly with the awareness of breathing. According to Alexander, breathing will normalize simply by relaxing the tensions found in the "pelvic musculature, perineum, diaphragm, intercostal muscles, shoulders, neck, hands, feet, the digestive and intestinal apparatus."[11] Alexander noticed that the breathing processes of an entire group will change simply by mentioning the word "breath." Conscious attention to the breath can also limit its "value as a source of information about the psychosomatic state of the pupil."[12] Other somatic therapies do approach breathing directly, but theorists use the term "breathing experiment" in order to convey that there is no one desired result of any intervention.

The spiritual schools mentioned do not hesitate to approach the breath directly, using a "practice" or method that is intended to lead to a desired goal. A practice, such as the one described by Thich Nhat Hanh, intervenes in the student's normal breathing pattern with a series of rhythms or manipulations, such as long and short, refined and rough, or through the right or left nostrils.

Some Sufi breathing pratices encourage the awareness of breath in a particular center, or *latifa,* of the body, for instance, breathing "in the heart."[13] By breaking the established rhythm of breathing, and changing the consciousness of the participant through the addition of a devotional, emotional focus, the spiritual practice will theoretically lead one to a more natural, full, or flexible breath. Breaking the pattern will lead to a new healthier pattern if one presumes, for instance, that the divine is helping one towards health, or that the body, as an expression of the sacred, knows what its own "natural state" should be.

By contrast, somatic therapy traditions generally focus on increasing one's awareness of the breathing wave itself. One simply observes the feeling of the breathing without intervening, becoming increasingly aware of the many, minute sensations and the emotions linked to them.

One of the primary findings of somatic research over the past seventy years (since Gindler and Reich) is that one can consciously develop a sensation of the position in space of joints, muscles, tissue, and organs on a very minute level. This so-called proprioceptive function of the body is not simply autonomic; it can be sensed and influenced by fine-tuning one's awareness.

The most famous story of this concerns Elsa Gindler. A teacher of *Gymnastik* in Germany during the 1920s, Gindler was diagnosed with fatal tuberculosis in one lung. By fine-tuning her sensory awareness, however, she taught herself to breathe solely in her healthy lung, thereby giving the diseased side a chance to heal. The fact that this was not simply labeled "spontaneous healing" by the medical establishment of the time was due to the fact that Gindler thereafter taught many others the same techniques, and started several schools of somatic therapy that still exist today.[14]

Breathing and Control: To Feel the Body or Not?

Reich also intervened in the breath of his patients with patterned breathing techniques that aimed to release their "vegetative" bodily impulses and breathing rhythms. Reich felt that Yoga breathing practices made it more difficult to find a naturally flexible breath; because such practices were sophisticated methods of holding the breath:

> The breathing technique taught by Yoga is the exact opposite of the breathing technique we use to reactivate the vegetative emotional excitations in our patients. The aim of the Yoga breathing is to combat affective impulses; its aim is to obtain peace.... That the Yoga technique was able to spread to Europe and America is ascribable to the fact that the people of these cultures seek a means of gaining control over their natural vegetative impulses and at the same time of eliminating conditions of anxiety. However; they are not that far from an inkling of the orgastic function of life.[15]

Writing in the 1940s, Reich was undoubtedly referring to the methods of extended, alternate nostril breathing and controlled holding of the breath practiced by the Patanjali school of Yoga, which were the best known in the West at that time. This school emphasizes holding fixed positions combined with fixed breathing patterns. These particular techniques; however; are not representative of Eastern breathing science as a whole and differ fundamentally from the oldest texts on yoga like the *Vijnana Bhairava Sutra,* according to Jaideva Singh. In the *Vijnana Bhairava Sutra,* says Singh, the goal of the practices given is not "isolation of the Self" from sensation and existence, as in the Patanjali school, but instead "realization of the universe as the expression of . . . spiritual energy."[16] That is, the object of the practice is not cessation from bodily sensation but exploration and integration of all sensation. This is illustrated by many of the brief practices in the sutra.

2. As breath turns from down to up, and again as breath curves from up to down—through both these turns, *realize.*
23. Feel your substance, bones, fleshy blood; saturated with cosmic essence.

38. Feel cosmos as translucent ever-living presence.
39. With utmost devotion, center on the two junctions of breath and know the knower.
40. Consider the plenum to be your own *body of bliss*.[17]

Paul Reps, who provided the above poetic translations of the sutra, felt that these practices influenced later ones of Zen Buddhism and included them in his collection *Zen Flesh; Zen Bones*, coauthored with the Rinzai Zen teacher Nygoen Senzaki.[18]

Returning to Gindler's work during the 1920s in Germany, one sees a remarkable similarity between her early recommendations for a breathing therapy and the primary practice of the *Vijnana Bhairava*:

> If one wishes to carry breathing all the way to completion, it is necessary to be able to carry through the four phases of breathing: inhalation, pause, exhalation, pause. These pauses and the conscious feeling of them are of the greatest importance. The pause, or rest, after exhalation must not be lifeless. It should never be a matter of holding the breath. On the contrary; it should most closely resemble the pause we experience in music—which is the vital preparation for what is to follow.[19]

Interpretation aside, all human beings experience, in some limited way, Gindler's four phases of breathing, and both somatic theory and spiritual practice ascribe value to experiencing them more fully.

The *Vijnana Bhairava Sutra* and Gindler also both propose that the whole person should kept in the field of awareness and sensation during a breathing practice: the world or universe is included in the practice or experiment, not denied. Attention to the breath can then lead the student deeper into ranges of sensation that habitual breathing patterns have prevented him or her from feeling.

Again, the distinction drawn between feeling and not feeling the "body" and the "world" may hinge on a language problem, the difference between the way various modalities use these words. The contemporary Sufi scholar Seyyed Hossein Nasr alludes to this in his discussion of Sufism's doctrine of Unity (*tawhid*) and how it relates to the practitioners' experience of the world:

Sufi doctrine does not assert that God is the world but that the world to the degree that it is real cannot be other than God; were it to be so it would become a totally independent reality, a deity of its own, and would destroy the absoluteness and the Oneness that belong to God alone.[20]

Integration and the Self: Who is Breathing?

The questions concerning feeling and perception of breathing raise deeper ones, in all of the traditions and modalities I surveyed: Who or what is doing the feeling and perceiving? Does the awareness of breathing help to build a healthy self, however defined, or does it lead to the dissolution of the self.

In the somatic field, Reich's analysis of this area is the most thorough and influential. Reich considered the detailed witnessing of small proprioceptive differences essential to his approach with patients. These differences included feelings of tension (called "armoring") in the muscles and connective tissue arranged in rings around the eyes, throat, chest, solar plexus, genitals and pelvic floor. Reich associated this armoring with a patient's subconscious attempts to suppress breathing, sensation, and feeling. In other patients, Reich found the reverse of armoring in these areas—an excessive softness (*hypotonia*) and lack of feeling. In these cases, Reich felt that patients' awareness of bodily sensations and feelings had become "split" from their sense of identity. In extreme cases, he felt that this splitting of body awareness from identity was the functional definition of schizophrenia.

He noted in an extensive case history of a schizophrenic patient in *Character Analysis*:

> [The] degree of clarity and oneness [of consciousness] depends, to judge from observations in schizophrenic processes, not so much on the strength or intensity of self perception, as on the more or less complete integration of the innumerable elements of self-perception into one single experience of the SELF.[21]
>
> Besides the abilities to see, hear, smell, taste, touch, there existed unmistakably in healthy individuals a sense of organ functions, an orgonotic sense, as it were, which

was completely lacking or was disturbed in biopathies. The
compulsion neurotic has lost this sixth sense completely. The
schizophrenic has displaced this sense and has transformed it
into certain patterns of his delusional system, such as "forces,"
"the devil," "voices," "electrical currents," "worms in the brain
or in the intestines," etc.[22]

What the schizophrenic experiences on the level of body awareness,
Reich maintained, is not so different from the experience of the inspired
poet or mystic:

> The functions which appear in the schizophrenic, if only one
> learns to read them accurately, are COSMIC FUNCTIONS;
> that is, functions of the cosmic orgone energy in undisguised
> form. . . . In schizophrenia, as well as in true religion and in
> true art and science, the awareness of these deep functions is
> great and overwhelming. The schizophrenic is distinguished
> from the great artist, scientist, or founder of religions in that
> his organism is not equipped or is too split up to accept and
> to carry the experience of this identity of functions inside and
> outside the organism.[23]

Apart from the experience of a great poet or mystic, which he felt
was unusual, Reich defined health as the everyday ability of a person
to love, work and learn without inhibition or anxiety. The motto with
which he prefaced all of his books was "Love, work and knowledge are
the wellsprings of our life. They should also govern it."

The splitting of the subconscious personality into multiple fragmented
I's is also a spiritual problem approached by several branches of Middle
Eastern mysticism, including Sufism. We could see Reich's orgonotic
"sixth sense" as comparable to the witnessing or gathering self in Middle
Eastern psychology. In Sufi psychology this is called the awareness of
"Reality" (haqiqa). In one interpretation of Jewish mystical psychology,
the same function is served by the "Sacred Sense" or "Holy Wisdom"
(hokhmah) which organizes the healthy sense of an I. Without this gathering or witnessing awareness, which is intimately tied up with the body's
proprioceptive awareness, the subconscious self (nafs in Arabic, nephesh
in Hebrew) splits into a multiplicity of discordant voices forgetful of the

divine Unity. This could be seen as a foundational view of the psyche that underlies the entire range of Middle Eastern mysticism.[24]

If this relative self or I has no ultimate existence outside of the ultimate Oneness, it is nonetheless not separate from that Oneness, according to the Sufi view. Nasr notes this in commenting upon a Sufi practitioner's progressive relationship to body awareness:

> Although at the beginning of man's awareness of the spiritual life he must separate himself from the body considered in its negative and passionate aspect, in the more advanced stages of the Path the aim is to keep oneself within the body and centered in the heart, that is, within the body considered in its positive aspect as the "temple" *(haykal)* of the spirit. . . . When Rumi writes in his Mathnawi that the adept must invoke in the spiritual retreat until his toes begin to say "Allah," he means precisely this final integration which includes the body as well as the mind and the soul.[25]

Another modern Sufi commentator and scientist Samuel L. Lewis (Sufi Ahmed Murad Chishti), whose work stemmed from both the Chishti Sufi and Buddhist traditions, makes similar comments to those of Reich and Nasr. In analyzing the psychophysical function of various breathing practices, he states that, without an integrating sense of feeling or "heart," held breathing practices can lead to psychological problems and even a schizophrenic breakdown. Lewis defined "meditation" as "heart-exercise" that leads to a greater ability to sense and feel in an integrated, compassionate fashion. This enlarged "heart" and unified perception of feeling created a greater capacity for the bioelectrical energy available through the awareness of breathing:

Every breath raises or lowers the electrical state of the body which can be demonstrated and proven scientifically. If this power is increased without augmenting the capacity many times more—which is done by meditation—the same thing will happen and does happen to the human body as occurs to the electrical system—a fuse blows out and you have trouble. Capacity is increased by meditation and, in general, by heart action, by maintaining the rhythm of the heartbeat, by feeling the consciousness in the heart, by directing all activity from the center to the circumference and by maintaining unity in feeling, thought, and action.[26]

In Lewis's estimation, an effective approach to the breath would combine awareness of breathing with physical movement and increased awareness of sensation in the heart. This combination would provide the "unity in feeling, thought and action" he recommended in order not to "burn out the fuses."

Up until the final stages of breathing practice, which emphasize liberation from individuality, Thich Nhat Hanh emphasizes the healthy development of an I existing in the present moment. He also comments on the ultimately nondual experience of breath, body, and world in his commentary on the *Sutra on the Full Awareness of Breathing*:

> Breathing and body are one. Breathing and mind are one. Mind and body are one. At the time of observation, mind is not an entity which exists independently, outside of your breathing and your body. The boundary between the subject of observation and the object of observation no longer exists. We observe "the body in the body."[27]

Like Lewis, Thich Nhat Hanh recommends the integration of breathing awareness with everyday life situations:

> Most of our daily activities can be accomplished while following our breath according to the instructions in the sutra. When our work demands special attentiveness in order to avoid confusion or an accident, we can unite Full Awareness of Breathing with the task itself. . . . In fact, it is not enough to combine awareness of breathing only with tasks which require so much attention. We must also combine Full Awareness of our Breathing with all the movements of our body: "I am breathing in and I am sitting." "I am breathing in and wiping the table." "I am breathing in and smiling at myself."[28]

From the somatic point of view, F. M. Alexander (1932) also advocated an integrated approach that emphasized body awareness, breathing, intention, and movement in unison, rather than specific corrective attempts to "breathe better" or "move better." He felt this was important due to the human tendency to place "end-gaining" over the awareness of the process itself. That is, one's desire to be more "healthy" or "liberated," for instance, would distract one's attention from the very process by which any progress or realization could be made: "[W]hen a person has reached a given stage of unsatisfactory use and functioning, his habit of "end-gaining" will prove to be the impeding factor in all his attempts to profit by any teaching method whatsoever."[29]

Conclusions

In conclusion, we have discussed the meeting points between Western and Eastern practices and opened a door for further exploration between somatic and spiritual practitioners regarding functional approaches to breathing experiments and practices.

1. The importance of breath, or breathing awareness, in the modalities and traditions surveyed in this chapter, focuses on flexible breathing as a functional goal, that is, on releasing inhibitions and blocks to "natural" functioning, however the final state of "health," "liberation," or "realization" is conceived.

2. It is important to consider that differing students and clients have differing needs, and that one breathwork form may be preferable to another according to these needs. Are the actual interpretations of what is going on, or what goals are projected, secondary to the client's or student's increased awareness of a more flexible or "natural" breath?

3. The differing strategies and goals between increasing body awareness and ignoring body awareness may again be a language problem. Can these differences be resolved by looking carefully at how each modality or tradition defines "body," "world," and "breath" in relation to the actual somatic sensations evoked?

4. Likewise the way that each tradition or modality defines the healthy or spiritual self may obscure the general agreement of the various voices that the integration of a healthy sense of I is a prerequisite for any somatic or spiritual progress. The adage that you can't lose a self that you never had is apropos here, and may provide the basis for further mutual inquiry.

5. Most of the voices surveyed here recommend the integration of the awareness of breathing with everyday life movement. If one works solely with a controlled breath over a prolonged period of time, without any attention to body sensation, does perception tend to split off in a schizophrenic fashion, and are certain types of clients or students vulnerable to this? Alternatively, when a change does occur from such an approach, does the habitual use of the body later reorient the breath to its old pattern, thereby making the somatic or spiritual state temporary? Likewise, does work on muscular tension or structural alignment alone (for instance, through massage or other somatic deep tissue work) tend to be temporary, since without integrating a spiritual-emotional change, the habitual use of the breath may recreate the habitual tension?

The most beneficial approach to breathing and breath experiments based on this brief survey would seem to be one in which the goal was not to "breathe better," but to increase self-awareness or self-knowledge. This intention alone might help to release breathing practices or experiments from what F. M. Alexander would call their habitual "end-gaining."

The issues around breathing, body awareness, and inclusion or exclusion of sensation, open to broader cultural views of nature, in which there may be greater differences between somatic and spiritual schools than any surveyed here. In one of the mystical schools of hermeneutics in Sufism, called ta'wil, for example, the use of a spiritual practice corresponds to an approach to one's own body as an expression of a natural, sacred cosmos. In this view, as Seyyed Hossein Nasr notes, the natural world can be considered a "second Qur'an," and in one's own body one may read the sacred scripture of nature.[30] He contrasts this approach with the prevailing attitude of mainstream Western culture and science, which places human beings in conflict with nature and their own bodies.

In other less metaphysical terms, Lao Tze relates the experience of living embedded in a cosmic ecology, in a relationship not based on fear, or its somatic equivalent—holding the breath:

The heaven, the earth and I share one breath, but each manages it individually. How could heaven and earth put me to death?[31]

Notes

1. Thomas Hanna (ed.), *Explorers of Humankind* (New York: Harper and Row, 1979); and Don Johnson, *Body* (Boston: Beacon Press, 1984).

2. Eisa Gindler, "Gymnastik for Working People," an unpublished translation of "Die Gymnastik des Berufsmenschen" in *Gymnastik* (Journal of the German Gymnastik Foundation), 1926: 38.

3. Wihelm Reich, *The Function of the Orgasm* (New York: Simon and Schuster, 1948), 333.

4. Ibid., p.360.

5. Thich Nhat Hanh, *The Sutra on the Full Awareness of Breathing* (Berkeley, CA: Parallax Press, 1988), 22.

6. Jaideva Singh, *Vijnana Bhairava or Divine Consciousness* (Delhi: Motilal Banarsidass, 1979).

7. Paul Reps and Nyogen Senzaki (eds.), *Zen Flesh, Zen Bones: A Collection of Zen and Pre-Zen Writings,* trans. Paul Reps (Garden City, NJ: Anchor, 1955), 161.

8. Early Islamic Mysticism: Sufi, Qur'an, Mi'raj, Poetic and Theological Writings, trans. Michael A. Sells (New York: Paulist Press, 1996), 142.

9. Hazrat Inayat Khan, *The Sufi Message,* vol. 8 (Shaftesbury: Element Books, 1991), 135, 140n.

10. F. Matthias Alexander, *The Resurrection of the Body: The Essential Writings of F. Matthias Alexander,* ed. Edward Maisel (Boston: Shambhala, 1986), 3.

11. Gerda Alexander, *Eutony: The Holistic Discovery of the Total Person* (New York: Felix Morrow, 1985), 24–25.

12. Ibid.

13. Carl W. Ernst, *The Shambhala Guide to Sufism* (Boston: Shambhala Publications, 1997), 107.

14. Charles V. W. Brooks, *Sensory Awareness: The Rediscovery of Experiencing* (Santa Barbara, CA: Ross-Erikson, 1982), 229ff.

15. Reich, *Function of the Orgasm,* 358–59.

16. Jaideva Singh, *Vijnana Bhairava or Divine Consciousness* (Delhi: Motilal Banarsidass, 1979), ix.

17. Reps and Senzaki, *Zen Flesh, Zen Bones,* 160–64.

18. Ibid.

19. Gindler, "Gymnastik for Working People," ""38.

20. Seyyed Hossein Nasr, *Sufi Essays* (Albany: SUNY Press, 1991), A5.

21. Wilhelm Reich, *Character Analysis.* New York: Farrar, Straus and Giroux, 1949), 442.

22. Ibid., 454.

23. Ibid., 442, 448

24. Neil Douglas-Klotz, *Desert Wisdom: Sacred Middle-Eastern Writings from the Goddess through the Sufis* (London: Thorsons, 1995).

25. Seyyed Hossein Nasr, *Sufi Essays* (Albany: SUNY Press, 1991), 50.

26. Samuel L. Lewis, 201 Suras on Breath (unpublished manuscript from the Archives at the Sufi Islamia Ruhaniat Society, the Mentorgarten, 410 Precita Avenue, San Francisco, CA), pp. 16, 28.

27. Thich Nhat Hanh, *The Sutra on the Full Awareness of Breathing* (Berkeley, CA: Parallax Press, 1988), A8.

28. Ibid., 44.

29. F. M. Alexander, *The Use of the Self* (New York: E. P. Dutton, 1932), 62.

30. Seyyed Hossein Nasr, *Man in Nature: The Spiritual Crisis in Modern Man* (London: Unwin, 1968), 95.

31. *The Primordial Breath, Volume I: An Ancient Chinese Way of Prolonging Life Through Breath Control,* trans. Jane Huang and Michael Wurmbrand (Torrance, CA: Original Books, 1987), 12.

15

Be Wary When You Breathe

Respecting Its Wisdom, Power, and Beauty

SHARON G. MIJARES

Introduction

The breath, the energizing expression of life itself, expands the conscious breather's awareness, allowing for a variety of experiential possibilities. In his poem "A Goat Kneels" the great thirteenth-century Persian Sufi poet Jelaluddin Rumi explains that:

> The inner being of a human being is a jungle,
> sometimes wolves dominate, sometimes wild hogs.
> *Be wary when you breath!*
>
> At one moment gentle, generous qualities,
> like Joseph's pass from one nature to another.
> The next moment vicious qualities
> move in hidden ways.
>
> A bear begins to dance.
> A goat kneels,[1]

This portion of the poem, included in the introduction to part IV, suggests that there is much to learn about the healing and awakening power of the breath. Its expanding possibilities have been addressed throughout this book. Obviously the breath's wisdom, power, and beauty manifests in many ways. This chapter will discuss the psychospiritual journey that sometimes brings the breather into difficult inner terrain, especially if she or he has not had the guidance of a teacher, trained in the powerful mysteries of the breath.

Sometimes the expanding breath brings forth positive, uplifting, and ecstatic experiences. At another period of development, the breath's movement may take one to the depths of despair or into the unknown. The breath has the ability to awaken neglected ego states, archetypal forces, and the greater Self at the center of our being. It has the power to affirm our unity with the Absolute. The breath can take us on a journey of awakening, an adventure laden with possibilities.

Psychological and spiritual problems can arise, and even more so if the individual holds unconscious traumatic memories, and related emotional states, deep within the body-mind. Restrained emotions such as hidden rage and grief, as well as the qualities of love and compassion, are often undetected by one's dominant ego. The breath is quite miraculous in its power to awaken what needs to be healed. Actually this was clearly described in the chapters on Western breathing practices. Every emotion is felt in the body. When we are stressed, our muscles tighten. The body becomes the receptacle for repressed emotional memories.

A person may have certain expectations in practicing Pranayama, rebirthing, Holotropic Breathwork, and other breathing techniques, but as other authors in this book have pointed out, the breath often takes its own unique course. It stimulates the neural pathways and cellular structures of the body, which oftentimes contain these unresolved emotional memories and developmental ego states. It can also evoke the archetypal forces of the collective unconscious. The breather's internal somatic consciousness may become chaotic, as the body begins to awaken from its slumber. Spontaneous sounds, energetic movements, and other phenomena begin, slowly revealing the hidden presence of a consciousness beyond one's ordinary egoic identity.[2] The journey is not all about light and beauty; it also requires traveling into the darker, unresolved parts of human nature.

Beyond Social and Religious Conditioning

The traditional yogic view of spiritual development has often been that psychic energy should rise from the three lower chakras to the four higher ones (see chapter 1 for clarification on each of the chakras). Many believe the "lower" chakras to be related to gross, materialistic consciousness, whereas the "higher" chakras are associated with light and spiritual consciousness. This is a hierarchical rather than a wholistic perspective, as there is spiritual development that needs to occur in each of these power centers. As the heart lifts in devotion and higher centers are activated, the tendency has been for the devotee to dissociate from ordinary, earthly life. The *ascent* to heaven brings the practitioner into spiritual awareness, transcending body consciousness. But sooner or later the body must be included or the spiritual realization will be incomplete. This is when the *descent* to heaven becomes the focus, for it provides the opportunity to unify heaven and earth. And, as noted above, the so-called higher chakras also need clearing. For example, mistrust can block the heart whereas restrained vocal expression maintains a tight control of the throat center, and until we have cleared our erroneous projections into the world, our sixth chakra of perception can be influenced by them. As the Spirit descends, unifying with the body, a yet deeper awakening takes place in the chakras. The spiritual work of purification in each of these seven centers is an important inner task, for each one offers specific attributes that facilitate full human development, as discussed in chapter 1. My own process with this awakening began many years ago. It provides an illustration of this process.

In 1985, when engaged in large group rebirthing sessions, I discovered the breath could be moved in a manner that slowly opened a channel through the chakra centers from the base of my spine up to the chakra at the crown of my head. This process had not been "thought out," rather it had begun on its own. A stream of energy began to slowly move through this path, although not on a regular basis.

In that period of my life I was fully devoted to an esoteric Christian tradition. This retreat center included sacred dance and devotional movement, which I found to be spiritually uplifting. All devotion was focused in *upward* movements. One evening I noticed something strange. The intensity of the devotional service enabled me to see spiritual light all around me, but I didn't see it in myself or the people around me. It seemed that something was amiss, for *everything* should be part of this light, including human beings. At that time I made a decision to focus my attention on the *body and the human relational field*, rather than focusing away from it with upwardly-focused spirituality.

Four years after the rebirthing experience, a friend taught me a process of circular breathing. This required breathing energy up the spine, over the crown of the head and down through the chakras. It was recommended that the exercise be confined to fifteen minutes twice a day, but I soon doubled, and then tripled the time given to this concentrated breathing process. This amounted to two 45-minute breathing sessions twice a day; an unwise practice to follow without a well-seasoned teacher. My stance was akin to a boat sailing without a rudder, as the flow of energy began increasing. The following pages illustrate why these breathing practices have been highly guarded by mystical traditions.

The 45-minute sessions encouraged deep trance states and related spiritual phenomena. In the meantime, my personal life was disturbed in that my daughter was having a difficult time with drug addiction. On the one hand my life was expanding, whereas on the other I was carrying much pain and concern for her. In fact, the trance states encouraged an alternative reality, as nonordinary states of consciousness were increasing. Often there was great heat around my belly. A stylish chain-link belt could become quite hot; sweat might pour down my sides as I breathed.

One night, after falling asleep, I found myself traveling into a dark hole in my belly. I literally "pushed" myself out of it and woke in terror. The same thing happened the following night. My ordinary defenses were dropped as I entered into sleep, and this deep awakening process took off on its own. The "out-of-control" state evoked intense fear, for it wasn't happening in a meditative state with some form of conscious agreement. Human beings are more apt to engage in the *known* than the *unknown*.

My friend suggested I reverse the direction of the circular breathing, breathing down the spine through the lower two chakras into the psychic energy center in the belly. Although this would eventually initiate deep disturbances, in the beginning it facilitated openings into a variety of nonordinary experiences. One of these was the ability to gain knowledge while I slept, for sleeping states allow for other ways of learning. In this manner I learned that my daughter had disappeared (related to drug use).

The average texts on chakras are quite limited; yogis have kept their secrets well. A chakra can actually open consciousness into other realms. It is well-known that people can leave their bodies through the crown chakra, but few are aware that an Australian aboriginal shaman may travel through the second chakra (in the genitals) to enter the Dreamtime,[3] whereas other shamans may enter these inner realms through the third chakra in the belly, and in so doing, meet their animal totems, move beyond fear, and acquire their shamanic healing gifts. Sufi mystics focus on the heart center that opens to reveal the divine Beloved. Even Jesus proclaimed, "The Kingdom of Heaven is within you." Where would this heaven be within us? There are many realms of nonordinary experience waiting to be accessed through the consciousness within, and beyond, the human body.

Following one's own path is not easy to do for we are inundated with introjected religious beliefs telling us how we are to experience religious and spiritual development. It takes a lot of strength to follow one's own beliefs. To illustrate this struggle and one result, I would like to share a moment when I was standing in the center aisle of the church questioning my process, worrying I might be "going astray." (This was the very same church in which I had seen light above me, but not in myself.) As I stood there I could see a substance that was part of everything. It was in me, it was in everyone around me, and it was in the space between us. Everything was included in this strange universal substance. It was also very neutral in its nature. But at the same time, I realized this new awareness was only a step on the path of inner discovery.

I began reading Carlos Castaneda's books, and in one story learned that Don Juan had sent his female disciples to their children with the mission of reclaiming lost parts of themselves. The explanation was that women who had birthed children had "holes" in them.

The Archetypal Task of Balancing Gender

My next breathing session deepened my understanding of this story. That morning, engaged in deep breathing, I suddenly thought of my daughter with concern. My head did a strange movement to the right as I began to shape-shift,[4] experiencing myself turning into an eagle. I felt its immense power, and also knew the eagle's ability *to see from a great distance and*

hone in on what was needed. Once again, this triggered intense fear due
to the loss of ego control. The ego tends to adhere to a fixed identity,
and the loss of this identity is experienced by the ego as a threat akin
to death. Yet despite this intense fear, I still proceeded to learn from the
experience. My daughter had been conceived and born at a time when
I lacked a sense of my identity as a whole woman. Her most troubling
issue was that her identity was dependent upon having a partner. She
lacked inner and outer self worth, and gender balance was part of the
needed healing. In the months that followed, I began to work on my own
lingering issues in this area—balancing my own feminine and masculine
expressions. This was the filling of the metaphorical *hole* described in
Castaneda's book. The gift of the eagle was the ability to see what was
needed. My daughter reappeared within a few months. During that time
she had also acquired an understanding that she needed to develop an
inner harmony between her masculine and feminine selves.

The task of balancing masculine and feminine archetypes is an important element in healing and balancing our lives. This has been acknowledged throughout this book, for example, the yoga practice of balancing
the ida (feminine) and pingala (masculine) expressions; Taoist methods
for integrating yin and yang energies; and Sufi ways for the alchemical task of unifying solar and lunar energies. Also, Native American[5]
and indigenous religious traditions also have stories relating this same
message. The imbalance of these archetypal influences is reflected in
our personal and relational lives The deeper side of religious traditions
recognizes the need for inner and outer gender balance in the process
of becoming spiritually whole. As we balance the energies manifesting
from these psychic energy centers (chakras), we also balance their unique
expressions.

Prana Has a Mind of Its Own

I was introduced to Holotropic Breathwork in late 1989, adding it to
my breathing regime. This required a change in the breathing pattern
as practitioners are asked to simply breathe faster and deeper than they
would normally breathe. For example, controlling the breath by bringing prana up or down the spine and so forth is not an emphasis in this
breath therapy. (The circling breath pattern was still being done twice a

day during this time.) Within a few months intense energy started moving through my body. For instance, when visiting the East West Book Store in Menlo Park I entered a room containing numerous shelves filled with bottles of flower remedies. My body began to quiver, vibrating in response to the healing energies surrounding me. At another time I had to move away from the counter when standing in a pharmacy for Chinese medicine. Energy movements (*kriyas*) quickly increased due to the healing energies within the various herbs. Large jolts of energy regularly bolted through my body. This concerned my friends, and, to say the least, awakened deep fears within myself.

Bonnie Greenwell describes kriyas in her book, *Energies of Transformation*[6] as "pranic activities," and notes that these behaviors include involuntary jerking, spasms, shaking, vibrating, unexpected movements, and spontaneous sounds. My experience was well underway by the time I had been introduced to Bonnie's book, one of many books recommended for people experiencing *spiritual emergence*. It simply confirmed my experience.

The Spiritual Emergence Network (SEN) was established by Christina Grof, in 1980, to assist the many people experiencing what they called *spiritual emergencies*.[7] Often these difficult experiences led to a spiritual emergence. Christina's efforts in this area were initiated by her own difficult Kundalini awakening. This spontaneous rising had occurred when engaged in Lamaze breathing to ease the pains and stress during the birth of her first child. Christina suffered greatly at the time, and also for many years thereafter, even though she understood she was experiencing a profound transformation. She and her husband, Stanislav, recognized that modern society failed to support spiritual phenomena, interpreting its symptoms as pathology. The average religious teacher, priest, or pastor, may speak about spiritual rebirth, with little, if any, idea of the many ways this may manifest. It is one thing to *talk* about spiritual realms, and yet another thing to *enter* a transcendent state wherein one actually experiences them. Therefore, the SEN represented a beneficial support system as the loss of one's ordinary ego consciousness, and ideas (illusions) of self-control can be quite frightening.

Shamanic cultures recognize a shaman-to-be may go through a form of psychosis, or a deep illness, obtaining extra sensory awareness, healing gifts and even the ability to travel into the lower and upper worlds to receive guidance or to help others. So what might appear to be pathological is, instead, honored in these traditions. The "second birth" or spiritual awakening takes many forms, and often one's ordinary ego identity may have trouble accepting and integrating them. For some it is a difficult journey. More likely, this is truer of Westerners due to poor and limited preparation, which included myself.

Since ego defenses weaken when sleeping, there were many nights when I would be awakened by large jolts of energy pounding against blocks in the back of the heart chakra and in the throat. My life felt threatened in the grip of this powerful force, but this was only the beginning stages of a deep, uncontrollable purification process.

Research led me to Gopi Krishna's book, *Kundalini: The Evolutionary Energy in Man*.[8] The book describes his horrific thirty-year journey with Kundalini awakening. He endured pain, despair, moodiness, and numerous biological symptoms. His diet had to be carefully monitored. Even a self-centered thought could provoke deep suffering. He was also awakened from sleep by restlessness and agitation.

His experience differed from mine in that the Kundalini was purifying his sixth chakra and causing strong visual disturbances, whereas my experience was focused in the body. The psychic energy (breath) was detained by strong energy blocks associated with unresolved trauma. One obvious difference was the fact that he had experienced years of yoga training, under the guidance of a teacher.

In his autobiography, Gopi Krishna explained, "The sudden awakening of Kundalini in one whose nervous system has reached the ripe stage of development as a result of favorable heredity, correct mode of living, and proper mental application, is often liable to create a most bewildering effect on the mind."[9] In applying these words to my own condition, it became obvious that my emergence process was not going to be easy as my own life was marked by the effects of childhood trauma, and a lack of proper preparation. "And, yet," I asked myself, "what inner knowledge enabled me to open that channel in the first place? Who and what was guiding me?" Perhaps everything was moving with a timing and manifestation of its own.

Dreams and trance states in between 1988 and 1990 were suggestive of unresolved, hidden trauma within my body, and also revealed a capacity for healing others through the atmosphere of the breath. In 1988 a dream alluded to this trauma in a metaphoric portrayal of the discovery "that a murder had occurred, and that the body was hidden in a locker in the locker room." A couple of years later I realized the "locker" and "locker room" referred to my own body, and its deep repressed memories of trauma. Next, in 1990, I woke from a dream in which I had opened a small coffin, because a small spot was burning in the wood, and discovered a very pure and innocent-looking child within. Her hands were cupped in a silver chalice, and covered with a rosary. Although her flesh was dead, I had the understanding in the dream that she could be reached through the breath. Within months, spontaneous sounds began, unconscious expressions manifesting of their own volition, separate from my conscious ego identity. At first these spontaneous sounds seemed to be a response to the waves of energy moving through my body. Eventually they took on a form and expression of their own as vocal expressions began to manifest from other ego states and archetypal presences within my body—and breath.

The Body Has a Life of Its Own

Scientists have never acknowledged a specific area for the unconscious mind. Somatic practitioners believe the unconscious mind to be related to the body, recognizing that it is not an inert mechanism. Rather it is a living formation, vibrating with feeling, and an intelligence of its own. Our dreams and our emotions both affect, and arise from and through, its cellular structures. The chakras are psychic energy centers, which are deeply enmeshed in the body, resonating with the subtle energies related to other realms of consciousness. It is a fact that scientists are slowly validating the presence of consciousness in the body, finding that the body-mind is a tapestry woven with rich communications systems.[10]

For example, in 1994, researchers Gerson, Kirchgessner, and Wade were able to validate an independent and complex nervous system influencing the bowels and internal organs. They called this the enteric nervous system (ENS),[11] and likened the ENS to "a brain in the gut." These researchers discovered that this brain in the gut is able to both send and receive messages, similarly to the brain in the head. The ENS initiates neurotransmitters related to anxiety and also neurotransmitters related to feelings of profound peace. This is the area of the Manipura, Sanskrit for the third chakra, associated with fear, centering and peace. Similarly, other researchers have been examining the intelligence of the human heart as neurotransmitters have been identified in the heart, as well as the brain and the ENS. Our bodies are laden with feelings, and these bodies also house various states of consciousness.

I became acutely aware of a long-neglected child self, subpersonalities, and warrior-like archetypal forces. Sudden sounds would erupt, sometimes subtle, and other times quite fearsome, forces announced their presence within this vast sea of consciousness within the body. This became my ongoing experience, for several years.

The late Italian psychiatrist Roberto Assagioli founded Psychosynthesis, which is a psychospiritual method for recognizing and working with subpersonalities to assist one's spiritual development. Assagioli recognized four phases in this process,[12]

> Crises preceding spiritual awakening
> Crises caused by the spiritual awakening
> Reactions following the spiritual awakening
> Phases of the process of transmutation.

The first phase represents the various life issues that bring us into a process of transformation. This could be discontent, an inner sense of dissatisfaction with one's life, escape from traumatic experiences and so forth. The second phase represents the ego confusion caused by experiencing a very different spiritual reality as when one has a realization of the higher Self and its spiritual energy. The third can include profound gratitude and a sense of harmony with the divine as a result of the spiritual presence, or problems can occur if the ego identity is unable to integrate these new spiritual energies. Assagioli recognized that,

> The energy transmitted by the Self is not sufficient to bring about the higher level of organization. The energy is then absorbed by the hidden blocks and patterns that prevent the higher integration. It has the effect of energizing them and thus bringing them to light, where they can be recognized and dealt with. In such cases, the experience is usually of a painful quality and its transpersonal origin often goes unrecognized. But in reality it is just as valuable, because it can show the individual the next steps he needs to make to achieve the same goals and states of being.[13]

My experience was truly valuable, for I was recognizing and slowly healing my soul. Jesus had advised that one must have the consciousness of a little child in order to enter into heaven. If our inner child was frozen in time, traumatized, and unwilling to trust, our hearts are unable to receive the grace of a unifying realization of the Divine.

Not Forcing Growth—Rather Let It Be Like a Flowing Stream

I had another dream related to this process. In it, a fire was billowing upward from the base of a large wall. In the dream, I simply walked over and watered a hanging plant, unharmed by the fire beneath it. The message was clear: I needed to quit intense breathing practices or any methods intended to force through the blocks, and, instead, follow a path of gentle, caretaking approaches. This was supported by the guidance I was now receiving through my Sufi guide, who recommended specific mantras and gentle healing breaths. Healing the neglected child state within me required a more sensitive and compassionate approach. My teacher encouraged me to use the Element Breaths, a subtle breath evoking the purifying energies of Earth, Water, Fire, and Air. This breath practice is used by members of the Inayati schools of Sufism, specifically the Sufi Ruhaniat International and Sufi Order International. The following form, "Element Purification Breaths," was advised by Saadi Neil Douglas-Klotz, and I have practiced it daily for over eighteen years.

> *Earth Breath*: Feel your bones, the foundation of your body. Breathe slowly and rhythmically in and out through your nose. Breathe into the bones.
>
> *Water Breath*: Visualize a fountain of water coming up your spine, bubbling out at the crown of your head and flowing down through all your muscles. The breath itself is a very refined—in the nose and out through softly pursed lips.
>
> *Fire Breath*: Feel a connection with the pulse of the universe, the beat of your heart. Breathe in through the mouth (and the solar plexus). The breath circles up and you breathe out through your nose (and the heart and circulatory system).

Air Breath: Feel the boundaries of your body—your skin. Sense the spaciousness within the boundaries of your skin and outside of you. Breathe a refined breath in and out through softly pursed lips.

Ether Breath: This breath integrates all of the above. You can breath in and out through nose, or simply settle into a natural breath, integrating all of the elements.

Each of these breath channels are done five times in a slow, gentle, rhythmic pattern. Then the breather sits silently for a few minutes absorbing, sensing and receiving.

These gentle element breaths naturally evoke healing, peace, and enhanced inner awareness.

The Soul Breathes into Me

Spiritual books and teachers explain that our egos are transitory, limited, and not who we really are. But often, it is difficult to identify with this teaching when one has never personally experienced it, although a moment in harmony with the breath can quickly illuminate one's understanding.

A divine breath can breathe into us and illuminate our understanding in a moment. In fact, this is what I experienced when expressing my appreciation to my guide on the sixth day of a spiritual workshop. It was time to leave. I was apologetic for my spontaneous and seemingly inappropriate kriyas. My eyes were in the sun, so he moved my position ever so slightly. The shift seemed to coincide with a spiritual awakening, in that suddenly I was the High Self. There was no dualism at all, and any descriptions come as a memory after the experience. He was letting me know that everything was okay. I touched a tear on his cheek, saying "but you cry." It felt like anything I touched would be blessed. I was *embodied compassion.* Then just like that it was gone, and I was back to my ordinary ego identity. I now knew it was true that we are not who we think we are. It was a fact that the High Self has none of the consciousness related to our every day struggles, and identities. I also realized this was only a hint of what was possible, and that it was a precious moment on the way to unity and wholeness.

"So what does one do about this?" I asked myself. There is really not much one can do, except follow spiritual practices and discern the best responses to life circumstances. Eventually we become more permeable to light, wisdom, and compassion. I felt a confirmation of my declaration that I would not look "upwards" toward a transcendent divinity, choosing instead to engage with the divine in life itself. The heart is the healer at the center of it all. As the body unites with spiritual energies, we mend the division between heaven and earth (spirit and form). True spiritual awakening includes the body.[14] This is one of the values of the feminist movement as women reclaimed the value of our bodies and the earth herself. As we honor spirit and form, we also honor gender balance.

Life is a journey, and every day it offers new learning, and opportunities to open to the breath that brings wisdom, power and beauty. The last portion of Rumi's poem explains that,

> At every moment a new species arises in the chest—
> now a demon, now an angel, now a wild animal.
>
> There are also those in this amazing jungle
> who can absorb you into their own surrender.
>
> If you have to stalk and steal something,
> steal from them![15]

There are presences and divine qualities within the breath that breathes us. They have the power to open our hearts, and lead us to the Divine Absolute.

Notes

1. *Delicious Laughter: Rambunctious Teaching Sories from the Mathnawi,* trans. Coleman Barks (Barnesville, GA: Maypop Books, 1990), 113.

2. Sharon G. Mijares, "Fragmented Self, Archetypal Forces and the Embodied Mind," 1995, The Union Institute, *Dissertation Abstracts International* 56(11)B (University Microfilms No. 9608330).

3. In aboriginal mythology, the Dreamtime is the place of the aboriginal ancestral past, where creation existed prior to the emergence of human beings. To return to this place, where totemic beings reside, is a journey of power and healing.

4. Shape-shifting is a Shamanic term for a complete identification with a totem animal or a spirit.

5. Many Native American tribes consider a homosexual to be a "two-spirit person" and therefore gifted, perhaps as a healer because of the obvious male and female representation. Terry Tafoya and Nick Ksoulas, "Dancing the Circle: Native American Concepts of Healing," in *Modern Psychology and Ancient Wisdom: Psychological Healing Practices from the World's Religious Traditions*, ed. Sharon G. Mijares (New York: Routledge Mental Health, 2003), 125–46.

6. Bonnie Greenwell, *Energies of Transformation: A Guide to the Kundalini Process* (Cupertino, CA: Shakti River Press, 1990), 31.

7. Stanislav and Christina Grof, *Spiritual Emergency: When Personal Transformation Becomes a Crisis,* (Los Angeles: Jeremy Tarcher, 1989).

8. Gopi Krishna, *Kundalini: The Evolutionary Energy in Man* (Boston: Shambhalla Publications, 1967).

9. Ibid., 46.

10. Sharon G. Mijares, "At every moment a new species arises in the chest," in *Walking in Two Worlds: The Relational Self in Theory, Practice and Community,* ed. Stephen Gilligan and Dvorah Simon (Phoenix, AZ: Zeig, Tucker and Theisen, 2004), 180–91.

11. M. D. Gerson, A. L. Kirchgessner, and P. R. Wade, "Functional anatomy of the enteric nervous system," in *Physiology of the Gastrointestinal Tract,* 3rd ed., edited by Leonard R. Johnson (New York: Raven Press. 1994), 381–422.

12. Roberto Assagioli, "Self-realization and psychological disturbances," in *Spiritual Emergency: When Personal Transformation Becomes a Crisis,* ed. Stanislav and Christina Grof (Los Angeles: Jeremy Tarcher, 1989), 27–48

13. Ibid., 38–39.

14. M. Washburn, *Transpersonal Psychology in Psychoanalytic Perspective* (Albany: SUNY Press, 1994).

15. *Delicious Laughter: Rambunctious Teaching Sories from the Mathnawi,* trans. Coleman Barks (Barnesville, GA: Maypop Books, 1990), 113.

16

Children Learning to Breathe

An Education for Our Future

KEN FRIEDMAN

Introduction

How can we help children retain the natural breath they were born with, and in so doing create a healthier humanity? Sadly, the majority of our schools have focused more on disciplining and molding children's intellects than their bodies and souls. For the most part, awareness of breath has not been part of the academic curriculum. This chapter will focus on the philosophy and teaching methods used in Waldorf schools, as its founder, Rudolf Steiner, recognized the value of the breath in education. Since our children represent humanity's future, it would be wise to educate them in a way that builds a healthier, and more wholistic, relationship with self and all of life.

In 1919, just months after the end of World War I, Rudolf Steiner was asked to create a new method of education that would help children develop into human beings who would be capable of bringing peace to the world. The developmental process was designed to gradually bring children into the world and each lesson is a thread in a great tapestry that has seeds for the future woven into it. The goals include helping children to become creative, independent, moral, freethinking individuals who are able to fulfill a purposeful self-destiny and transform the world. Freethinking, in this case, suggests an inner will, or self-motivation, to freely do what is best for oneself and the world community.

In Rudolf Steiner's lectures to the first teachers, he said, "In observing children, we must say ... they have not yet learned to breathe so that breathing properly supports the nerve-sense process. The most important educational deeds lie in the observation of everything that properly organizes the breathing process ... and that education consists in teaching proper breathing."[1] Annual, seasonal, monthly, weekly, and daily rhythms, and more, are part of the design for teaching children to breath.

Many current educational methods have cut out the heart and breath from our children and teach directly to their heads. This has placed a strict limitation of the child's innate capacity for a fuller life and expression. For this reason, the breathing practices in the following pages should not be limited to Waldorf education. It is important to keep in mind that these examples can be implemented into both public and private schools, beginning with the teacher's awareness of breath and its importance. Teachers, and parents, can find creative ways to integrate and use these examples.

First we will look at how education can help us breath again and how we can reconnect our thinking with our heart realm through joy, enthusiasm, and love. Secondly, a scattered daily life can literally exhaust the breath from children and adults, and so we must look at ways we can create rhythms that will assist with breathing in our home life.

Rather than saying to children, "Now breathe in and out slowly," or "Count how long each in and out breath is." Daily activities can stimulate our breathing in such a way that we alternate more inward times, which are like in breaths, with more active times, which are like out breaths.

A key element in Waldorf education is to teach from "the whole to the parts." Breathing from the whole to the parts starts with being attuned to the natural rhythms found in nature. Nature's rhythms permeate our being with rhythmic cycles that surround us with a steady stream of expansion and contraction, or in a grand sense, a breath.

The cycles of the sun rising and falling and moon waxing and waning create a relationship with the earth that is the source of a great breathing process that supports life on the earth. The sun's light and warmth guides us to expand into the summer season and contract during the colder winter months. The moon affects the tides and movements of fluids and is a source of monthly rhythms. Animal lives are directly affected by nature's cycles, and they migrate, hibernate, and search for food depending upon the cycles of nature. Plants blossom, develop fruit, drop their seeds, and of course, literally breathe.

Breathing in this greater sense of the word suggests alternating between something more inward and something more outward. For much of humanity's existence we lived closely with nature and the rhythms of life, and felt ourselves to be part of nature. Through technology and our modern way of life we have lost much of our connection with nature's rhythms, and in this way have lost touch with one aspect of our breathing.

Reenlivening our life and reconnecting with the seasons through annual festivals reintroduces life's rhythms with a sense of delight. The anticipation for these annual autumn, winter, and spring festivals also connects the children with nature's cycles. Reenlivening our life and reconnecting with the seasons through annual festivals reintroduces life's rhythms with a sense of delight.

The Honolulu Waldorf School, which has been open for more than forty-five years, wrote in its school paper, "Harvest time, the autumn equinox was once an occasion to show gratitude as well as prepare for future challenges such as the winter ahead that some might not survive. The world is currently faced with new fears, and this festival can help us recognize, conquer, and tame the fears we face. The children may learn that even the smallest good deed is never lost, whether noticed or not, and that all good deeds bring healing into the world."[2]

Festivals breathe new life into those who join in and may have powerful, harmonizing effects. Whereas the tasks of our time may feel overwhelming, festivals have the potential to spark hope and a sense we are making some contribution. The alternating between concerns and hope, between fears and acknowledging, and symbolically facing a fear, and taking some action with those in our lives, may rekindle the meaning that lives in seasonal festivals.

Annual plays performed by every class, every year are another hallmark of the progress of each class, and a highlight of the year for the children and the community. The plays are related to the curriculum for each grade and some times the plays are written by the teacher. The children enjoy seeing the plays supporting their schoolmates and gain self-confidence by performing before the school community. There is great excitement, and thus breathing, for the class during the month the play is learned and rehearsed, and costumes and props are made or put together.

This is an opportunity for each student to mature in the way they hold themselves by listening and waiting for the appropriate times to speak while learning and then performing the play. Usually everyone knows all of the lines in the whole play and could speak any of the parts. Everyone learns together and the children who excel help those who might struggle on their own. The plays are a wonderful opportunity for a great out-breath (releasing energy) during the year and supports the breathing of the class from year to year.

Another aspect of the breath that is often missing in our society is found in conversations that breathe between speaker and listener. Waldorf classrooms often include lively conversations and discussions between the children and the teacher. The children's hands fly up to answer questions, such as, "Would you have given the poor couple food and invited them into your house?" From this initial question and additional questions as the conversation deepened, the children listened to each other's compassion for a poor couple and the concerns of letting strangers into your house.

Quality conversations can develop aspects of thinking and under-standing that are useful life skills. "Where in the world are we taught how to have a conversation?" I asked this in the first section of my book *From Turtles to Rainbows*, noting that "We mostly learn communication skills by imitating our parents and family when young, and our teachers and peers during our school years."[3] I believe many, if not most, conversations miss having people feel understood and heard and instead have the undertone of a jousting match. By asking quality questions and delving deeper into discussions at school, the interaction between listening and speaking will teach how conversations breathe, and perhaps when we develop an ease with conversations, we will be able to listen and work through deeper, emotional issues with our friends and loved ones.

Modeling this approach during daily conversations in the classroom and at home sets the tone for a future when we will naturally listen with greater care and compassion. With each additional question, con-versations will often go deeper than the superficial level and penetrate into how we feel about something. Hopefully, by developing conversation skills as part of the classroom environment, we will develop skills that will lead to a more compassionate and peaceful world.

The feeling in the classroom during class discussions, when children listen to each other, also helps balance the social dynamics of the class. The living quality and rhythm of conversations are missing when we talk through electronics. The vibration of the human voice is vital to the development of children and learning language skills. During class discussions I have a sense that the whole room is breathing.

Another art that is intimately connected with the breath is the art of speech. In its most widely recognized form speech involves reciting poetry or dramatic recitation in plays. Recitation on a daily basis has shrunken from our culture but is an active and significant part of every day at a Waldorf school.

Eurythmy, a relatively new movement art, which is available at most Waldorf schools, is an ideal form of movement for supporting children to move and breathe individually and as a group. Singing is also a daily activity at Waldorf schools. The whole class is breathing together while creating something beautiful. Since every child sings every day beginning in kindergarten, children are usually less sensitive to how they sound and join together with the class enthusiastically. Breathing together through speech, eurythmy, and singing has the effect of helping to harmonize the group and works deeply into their social interactions.

Waldorf schools select songs according to developmental guidelines. The early grades begin with the open, airy-sounding "mood of the fifth" and pentatonic songs related to the seasons and the curriculum. Each year singing progresses by quality and difficulty. Reciting poetry by heart and singing also develops excellent listening skills and memory as well as exercising the breath.

Change and transitions, which can be unsettling for many of us, can be harmonized and smoothed with a song or poem. The children at school know when a class is beginning, and mostly sit quietly, when a certain song is sung. Other songs give directions or help to children stand up and get in line without speaking. Familiarity helps a group move easily as a whole through transitions, and the singing helps the children breathe.

Each year singing and musical instruments are played almost every day and become progressively more challenging to meet the interests and developmental stages of the children. By seventh grade the children are singing four-part choral works and playing band and orchestra pieces. Music may be one of the richest ways to help individuals, classes, and communities breathe together.

In *Uncovering the Voice*, Valborg Werbeck-Svardstrom says, "For a true understanding of the respiration process, it is essential to grasp that in the activity of singing, respiration should not be anything more special for us than it is in our usual every day activities—without bringing attention to breathing and without giving children breathing exercises."[4] By integrating music into each school day, breathing becomes as much a part of our usual, every day activity as does eating, walking and talking—especially when the children start at an early age.

Breathing also comes naturally during movement classes such as Spacial Dynamics, which integrates games and what many call physical education into a movement class that supports breathing, and social and spatial development. Currently, movement is often too robotic, or competitive, and does not integrate moral thinking into the movements. Also, many movements develop cause and effect thinking at a premature stage of development. Look at a movement, game, or artistic activity and ask, What is this teaching? How do the children breath individually and as a group, and what are the social dynamics? If we include these intentions, then, perhaps, we will develop classes and children who enjoy moving and breathing in ways that are more social and even peaceful.

We must deepen our teaching even farther by bringing lessons imbued with the heart and art. Many excellent teachers all around the world use activities and lessons in their classrooms, such as singing, poetry, painting, and drawing. However, there are deeper levels related to the presentation and the type of materials used. Songs and poems learned by listening to someone who has learned the pieces by heart, and who presents the work orally, penetrates into the heart and has a living quality that enlivens the class.

Listening to stories recited by heart (with feeling) can convey the words such that living pictures are painted inside the children's hearts and minds. When key aspects of the academic work are represented artistically, we can take hold of what is living inside the children by doing drawings, paintings, modeling with beeswax or clay, knitting, and other artistic renderings. The academics become integrated with "heartistic" love. Cutting out or reducing these components has had the effect of cutting the heart out of children's education and may be partly responsible for creating a less loving and more socially and emotionally disabled world.

When all lessons include a balance of physical movement, social-artisitc work, and thinking, in varying degrees depending on the age of the child, the lessons will be well-rounded. As a child integrates the lesson she naturally becomes more well-rounded by joining in with the daily activities. When every lesson is designed with a developmentally appropriate mixture of physical movement, artistic expression, which includes social dynamics and academic thinking, and these these aspects are balanced, we will transform human beings throughout the world.

On the other hand, when curriculums make cognitive development the primary focus for children, the joy and love for people and the world becomes less important than knowing about them. Subjects that are too detailed at an early age can make the student separate from the subject rather than feeling interconnected with it. By harmonizing thinking, feeling, and actions—also phrased as head, heart, and hands—our intellect, which is so highly valued in the world today, will be enlivened with vibrant soul qualities.

The daily, weekly, and monthly schedules and rhythms are a key aspect of the Waldorf curriculum. The daily and weekly class schedules are carefully designed so the class activities help the children maintain harmony with their breath. In the morning before lunch when the children are usually more alert, the more academic classes are scheduled. Though more oriented toward thinking, the academic classes are, as mentioned, enlivened with art and movement. Even adults are often more focused at lectures, work, or workshops during the morning and then do better with some type of interactive activities after lunch. Ideally, we would probably enjoy taking the afternoon off and taking a walk in the park or a nap. Children can remain energized and attentive, and even feel the day has flown by, when the daily and weekly schedules breathe.

Each lesson is balanced between activities that are quieter and more inward with activities that are more active and outgoing. In the early grades mathematics and language arts lessons may include jumping rope, clapping games, circle activities, and games that bring joy, as well as breath, to the lessons. In the middle grades geometry may be experienced through physical movements such as Bothmer Gymnastics and art projects. The upper grades, though ready for more abstract thinking and pure academics, are still imbued with activities and lectures with an experiential nature that keep learning engaging and alive. A Goethean science approach is used to observe phenomena and relate plants and animals to others within their species, study their metamorphosis as they change and grow in relation to themselves, and relate what is found in nature to qualities found in humans. Of course, the songs and the poetry that are a natural part of every day, relate to the lessons being presented and progress from kindergarten to eighth grade, or twelfth in the Waldorf, that each subject stays fresh and enthusiasm, or at least interest, is kept alive.

Another purpose is to let what is learned "rest or sleep." Much of the Waldorf philosophy is based upon having children sleep overnight on what is learned before working with the material, and then letting the material sleep for a month before adding an additional layer with new information.

Letting an activity done with the limbs sink in overnight is preferable than asking our thinking to be so awake that we rush to work with new information immediately. Many adults also learn better by doing it themselves a number of times and allow the skill to sink in so they know more than imitating it, but rather make it their own. We may take what we learn deeper when we do not ask to have something repeated back, or test, what has been heard or learned for the first time that day.

Often during the first week of a block we will review the previous block, and rather than, "Oh no, not that subject again," there is a sense of welcoming back an old friend. During the intervening month there may be practice periods and the upper grades may have some ongoing classes, but still the essential idea of letting new material sleep is maintained.

The three-day rhythm used at Waldorf schools introduces new material the first day, then discusses and works artistically with what was presented the second day, and the third day the children take it into their hands and do something with the material that makes it their own. The alternating between blocks and letting lessons sleep creates an ongoing breathing that continues for years. The layering and resting process may be compared to the art of dying cloth that was used long ago. The fabric would be dipped in the dye and left to dry each day for months so the color would deepen. More modern techniques may dye the material for a long time, but all at once. More is not always better. The lengthier process may have a quality that will hold up longer and have an intangible quality that enriches those who see the work. As noted, we do this because we believe the monthly blocks and three-day rhythm will help deepen the quality of the children's education, and the rhythm will help harmonize their breathing.

All of this is done by every teacher in every Waldorf school around the world. Though each teacher brings his or her creative touches, we are all following an architecturally planned design, purposefully and specifically laid out to lead us transforming our world by educating children to be world citizens who breathe and are capable of thinking out of flexibility and freedom.

Child Development

The child development picture used at Waldorf schools is at the heart of consciously working toward creating a world filled with physically, emotionally and spiritually healthy human beings. Many of the current models push academics on young children and learning more and faster is considered better. In many respects, from clothing to sports and many social behaviors, societies are treating children as little adults. Although children may be capable of adult skills and behaviors, is it possible that steps are being missed that could create healthier, more fruitful adults and a healthier society or a society with fewer ills?

Fruit trees that are forced to bear fruit as soon as possible have fewer years of production. Educational approaches that focused on thinking may have less depth and breath. The indications for Bio-Dynamic agriculture were introduced by Rudolf Steiner soon after he designed Waldorf education. This quote from Bio-Dynamics may reflect the comparison of our choice to offer an education that may bear fruit throughout our adult life or one that is seeking more immediate results, "Long-bearing trees, which will grow 30, 40 and 50 or more years, are the kinds we have inherited from our fathers and grandfathers. The modern economy tends toward a faster rate of turnover and prefers dwarf varieties. These bear fruit earlier and are easier to harvest and treat, but their life cycle is shorter, perhaps fifteen to twenty-five years. No spray or fertilizer will make them live longer than their life cycle allows."[5]

The child development picture, that is part of the foundation of Waldorf education, has the intention to gradually bring children into the world so they will bear fruit as healthy, freethinking adult world citizens. The curriculum seeks a harmonious balance for each child with the child's physical education as a foundation for their social and emotional life, which will then support academic thinking.

Every seven years of life has a primary focus. The first seven years of life learning is more from doing activities with the limbs. Crawling, walking, touching nature's surfaces, and free play are thinking with the body and lay the foundation for thinking with our mind. The curious young scientists feels the textures of sand, rocks, and mud and develops a sense of balance by running, rolling, twisting, twirling, and falling over and over again. The experience from these physics experiments shape their bodies, hearts, and minds.

Natural materials, such as wool, wood, cotton, and silk, can be used for inside play. However, in our modern world we must accept every child will have more than a fair share of plastic, flat floors, sidewalks, carpet, and other manufactured surfaces. What a child feels and senses can affect their breathing, and there are positive benefits such as a more natural breath and a well grounded connection to all life when natural materials are used.

Science projects involve the elements: earth, water, fire, and air. The youngest children experience these elements firsthand. Their education begins when they splash about in the water, make mud pies, run in the fields, feel the wind, and listen to the leaves rustling, feel the snow while making snowballs and snowmen, feel the warmth of a fire to warm hands or the sun on hot days. Play brings joy to the exploration, though as my two-year old who loves to climb, move, and throw rocks; dig in the sand, water, and snow; and rolls, runs, and twirls, he gets a bunch of bumps and bruises too. Everything opens a gate to learning through the limbs and the heart.

Throughout all of their play, children are doing great scientific experiments in physics, geology, botany, and more. The young body is calculating the distance for a jump, the force required, and the results, depending on whether he reached the sand or splashed in the water. Instilling an education that lives in the limbs, as well as our social, artistic heart realm, helps us learn with our whole body. This goes beyond learning with only our head and intellect.

During the second seven years, from age seven until fourteen, the emphasis for learning is directed to the rhythmic system, the heart and lungs with rich mental pictures, joy, enthusiasm, daily rhythms, and a love for the world. During this time adults can help by modeling kind, caring, social behaviors. Saving the forests, animals, and the earth and solving the political, social, and personal issues of our time may be accomplished, again dynamically, though gradually, during the school years when children are between the ages of seven and fourteen. When we connect children with these issues through delight, compassion, and enthusiasm, we lay the foundation for love to be the basis for thinking. Less emphasis is given to directly studying and talking about the topics because when we analyze something we become separate from it and can categorize, dissect, and even kill the thing we are studying. Throughout history great human beings such as Saint Francis have called all of nature brothers and sisters. When we love a plant, animal, or person, we are more likely to protect and care for it with compassion.

When children receive this type of modeling, it provides a foundation that helps them deal with the more emotionally-charged years from fourteen to twenty-one. This is because the children have been prepared to think for themselves. Hopefully, the time and effort of the earlier years will reap benefits, such as being more emotionally stable, and that during the first fourteen years they will have developed bodies and hearts for their thinking to ride on. Bringing children into the world gradually may be similar to planting seeds in rich, fertile soil that will create a strong, vibrant plant that will bear fruit for many years.

Even with all the good work being done by teachers and parents, transforming our world is going to be a gradual process. The effects of the preparations sprayed on plants used in Bio-Dynamic gardening have subtle but dynamic influences on the plant's growth. Similarly, the daily influences of a rhythmic, breathing education will influence the growth of humanity one day at a time. These approaches are dynamic, but not necessarily immediate. The processes are working day by day and breath by breath to transform humanity.

In Waldorf schools, as in all schools, there are children who excel and those who develop more slowly or differently than other children. Were we to grade them for their academic, social-artistic, and physical progress we could look at how each child is balanced among these three aspects, we would see that each child has strengths and weaknesses in varying degrees.

Many of the physical, social, and behavioral skills start at home and each family's and society's choices for food, entertainment, games, and activities have a great impact upon how the children will be when they start school. Bringing lessons that develop all three of these aspects will gradually help harmonize each child. I cannot stress the importance of this enough as our children represent the future of our humanity.

Transforming the current state of the world will truly be a process and not a quick fix. Our task is not hopeless, but we must remember that it took thousands of years to create our current habits and we may require several generations or more before we begin demonstrating the changes we are now beginning.

Breathing in All Phases of Life

How can we reconnect with monthly, weekly, and daily rhythms that also feel scattered and out of breath in our modern lifestyle? Sometimes with all of the running around and rushing we can literally be out of breath. Having regular mealtimes, when everyone helps prepare the meal or set the table, sits down together and talks, and then plays games together or reads before the regular bedtime routine begins, greatly helps the children feel the daily rhythm and get enough rest to be alert in school. Unfortunately, many children have irregular home schedules due to the parents' work schedules and sometimes a full schedule of after school activities. Some children's bedrooms even have stimulating electronic entertainment instead of being a place for bedtime stories and sleep. A life rhythm that includes a good night's sleep, and a rhythmic home life, can either support our children or strain their rhythms and breath. Instead, many children are rushed from one event to the next, and far too much attention is being given to intellectual development at the expense of the whole child.

In her book *Endangered Minds: Why Our Children Can't Think and What We Can Do About It*, Dr. Jane Healy indicates that premature intellectual activity may harm the child's future intellectual development. Drawing on the latest findings about the development of the human brain, she cites that early exposure to computers, computer games, and television are a prime cause, along with premature academics, of the attention, learning, and behavioral problems that afflict many children today.[6] This is a prime example of unnatural rhythm and restricted breath.

We need to change our current approach to education and limit our excessive use of electronic entertainment. We need to protect our children and safeguard their development. Though there are specially designed Waldorf remedial programs available, the daily work in the classroom, and support in the home environment, can model and guide the children each day. Rhythm and breath in all of our endeavors and relationships creates the foundation for a balance in intellectual development, empathy, and love.

The solutions are easy—and almost impossible. All that is required is for us to change our way of life. Preventative change is preferable than facing a crisis or threat with no choice. The inner motivation to do what will improve a situation is another key aspect of Waldorf education. Rather than threatening, offering rewards or other external motivations, the will to do something well must come from within the children. Inner motivation is developed in many ways, and all efforts along this path will hopefully lead each child to develop his or her inner motivation. As these children begin to shape the future of our world, they will have the interest and capability to take an idea or task to completion. Acquiring this type of skill will help change come from free will and a sense of joy for creating a world we will love.

Today's children will become our future leaders, and their education can continue to produce dense, materialistically oriented thinking or change to be compassionate and connected. When our education is developed out of a more socially conscious and less dense approach, we will lighten up and create a society that is more loving and compassionate.

Education is a slow process and not a quick fix solution for world change. The children face a daunting task of redirecting this world with its ingrained habits. Perhaps it will take generations of children who support a more loving relationship with the world before we will see the results. For this reason we must continue nourishing the seeds of our future.

When an architect designs a beautiful, finely crafted house, he or she would plan for the finest craftspeople to do the construction and that the finest materials be used. The finished house would need to have the workers arrive in the proper sequence so the foundation, frame, and insides are ready and completed in the proper order and in a timely fashion. Waldorf education is an architectural design for an educational system that brings the finest materials in a sequence that children can receive an education for our future—one that breathes in harmony with all of life. Hopefully, we will choose available educational methods that allow children to maintain the natural breath. In so doing, we can transform our schools to nurture the development of compassionate families and communities—and children who will have a future that is centered in love.

Notes

1. Rudolf Steiner, *The Foundations of Human Experience* (formerly The Study of Man) (Hudson, NY: Anthroposophic Press, 1996), 40–41.

2. The Honolulu Waldorf School newsletter, September 2000 issue.

3. Ken Friedman, *From Turtles to Rainbows* (Victoria, BC: Trafford Publishing, 2005), 4.

4. Valborg Werbeck-Svardstrom, Uncovering The Voice (East Sussex: Rudolf Steiner Press, 2002).

5. Ehrenfried E. Pfeiffer, The Biodynamic Treatment of Fruit Trees, Berries and Shrubs, issues 42–43 (Springfield, IL: Bio-Dynamics, Bio-Dynamic Farming and Gardening Association, 1976). Bio-Dynamic Farming and Gardening Assoc., Inc. (1957) p. 5 (pamphlet).

6. Jane Healy, *Endangered Minds: Why Our Children Can't Think and What We Can Do About It* (New York: Simon and Schuster, 1990).

17

Breathing for a Better World
Final Thoughts on the Healing Power of the Breath

Puran Bair

Breath is Life

Breath is life, and the act of breathing is our most fundamental inter-action with life. Not only does breath give us life, the way we breathe determines the way we live. This might be considered the fundamental faith of the mystic—the pattern of life is created by the pattern of breath. If we take this idea seriously, we should breathe in such a way that reflects our deepest world view and advances our purpose in life.

Conscious and Unconscious Breath

Breathing is a unique activity for the body as it is the only function that can be done either consciously or unconsciously. When breath-ing becomes conscious, a neurological shift occurs; a different part of the brain, different nerves and different muscles are engaged. The part of the brain that was responsible for unconscious breathing is freed; it then takes on a new role—it becomes the gateway between the conscious and unconscious mind. Consequently, a flood of creativity and unconscious memory emerges in the conscious mind after a few minutes of conscious breathing.

People often tell me they can't meditate because they can't shut off their mind. I say one should not expect the mind to be free of thoughts; the question is whether one's thoughts are the ordinary, uninspired variety that comes with an unconscious breath, or the revelatory, inspired thoughts that come with a conscious breath. Inspiration (ideas) comes from conscious inspiration (breath).

Conversely, the unconscious can be programmed by conscious intention and repetition through the same open gateway. When you learn something "by heart," you are programming your unconscious. You can recall, from learning to play the piano or drive a car, that it required repetition. Usually, the task being learned takes up all of one's attention, so the breath goes unconscious and many repetitions are necessary to knock at the closed door. But if you can stay aware of your breath, learning becomes rapid because the conscious intention enters the unconscious memory directly through the open gateway caused by conscious breathing.

Breath Pattern <=> Life Pattern

We have all experienced the many ways the breath affects our physical state; by breathing in a certain way we can put ourselves to sleep, get excited, become calm, relax, become alert, even access unusual strength and endurance. Our emotional state is also powerfully affected by the breath. Your heart is touched by a sigh, or excited by a sharp intake in the breath. Our emotions are caused by the action of our breath flowing in a certain direction, which causes a corresponding movement of energy within the heart.

It's also true that your physical and emotional state affects your breath—when you're tired, you yawn, which emphasizes the inhalation, and when you're exhausted, you let your breath out audibly—the link between your breath and your state of being works both ways. You can see your physical and emotional condition by watching the pattern of your breath, and you can change your condition by changing your breath. When you are unaware of your breath, you unconsciously *receive* the influence of your environment; when you are aware of your breath, you become conscious of the interaction *between* your inner state and your environment, and when you control your breath, you direct your inner state and create an influence *upon* your environment.

The way we breathe both indicates our state of being and produces our state of being. The pattern and rhythm of the breath is formed by the time of the inhalation, exhalation, and any time when the breath is still, within one breath cycle. Some place a greater emphasis on the inhale, some on the exhale. Some hold the exhale, others hold the inhale. All of these patterns affect one's spiritual condition, emotional state, thought stream, relationships, career, physical body, and every aspect of life. For example, inhalation gives glorification, while exhalation gives surrender, the two great emotions from which all other emotions flow. Inhalation makes one sensitive, while the exhalation makes one influential. Holding the exhalation takes one out of life, while holding the inhalation holds life in the center of your being. A slow breath is helpful for poetry, music, and all creative activities. A faster breath is necessary to give force to physical or mental exertion, but too fast a breath produces confusion and exhaustion.

I used to put my children to sleep by lying next to them and breathing the "sleepy breath": a quickly falling out-breath that releases all concerns and tensions. Children are very sensitive to the breath of others, so my sons would usually fall asleep before I would. The power of a rhythmic breath can also be seen in runners—when the rhythm is even, runners can perform at a high level of exertion, but if the breathing rhythm becomes too fast, erratic, or interrupted, fatigue sets in quickly.

Breath Entrainment

An simple way to ensure that your breath has the appropriate speed for the physical and emotional situation of the moment is to time your breath to your heartbeat. This is called entrainment of the breath. Usually, your breath rate and your heart rate are completely independent, but you can synchronize them by breathing six heartbeats in and six heartbeats out. Perhaps you can feel your heartbeat when you sit still; some people can. Most people can't, so you can also use your pulse, the echo of your heartbeat. You can feel your pulse at your wrist, or in your thumb and finger pressed together. Keep looking for your heartbeat in your chest; it will reveal itself eventually. When you get used to six, a little longer count, like eight or ten heartbeats, will feel more comfortable. There are many other benefits of entrainment, which synchronizes the two main biological oscillators, or clocks, of the body. Emotionally, it makes one feel whole and centered. It creates integrity: all parts of the self are working together in the same rhythm.

The Breath Stream Creates Individuality

Breath affects us at different levels—physically, mentally, emotionally and spiritually—because breath is a stream of energy that unites the realms of body, mind, heart, and soul. These realms are not unique in themselves, it's their unique combination that makes an individual. The essence of one's individuality is a singular stream of the One Breath that enlivens each of the levels of reality in a unique way. You are being continuously created by the out-breath of the One Who Becomes, and all that you have become is absorbed on the in-breath of the One Who Is. Therefore being aware of breath is fundamental to knowing all the levels of yourself and is essential to meditation, the exploration of the self and the All.

Two Currents of Breath

There are two currents of breath, the air stream and the energy stream, which flow in and out synchronously. The air stream can be directed in and out through the mouth or nose in four different combinations, each of which stimulates one of the four "Elements" (Air, Fire, Water, and Earth), which are actually different types of subtle energy. As the air stream flows in and out, the energy stream of the breath rides on the air stream. The Elements of the energy stream can then be directed into and out of any meridian, chakra, or any place in the body. It is the combination of the breath timing, the position the body is held in—spine, head, shoulders, arms, hands, legs and feet—the visualization and placement of the two breath streams, together with intention and invocation, that form the basis of the various types of meditation in the world's traditions.

Concentrating the mind on a certain image, object, or event gives it power from attention. By holding a thought while maintaining a concentration on the breath, the breath is naturally directed toward that which we visualize. Invocation is calling upon a quality of the One Being—Peace, Love, Truth, Wisdom, etc.—that we may receive (inhalation) or manifest (exhalation) that quality in ourselves. The posture of the body and the kind of movement or stillness of the body also affects, and is affected by, the breath. This is the foundation of hatha yoga, the art of meditating in different postures, called asanas. As discussed by Dr. Tong in Chapter Three, T'ai Chi Ch'uan and Chi Gong also use movement in rhythm with the breath to control the direction and flow of the energetic stream of the breath.

Upward and Downward Breaths

Upward forms of meditation use the breath to lift the consciousness out of the body, allowing one to experience the timeless, eternal, nature of our being separate from the body, mind, and heart that we know. Downward forms of meditation bring the experience of infinity into the heart, into the mind, and into the body itself. All of this is the result of different directions of the breath.[1] In our school, The Institute for Applied Meditation, we want to affect the world, so we use the downward form of meditation. The principle meditation of this type is called Heart Rhythm Meditation.[2]

Exhale into the World

One's exhalation is one's primary means of affecting the world. The out-breath takes what is within a person and sends it out to the world. When the exhalation is powerful and complete, one's magnetism is strong, one's influence is wide, and one's accomplishments are great. One can observe the power of the exhalation in the martial artist who uses a forceful exhale, perhaps combined with a shout, to break blocks of solid concrete. The fullness of the exhalation gives one the energy to start a project, and follow it through to its conclusion.

The exhalation also reaches deep into the heart—the end of the exhalation gives access to the deepest feelings of the heart and the ability to express them. Without a deep breath, one's depth is impenetrable; with a deep exhalation, one can reach within oneself the emotions that all people share and the common connection between all beings.

Inhale the World into Yourself

By one's inhalation one experiences the outer world, which is brought into the lungs and circulates throughout the mind and body. Inhalation also gives us inspiration and joy. But we can't increase our inhalation without first making room for fresh breath. To inspire, you must first expire. This is expressed in the Christian teaching that we must first give in order to receive.

The inhalation develops sensitivity, perceptiveness, insight, and intuition. When the inhalation is deep, one's ability to receive impressions of all kinds—joy, pain, beauty, love, sadness, kindness, and so forth—becomes full and rich.

The Full Breath

A full breath is expressive of the Sufi maxim: "Accept all that is given to you and give all that your heart contains." A full breath is necessary to live life fully. The Sufi master Hazrat Inayat Khan[3] said, "Do you know why some people have a full life and others seem to have half a life? They have half a breath." When a person is unable to finish a task they have taken up, they may blame tiredness, lack of enthusiasm or loss of memory, when it is often the lack of a regular and full breath. A full breath starts with a full exhalation, which requires an exertion of the abdominal muscles for a few seconds; the diaphragm muscle will not empty the lungs. Then the inhalation that follows rushes into your depth and fills your being like a new beginning, giving fresh inspiration.

This is our aspiration: to take every in-breath from the beginning, without any left-over breath from before. This allows us to be fully engaged with the life around us, having maximum awareness of others and maximum influence upon events, without baggage from the past. Breathing fully is not only a physical training; it is an emotional training as well to allow a deep surrender in expiration and a full experience of joy in inspiration.

But if your body is still, a full breath must be taken slowly, no more than eight a minute, to avoid hyperventilation. This is never a problem in Heart Rhythm Meditation because the breath is entrained to the heartbeat. As long as the heart rate is 96 or less, using a count of six heartbeats or more for each inhalation and exhalation yields eight or less breaths per minute.

The Shallow Breath Problem

The most common breath problem is shallow breathing, and it is very common. A shallow breath is a small, unconscious breath taken ten or more times a minute into the upper part of the lungs with a very slight physical movement. Of the five-liter capacity of the lungs, the shallow breath moves perhaps one-half liter, or ten percent. This breath produces a low-level of oxygenation in the brain and other organs of the body, resulting in chronic fatigue and weakening, over time, of the lungs, heart and nervous system. The shallow breath is a defense mechanism to either avoid absorption of the inharmonious vibrations of others or to avoid the fear of death that one touches during a full expiration. But breathing in a shallow way makes one shallow, diminishes one's enthusiasm and concentration, and makes one's life mundane and mediocre. There is not enough life energy in a shallow breath to power the attainment of the extraordinary states of meditation. When people try to meditate while maintaining the defensive shield of a shallow breath, they typically go to sleep.

The Death Breath Problem

The second most common breathing problem is holding the exhalation: after breathing out, but not completely, the breath stops for several seconds. This is a physical expression of the emotion that says, "I don't want to be here, as I am, doing this." We call it the "death breath," as it is an unconscious wish to be without life. Breath is life.

My friend Simon used to regularly feel as though he was about to fall asleep during important meetings. In spite of many doses of caffeine and sugar, in many meetings he felt it was all he could do to stay awake, which impaired his ability to pay attention to the issues under discussion. After learning meditation, he realized he had been holding his exhalation, perhaps because the meetings both bored him with their endless discussion, and stressed him out because he felt his career was on the line. Practicing meditation allowed him to notice when he interrupted his breathing in this way, and to respond by extending his exhalation to the end. When the out-breath is completed, one automatically breathes in again, and that inhalation gives an energizing blast of oxygen to the mind and the whole body. By keeping his breath deep and regular, he could stay alert and sharp.

In the death breath, the exhalation pauses before the out-breath is complete. Sleep apnea, which can be life threatening, is also an incomplete exhalation followed by an extended pause; literally a "death breath." It can be cured by breath training in which one learns in meditation to make a fully conscious breath that reaches the real end of the exhalation. This breath pattern then carries over into one's day, and even into sleep if one meditates before bed.

Balanced Breath

I recommend a balanced breath, with equal length inhalation and exhalation. If the inhalation is longer, one develops the ability to feel and see what must be done without the strength to do it. If the exhalation is longer, one develops the ability to accomplish things without the insight needed to direct that power. With a balanced breath, one walks through life with a rhythm: one step in insight, one step in power. Then neither does one become exhausted nor uninspired.

Generating Magnetic Waves

Every heartbeat generates a powerful magnetic wave that radiates into the space around you and affects the brain waves and other aspects of people in your vicinity.

When your breath is entrained to your heart, and your breath is full and slow, several physiological changes occur. The metabolic rate increases, blood pressure and heart rate decrease, and the Heart Rate Variability (HRV) becomes a smooth wave. Breath control gives regulation of these autonomic functions that can't be controlled directly. Raising the metabolic rate demonstrates that oxygenation has increased; this is also helpful in weight control. Lowering the blood pressure and heart rate gives an increased capacity to handle stress.

Most importantly, regulating HRV as we do it in Heart Rhythm Meditation creates a single, low-frequency transmission from the heart below 0.13 Hz., well within what is considered a heart-healthy frequency range of 0.03 Hz. to 0.15 Hz. Heart arrhythmia is eliminated. Without breath control, the transmission power of the heart is spread across many frequencies, some as high as 0.5 Hz, where the heart is significantly stressed. The wide frequency distribution caused by unconscious breath reduces the transmission of the heart to noise without any content.

With a slow, full, balanced and entrained breath, as in Heart Rhythm Meditation, the magnetic transmission of the heart is focused into a synchronous beam of low frequencies; this means the magnetic field can extend quite far, like an FM radio broadcast, and the message carried on this wave is a very simple and coherent message: peace and harmony.

Radiating Waves of Peace into the World

The ultimate purpose for breath control is not to increase the capacity and health of your lungs, heart and nervous system, nor to increase your capacity for stress, nor to make your work more creative and productive. Breath control will do these things, but its real purpose is to increase the gift of your harmonious heart to others and the whole world. When the breath is entrained with the heartbeat, the magnetic pulse generated by the heart carries a powerful message of spiritual harmony and peace. Magnetic fields extend into space indefinitely, influencing all other fields they contact. It has been shown that people receive information from the magnetic fields of others. Those who receive the heart's harmonious transmission absorb its message and become more harmonious within themselves and with others. *Thus the heart-centered breath is a direct way of creating peaceful, harmonious changes to improve the condition of the world at a fundamental level.*

Expansion and Contraction

Observing and regulating your breath makes you conscious of the fundamental movement of the universe: the movement of expansion and contraction. This is the motion of all things, and you activate your cosmic consciousness when you see this cycle in yourself. When you sit still and look within, you notice two forms of this movement: your heart is expanding and contracting with every beat, and your lungs are expanding and contracting with every breath. It's exhilarating to experience consciously the expansion and contraction of the universe operating within yourself. Reflecting upon the stages of your life, you can also see steps of expansion interspersed with steps of contraction as breakthroughs and breakdowns alternate. Your life as a whole is also an example: the universe contracted itself to create you as its microcosm, and your life experience contributes to an expansion of the self-discovery of the whole universe.

Everything has expansion and contraction; it is unrealistic of us to expect that expansion will persist without a contraction. On a personal level, we need a period of rest between periods of activity, of consolidation after gains, and of reflection after risk-taking. Society also has cycles of expansion and contraction. The USA had an incredible economic expansion from 1982 to 2007, as the Dow Jones Industrial Average (DJIA) went from 822 to 14,279, a gain of 17.4 times in 25 years. In the previous 28 years, from 1954 to 1982, the DJIA moved from 360 to only 822, a gain of 2.3. This relatively flat period was preceded by the contraction from July 1929 to July 1954; it took 25 years for the DJIA to regain its high of 381 just before the financial crash of 1929 that took the DJIA down to 41 in 1932, a loss of 89%. Before 1929, the previous 22 years from the "Panic of 1907"[4] showed a gain of 7.2 times. These four phases—up 7.2 X, down 89%, flat 2.3 X, up 17.4 X—look like a breath of exhale, inhale, hold, exhale, with approximately 25-year periods, like the breath of a generation. Is another 25-year, 90% contraction coming? I think so, although if hyperinflation occurs the DJIA may actually go up during this depression, as in the Weimar Republic. This necessary contraction cycle may be considerably shortened if the contraction is honored, not resisted, and if expanded consciousness can then be applied on a large scale.

A cycle must finish one phase before it can start the next. At the end of a contraction, people can hardly remember the expansion, and at the end of an expansion, people can hardly remember the contraction. Until recently, people thought that real estate can only go up and that the stock market is always a good investment if you just hold your position. I worked with portfolio managers in the 90's that had never seen a contracting market. During a personal depression, a person can hardly remember the good times and during a personally successful phase, the caution and appreciation for simple things that one had experienced in hard times is long gone.

A major contraction is already in process in the American economy, in America's world standing, and in American's trust in government and large institutions. Our standard-of-living will fall dramatically as a predictable reaction to living on individual, corporate and government debt and inflating our paper currency for decades. We have benefited materially from the expansion and we will benefit spiritually from the contraction. As soon as this period of contraction is over, another period of even greater expansion will follow. Our goal should be to complete the contraction fully, consciously, with appreciation for its benefits, and then start the expansion as soon as possible. This is the full breath.

Listening with Your Heart

With a conscious breath, experiencing expansion and contraction, you are aware of the cycles of life—the very short cycles of the heartbeat, the cycles of a breath in and out, the longer cycles of the moon and sun that resonate within our bodies and emotions, and the generational cycles of the culture. The stock market cycles noted above are about a generation in length. The periods of war and peace in the United States also have had a generational rhythm. This awareness of the cycles of life allows us to anticipate and honor each phase, for progress is made, like the motion of an inchworm, by the combination of expansion and contraction. Neither is contraction bad nor expansion good; both have their purpose, like inhaling and exhaling. Success comes by taking action appropriate to the cycle. Those who can use the energy of contraction will be able to contribute in the coming time, while others who are attempting expansion-appropriate activity will experience loss.

What are appropriate activities during a contraction cycle? Simplification and purity; appreciation of natural beauty; care of the environment; consolidation and research; reflection upon the lessons of life; local focus toward communities, small work groups and family; inner spirituality; meaningful work; and close cooperation with others along strongly-held values and common purpose. What activities are inappropriate for a contraction cycle? Globalization, outsourcing to people you don't know, debt, busy-ness, work without joy, and competition. During times of expansion, when nearly every area of life is increasing, one doesn't need to examine one's values. Expansion is its own purpose. "A rising tide lifts all boats," so most strategies work during expansion. Engrossed in outer activity, the inner world is lost to view; morality and compassion fall to greed and fear. During contraction, values are re-examined; when most outer-directed activities become difficult, people look for an inner happiness that can't be counted or measured. The inherent belief in an individual purpose in life gains strength while dogmas fall away.

Use Your Breath to Help Others

In the difficult years of the coming period of contraction, your breath can help you help others in two ways. (1) Your inhalation gives you guidance and inner conviction as you draw in spirit as a subtle energy. Your in-breath will also carry into your heart the condition and needs of others so you'll know where help is needed. Feeling your inner rhythms will bring awareness of the cycles that influence you so you can tune your actions appropriately. (2) Your exhalation will send waves of peace and harmony into the hearts of others, as described earlier. Your inner confidence will emanate as hope and optimism that can sustain others.

As you breathe in, be aware of a flow of inspiration entering your heart from behind, between your shoulder blades. This is your spiritual inheritance, like a hand on your back, continually energizing and guiding you. As you breathe out, send an energy stream from your heart forward, opening and illuminating the path in front of you. The key to using the breath is to send out into the world the same energy you would like to have more of. Breath is a stream; the more that flows out, the more that can flow in.

With your awareness of breath, which is spirit and subtle energy, in the rhythms of expanding and contracting cycles without and within, and with the power to transmit waves of peace and harmony through your exhalation, you can have a greater effect upon the world than the world has upon you. We all need your help to keep spirit flowing through the cycle of contraction and into expansion again. Honor every breath; entrain your breath to your heartbeat; live from your heart.

Notes

1. Puran and Susanna Bair. *Energize Your Heart in Four Dimensions*, Living Heart Media, 2007.

2. Puran Bair, *Living from the Heart*, Three Rivers Press, NY: Random House, 1998.

3. Hazrat Inayat Khan. *The Sufi Message, Volume 13, The Gathas*, Alamedia, CA: Hunter House, 1982.

4. http://en.wikipedia.org/wiki/Panic_of_1907

Final Words

Breath nourishes your body and fuels physical life.
Conscious Breathing heals and clears emotions.
Even Breathing relaxes the mind, allowing greater focus and
    peace.
Breath unites you with the Divine.

Therefore, Breathe into this one precious moment.
Breathe! And claim your life!

—Sharon G. Mijares, May 2009

Contributors

Editor/Author

Sharon G. Mijares, Ph.D., is a Licensed Psychologist and a graduate of the Union Institute and University. She is a member of the Sufi Ruhaniat International, the International Association of Sufism's Sufi Women's Organization and the American Anthropological Association's Society for the Anthropology of Consciousness, and is an ordained Sufi Minister of Universal Worship. She also has a black belt (Shodan) in Aikido. She teaches Comparative Religions at the California Institute for Human Science, is a certified core faculty at National University and also a core member of Brandman University's Counseling Psychology program, and has served on several doctoral committees as adjunct faculty of the Union Institute and University. Sharon is the primary author of *The Root of All Evil: An Exposition of Prejudice, Fundamentalism and Gender Imbalance* (Imprint Academic, 2007) with Aliaa Rafea, Rachel Falik and Jenny Eda Schipper. She edited *Modern Psychology and Ancient Wisdom: Psychological Healing Practices from the World's Religious Traditions* (Haworth, 2003), and co-edited *The Psychospiritual Clinician's Handbook: Alternative Methods for Understanding and Treating Mental Disorders* with Gurucharan Singh Khalsa (2005). She has authored several articles and contributed a chapter "At every moment a new species arises in the chest" in Stephen Gilligan's and Dvorah Simonds edited book *Walking in Two Worlds: Theory and Practice of Self Relations* (2004). She can be contacted at (760) 436-3518, through her website www.psychospiritual. org or email at sharonmijares@aol.com.

Foreword

Shah Nazar Seyyed Ali Kianfar, Ph.D., is the co-founder and co-director of the International Association of Sufism and the Editor-in-Chief of the journal *Sufism: An Inquiry.* An internationally published author and lecturer, he was appointed to teach Sufism by his Sufi Master of the Uwaiysi Tariqat, Hazrat Moulana Shah Maghsoud.

Dr. Kianfar has taught Sufism, Islamic philosophy, mysticism and psychology in many cultures throughout the world for over forty years. He represented the United States at the UNESCO Culture of Peace conference in Uzbekistan. He recently represented International Association of Sufism in a cooperative educational program with the Al-Azhar University in Cairo. He has lectured and taught at many universities and conferences, has published numerous articles and several books including *Seasons of the Soul, Fatemah* (in Farsi), *Uwaiyse Gharani* (in Farsi), *Introduction to Religion*, and *Zikr*, which has been reprinted numerous times. He has worked locally and internationally to raise awareness about the peaceful dimensions of Islam and spirituality and to open the lines of communication for a better understanding of humanity.

Contributing Authors

Puran Khan Bair is a co-founder of The Institute for Applied Meditation (IAM), an international school. He is an American mystic, one of the foremost meditation teachers with 37 years of experience, a pioneer in bringing heart-based meditation to the public and one of the successors of Hazrat Inayat Khan. Puran is the author of *Living from the Heart*, (Random House, 1998), which has been hailed as a classic text in meditation. It introduced "Heart Rhythm Meditation," based on the practice of the Apostles of Christ. His second book, co-authored with his wife, Susanna, is *Energize Your Heart in Four Dimensions*, (Living Heart Media, 2007). It describes an energetic model of the heart and methods for opening and applying the heart to life. A frequent presenter at conferences and seminars internationally, Puran has worked with leading researchers to document the physiological changes that occur during meditation, including metabolism, heart rhythm, brain waves, light emission and electromagnetism. His background is in technology (MS in Computer Science from Univ. of Penn.) and business (V.P. of MFS, a mutual fund company).

Sensei Darrell Bluhm Chief Instructor Darrell Bluhm holds a degree of 6th dan (black belt) and Shihan (master instructor) certification in Aikido and is a member of the Birankai North America Senior Council. In conjunction with his training in the martial arts, Darrell Bluhm is a Licensed Massage Therapist, active in practicing and teaching a variety of bodywork methods for over twenty-five years. He is a Certified Feldenkrais Practitioner.

Dr Neil Douglas-Klotz directs the Edinburgh Institute for Advanced Learning and co-founded the Edinburgh International Festival of Middle Eastern Spirituality and Peace. He is the former co-chair of the Mysticism Group of the American Academy of Religion and has published several books on Middle Eastern spirituality and peace, including *Prayers of the Cosmos, Desert Wisdom, The Hidden Gospel, The Genesis Meditations, The Sufi Book of Life, Blessings of the Cosmos* and *The Tent of Abraham,* the latter authored with Rabbi Arthur Waskow and Sr. Joan Chittister. In 2005 he was awarded the Kessler-Keener Foundation Peacemaker of the Year award for his work in area of Middle Eastern peace and reconciliation. Information about his work can be found at www.abwoon.com and www.eial.org, the websites of the Abwoon Circles and the Edinburgh Institute for Advanced Learning.

Michael Essex. M.D., received a Master Degree in Anatomy in 1984 and Doctor of Medicine in 1985 from the University of Nebraska College of Medicine. His residency training was at Sheppard and Enoch Pratt Hospital, Towson, MD. He is board certified in Psychiatry. He is currently acting Medical Director for VA mental health services in North San Diego County and (Health Sciences) Assistant Clinical Professor, Non-Salaried, at UCSD. He began seriously studying Tibetan Buddhism in 1985 at the Tibetan Meditation Center in Washington, DC. Under Khenchen Rinpoche, he studied meditation and Buddhist philosophy, with special emphasis on the Jewel Ornament of Liberation. He developed a system for computer publishing bilingual Tibetan and English meditation texts, and has been involved in publishing and translating many Tibetan meditation manuals. He has studied with Drupon Samten since he arrrived in the USA in 1987.

Ken Friedman is a renaissance man—an artist, musician, business person, author, dance leader, a husband and father and a Waldorf teacher.

His sparkling blue eyes and smile show his clarity and joy of life. Ken has led workshops for over 20 years that include: business and personal planning, decision-making, retirement and life-choices planning for individuals in corporate settings and workshop classes, meditation, yoga and chi gung, creative writing and journaling, goal-setting marketing and investing—especially in one's self. He lives in Ashland, Oregon. Ken has published two books, *From Turtles to Rainbows, A Treasure Chest of Personal Growth Guides* and a novel, *The Decision Tree,* and two CDs of his music.

Orion Garland is a sufi dervish with the Rufa'i Marufi Order of America. She has been studying meditation, yoga, and martial arts for over ten years. She has completed an intensive twelve-week course taught by world-record-holding freedivers. This involved being part of a study at Simon Fraser University on the body's physiological adaptation to apnea training. She also participated in a study on the effects of decompression in freedivers. She has competed in freediving at the regional level, and also has experience safetying for competitions. She completed her Bachelor of Arts in Psychology and English at the University of British Columbia, and is currently working on a Masters degree in Public Health.

Sonia Leon Gilbert For thirty-four years, Sonia Leon Gilbert has been a president of the Bawa Muhaiyaddeen Fellowship and Mosque with fourteen branches in the USA, Canada, England and Sri Lanka. In that time, the study of the Sufi Way, as exemplified by her exalted teacher, M.R. Bawa Muhaiyaddeen (ral.) has been her focus and her work. Wisdom gained thereby is included in her many speeches and is her guide to continued enthusiastic engagement in numerous Interfaith Dialogues. She is a regular speaker at Sufi Symposiums and an ardent supporter of Interfaith Endeavors. In earlier years, Sonia Leon was a voice graduate of the revered Curtis Institute of Music in Philadelphia, Pennsylvania. Her operatic career spanned the concert stage, radio, television, performing with some of the greatest singers of the latter 20th century. From 1986 to 1998 she was the owner of two gem magazines, notably the international publication *Lapidary Journal.* In addition to these two mineral and jewelry arts magazines, she co-founded a third gem news magazine, *Colored Stone,* in 1987. Concerns for the spiritual, socio-political and physical environment has also led to a partnership in One Light Pictures

LLC, a company involved in documentary film productions.

Stanislav Grof, M.D., Ph.D., is a psychiatrist with more than fifty years experience researching the healing and transformative potential of non-ordinary states of consciousness. His groundbreaking theories influenced the integration of Western science with his brilliant mapping of the transpersonal dimension. On October 5, 2007 Dr. Grof received the prestigious VISION 97 award granted by the Foundation of Dagmar and Vaclav Havel in Prague. He is one of the founders and chief theoreticians of Transpersonal Psychology and founder of the International Transpersonal Association (ITA). He is Professor of Psychology at the California Institute of Integral Studies (CIIS) in the Department of Philosophy, Cosmology, and Consciousness, and teaches at the Pacifica Graduate Institute in Santa Barbara, CA. Among his publications are over 150 papers in professional journals and many books including *Beyond the Brain, LSD Psychotherapy, Psychology of the Future, The Cosmic Game,* and *When the Impossible Happens* and *The Ultimate Journey.* Many of Grof's articles are on his website at www.stanislavgrof.com.

Sheldon Z. Kramer, Ph.D. Dr. Kramer has a PhD in Clinical Psychology and is in full time practice in San Diego, California with offices in Del Mar and La Mesa. He is the author of two books that integrates perennial wisdom and ancient spirituality with modern day psychology. He is an international trainer in Transpersonal Psychology, Mind-Body Medicine and Coordinates the Spiritual Dimension with his work in Business Consulting/ Executive Coaching as well as in Integrating Individual and Couples/Family Counseling. His website is www.szkramerphd.com.

Timothy Laporte, M.A., is a doctoral student in Religion and Philosophy at the California Institute for Human Science (Encinitas, CA), where he studies closely with Dr. Hiroshi Motoyama, the school's founder. He earned an A.B. in Religion from Princeton University (2005), specializing in Buddhist Studies, where he complemented his work in the classroom with personal exposure to the experience of Buddhism in its Asian context while studying abroad in Bodh Gaya, India in 2004. An avid meditator, he has received instruction from experienced teachers of the Theravâda, Zen, and Tibetan Buddhist traditions, as well as from highly regarded instructors of Hindu Yoga and Japanese Shintoism. His research focuses on the potential value of Eastern religious ontologies in easing or resolving many of the intractable challenges and paradoxes facing the present-day scientific worldview, such as the "hard problem" of consciousness and the mysteries of cosmology and quantum physics.

Ilse Middendorf. Professor Middendorf began practicing her work in 1935. Ilse was searching for the essence of a person's Self within movements, and for a medium to relate to that essence or to create a connection to it. An intuition from her childhood and her deep conviction made her want to follow the path of breath, and what it had to teach her. It was clear for her that connecting with breath in depth meant connecting with the essence of Self and its creative and inspiring nature. In 1965, after many years of research and practice, she founded the Institute for The Perceptible Breath in Berlin, Germany, to train practitioners in her artistic form of breath education—which she now calls The Experience of Breath or breathexperience. From 1965 through 1975, Ilse was also a teacher at the Berlin Academy for Music and Performing Arts. Since its inception, her work has achieved international attention for its effectiveness as a process leading to therapeutic, artistic, and personal growth as well as a way to support the healing and re-balancing processes of one's self as a physical, emotional, and spiritual being. In her mid-nineties, Ilse still lives and works in Berlin, Germany. She has maintained a full schedule—leading workshops and training practitioners throughout the world. In June, 2005 she held The Experience of Breath Congress in Berlin.

Maura Richman, MS. Her original education and training was in education and guidance and counseling. Over the years, she has participated in a number of psycho-spiritual growth activities and has led spiritual study and meditation groups. Maura is a trained Jewish Spiritual Director through the Yedidya Center for Jewish Spiritual Direction. She offers spiritual direction to individuals and groups from various walks of life and faith backgrounds. For more information about Spiritual Direction or to contact her, please see her web site www.maurarichman.com

Juerg Roffler. Director and founder of the U.S. Middendorf Breath Institute, The Experience of Breath, in Berkeley, California. He was a former instructor in the professional training program at the central institute in Berlin for many years before coming to the United States. In 1986 Advanced Seminars invited Ilse Middendorf and Juerg Roffler to introduce The Experience of Breath to the U.S. in Berkeley, California. In 1991 Juerg founded The U.S. Middendorf Breath Institute in San Francisco, now in Berkeley. Juerg has developed The Experience of Breath further in its natural evolution, Breathexperience in Relationship™, a program to uncover, clarify, resolve conflicts, and deepen and transform relationships. Besides his active role as director of the institute in Berkeley, he is an author, and also maintains his private practice and conducts breathexperience™ workshops on a regular basis throughout the United States, Europe, and other international locations. He is a regular presenter at national and international conferences such as USABP (United States Association for Body Psychotherapy), International Somatics Congress, etc. Juerg participated in a research study at the Osher Clinic for Integrative Medicine at UCSF San Francisco. He is a founding member of The Breath Center of San Francisco (BCSF), a non-profit organization for the advancement of The Experience of Breath. He currently serves as a member of the Advisory Board. Contacts: Middendorf Institute for Breathexperience, Berkeley, CA 94710, (510) 981 1710, www. breathexperience.com.

Drupon Samten, Rinpoche, was born on March 25th, 1958, in Lamayuru, Ladakh, India. At the age of six, he entered the Drikung Kagyu Monastery. He studied with many accomplished teachers for many years. His studies included Buddhist philosophy, butter sculpture, painting, music, lama dance, healing, astrology and the traditional religious texts. Drupon Samten completed these studies when he was 21 years old. In 1975, he met His Holiness the Drikung Kyabgon Chetsang Rinpoche,(the lineage holder of the Drikung Kagyu school of Tibetan Buddhism), and since that time, he has served him faithfully. When Drupon Samten was 22 years old, he met the Very Venerable Khyunga Rinpoche, the great retreat master. Under the guidance of the Very Venerable Khyunga Rinpoche, Drupon Samten went into retreat. He completed the Three Year Retreat and the Six Yogas of Naropa. After completing his retreat, he was fully qualified and authorized to teach the Dharma to others. In 1987, His Holiness Drikung Kyabgon Chetsang sent him to the United States to teach the Dharma. On January 20th, 2001, he was enthroned by His

Holiness Drikung Kyabgon Chetsang in India, in front of over 800 monks attending the Snake Year teachings at Jang Chubling Monastery, and received the title Drupon Samten Rinpoche, the Vajra Meditation Master. Drupon Samten has been teaching in the U.S., Taiwan, Malaysia and Chile since 1987. He has obtained a very good command of the English language. He teaches with clarity, compassion and wisdom, and is open to help everyone he meets. Drupon Samten Rinpoche is the resident Lama in Escondido.

Vincentia Schroeter, Ph.D, has been a Certified Bioenergetic Analyst since 1980. She is the Coordinating Trainer for the San Diego Institute for Bioenergetic Analysis, is on the Faculty of the International Institute of Bioenergetic Analysis, and is on the Editorial Board of the IIBA journal. She has twice been named outstanding chapter leader as Professional Development Chair of the California Association of Marriage and Family Therapists. She is an adjunct faculty member of the Pacific College of Oriental Medicine. She has presented several papers on bioenergetics and its role in treating mental illness and improving sensory awareness. Published articles include "The Role of Sensory Styles in Psychotherapy: Synopsis of Research," "The Grief of Infertility: One Therapist's Journey;" and "Improving Bonding using Bioenergetics and Sensory Assessments: A Clinical Case Report." www.vincentiaschroeterphd.com

Michael Sky is the author of *Dancing With the Fire*, a comprehensive exploration of the scientific, psychological, and spiritual teachings of fire; *Breathing*, a definitive book on the use of breath for therapeutic and spiritual benefits; *Sexual Peace,* a practical guide for moving from aggression, violence and competition to peace, cooperation and genuine partnership; and, *The Power of Emotion*, his follow-up to *Breathing*, in which he details four potent tools to aid in the productive channeling of powerful emotional energy.

Since 1976, he maintained a private practice as a therapist and bodyworker focusing on breath, life-energy, and the resolution of suppressed emotions. He travels throughout the United States and Japan leading workshops in breathing, firewalking, bodywork, ritual, and the effective practice of partnership. He also works as a web designer and manages dozens of sites, including *energybreath.com* and *thinkingpeace. com.*

Michael lives with his wife and daughter on a small green island in the Pacific Northwest.

Russell and Jennifer Stark (husband and wife team) trained as Buteyko practitioners in 1993 with Russian trained Alexander Stalmatski, and later did additional training with the Buteyko founder, Dr. Konstantin Pavlovich Buteyko. Their son Robert had severe asthma that was unrelenting in spite of following all conventional medical treatments recommended by their doctors, and they turned to the Buteyko Breathing Techniques in desperation.Buteyko provided them with such a complete change of health that they decided to train as practitioners and help others as they had been helped. They took the Buteyko method to New Zealand in 1994, and they have been instrumental in propagating Buteyko not only there, but also in USA, the UK, Canada, Israel and the Netherlands. They have taught more than 7000 people with breathing problems to use the techniques so that they can improve their own health in a natural way, and have also trained more than 60 new practitioners. The Starks have taught the techniques in clinical trials and studies in New Zealand, Canada and the UK. They hosted the first international Buteyko conference in the world, where 45 delegates came to New Zealand to celebrate Buteyko and to learn more about the method.

Kylea Taylor, M.S., M.F.T., is a writer and therapist who has studied with Stanislav Grof since 1984 and served on the training staff of the Grof Transpersonal Training for seven years. She has written the books: *The Breathwork Experience, The Holotropic Breathwork Facilitator's Manual,* and *Considering Holotropic Breathwork*, and edited *Exploring Holotropic Breathwork*. She is interested in the ways in which rapid psycho-spiritual development is precipitated by non-ordinary states of consciousness, as well as the ways in which the gifts from that tumultuous process may be integrated back into ordinary life. In her therapy practice she has worked with many adults who were recovering from childhood trauma. Taylor wrote the ground-breaking book, *The Ethics of Caring*, which explores the compelling ethical issues unique to working with clients in non-ordinary states of consciousness. Her work now also includes managing the development of SoulCollage˙, an intuitive collage process now facilitated throughout the world and often used as an art process complementary to work in non-ordinary states of consciousness. www.hanfordmead.com.

Benjamin R. Tong, Ph.D., holds the rank of Professor in the Clinical Psychology Psy.D. Program at the California Institute of Integral Studies, San Francisco. An emeritus faculty member of the Asian American Studies Department at San Francisco State University, he is Executive Director of the Institute for Cross-Cultural Research, a nonprofit organization dedicated to the proper explication, validation and utilization of indigenous health and healing practices. Dr. Tong is Director and Head Instructor of the School of Taoist Internal Arts which offers a program that includes Taoist studies, Tai Chi Chuan and Chi Gung. He also maintains a private practice in psychotherapy and organizational development. He authored a chapter on Taoist healing practices, Taoist Mind-Body Resources for Psychological Health and Healing, in *Modern Psychology and Ancient Wisdom: Psychological Healing Practices from the World's Religious Traditions.* Website:http://drbenjaminrtong.com/ E-mail: lohfu@yahoo.com.

Index

Deuteronomy, 163
devekut (Hebrew), 158. *See also*
    merging
Devi (Sanskrit), 197
devil, 204
devotee, 3, 14, 20–22, 178, 213
dharmakaya (Sanskrit), 31
dharana, 14. *See also* concentration
Dhikr (Arabic), 183–184. See also
    Zikr; remembrance
dhyana, 14. *See also* meditation
dialogue, viii, 142–143, 146–147, 195,
    197
diaphragmatic, 45, 74, 122, 183
dbugs (Tibetan), 29. *See also*
    respiration
digestive system, 13
discipline, 2, 8, 16, 18, 22, 38, 57,
    59–60, 109, 113
diseased, 179, 200
disembodied, 195
diversity, xiii, 54, 175
divine, xiii–xiv, 3–4, 12–13, 15–17,
    21–22, 44, 116, 152–153, 156–
    158, 160, 198–200, 205, 215, 220,
    223; breath, xv, 152, 257, 222;
    nature, 11–12, 21; emanation,
    153
Divine, 1, 14–15, 19, 21–22, 44,
    136, 181, 187–188, 221, 223;
    vibration, viii, 181; wisdom,
    182; widsom within wisdom,
    182; luminous, 183–184; state
    of consciousness, 186. *See also*
    vibration
Divine Absolute. *See* absolute
Divine Self, 14
diving reflex, 109
do-in (Japanese), 59. *See also* dao-yin
Don Juan, 215
Dow Jones Industrial Average, 248
dualism, 72, 195, 222
dualist, 15
dualistic, 14; view, 14–15

dysfunctional breathing, 69–70

earth, 44, 46, 51, 53, 64–65, 80, 145,
    156, 175–178, 187, 208, 223, 226,
    235; elements of, 4, 31, 91, 192,
    221, 235, 242; and heaven, 18,
    21, 44, 151, 213, 223. *See also*
    elements
Eastern, 2–5, 68, 72, 75, 207;
    breath, vii–viii, 8, 192, 195, 201;
    spirituality, viii 4, 76, 96, 142,
    195; tradition, 8–9, 68–69, 76,
    152, 196
Eastern Church, 168
East West Bookstore, 217
ebal, 174
economy, 233, 249
education, ix, 34, 62, 134–135, 137,
    192, 196, 225–226, 230, 232–237
ego: as identity, 102, 212, 216–222;
    ego-states, 3, 212, 219; as way
    of breathing, 145, 212. See also
    nafs; *naphsha*; *nefesh*
eight-limbed path, 14
Einstein, Albert, xiv, 90
electrical, 204–205
element, xii, 4, 9, 15, 47, 58–59, 96,
    203, 216, 226, 243; as earth, 4,
    29, 31, 234, 242; as Aikido, 54,
    59–60, 62, 65; as breath, 103,
    152, 192, 221–222. *See also*
    Aikido; earth
embodied, 8, 147, 170, 195, 222
emotional, 21, 57, 68, 72, 74, 79, 87,
    90, 96–98, 100, 122, 136, 139,
    146, 148, 157, 173–174, 176, 192,
    200–201, 208, 229, 231, 234–235,
    240, 244, 257, 260; memories,
    88, 212; a psychosomatic state,
    96, 98–102; a state or condition,
    212, 240–241. *See also* mental;
    psychosomatic disorders
energy, 7–8, 13, 17–19, 23, 22, 39, 44,
    47, 49, 59, 64, 73, 75–76, 78–81,